THE DORSEY SERIES IN POLITICAL SCIENCE

American Foreign Policy
RESPONSE TO A SENSE OF THREAT

HENRY T. NASH

Associate Professor of Politics
Hollins College, Virginia

1973

THE DORSEY PRESS   Homewood, Illinois 60430
Irwin-Dorsey Limited, Georgetown, Ontario

First Printing, March 1973

ISBN 0-256-01419-1
Library of Congress Catalog Card No. 72–96524
Printed in the United States of America

To Valery

Preface

This book is designed to examine the following hypothesis:

Since World War II America's foreign policy has been a response to a sense of threat. The basic guiding principles of this policy were formulated immediately following the war in response to the threat of Communism and have remained fundamentally intact for a quarter of a century. Now, however, in the early 1970s, there are indications of serious consideration being given to cautious policy innovation. This suggests that American foreign policy may have reached a significant turning point.

The examination of this hypothesis focuses on the President's foreign policy role. The book analyzes the foreign policy implications of the influence exercised by specific executive agencies in the process of assisting the President to fulfill his decision-making responsibilities. The analysis of the relationship between the President and his foreign affairs advisers provides insights into questions such as why America's foreign policy assumed certain characteristics; why specific policies and actions developed so rapidly and persisted so long following the war; and why policy change, if it is to occur, must be preceded by altered official perceptions of the world and of America's role in the world.

The approach of this study of American foreign policy is based largely on the design used in my undergraduate course in this subject. The organization of the book and the emphasis given to specific topics within this organization evolved largely through classroom discussions over the past six years. These classroom discussions tended to be guided by two basic lines of thought, each qualitatively different and each transplanted from the classroom to the body of this book. The first line of thought is directed toward an effort to identify and describe the most important actual and potential sources of influence in the process of formulating and implementing American foreign policy. The second line of thought is more speculative. After identifying sources of influence, these sources are analyzed in terms of their strengths and weaknesses, their source of power and means of exercising influence, and the trends evident in gradually changing considerations and shifting power relationships within Washington's foreign affairs bureaucracy. It is assumed that if such speculation and theorizing "worked" in the classroom, they should be equally effective in helping the reader gain useful insights into how American foreign policy is made—how the system operates.

In expressing appreciation to those who made contributions to this book, it follows from the above that there is a deep indebtedness to my students of foreign policy for the many useful observations and insights they provided. In addition, I should like to express my gratitude to Professor Norton E. Long for encouraging me to undertake the preparation of this book, and to Professor Wayne G. Reilly for his helpful comments concerning many of the topics discussed in the chapters which follow. Finally, there are two individuals to whom special appreciation is extended for the help they provided. First, to Sallie Crenshaw who worked with me during the entire process of "building" this book. Her ideas, fact-finding skills, and support were invaluable. Second, to Valery Nash who scrupulously reviewed each chapter and, as a result, brought to the book a clarity and unity which it otherwise would have lacked.

February 1973   HENRY T. NASH

Contents

List of Figures

Introduction

This book is concerned with American foreign policy during the span of approximately 25 years since the end of World War II. In this period America's foreign policy rapidly shifted from an attitude of anticipated international cooperation to a fixed Cold War posture that was rigorously adhered to for almost a quarter century, and then with the late 1960s, reflected restrained but significant signs of an official disposition toward altered forms of behavior—actions toward other nations that were more conciliatory, slightly more flexible, and less hard-line in their reactions to communism. This book analyzes these postwar changes to identify attitudes that account for America's perception of international threats and to describe the organizational alterations that occurred within the government to contend with these threats.

In a basic sense, the book is divided into two broad yet related areas of discussion—first, the events that shaped policy for over two decades, the policy itself, and the effect of this policy on the government's foreign affairs institutions; second, the indicators that suggest that American officials began to view with some skepticism the appropriateness of the policies of the past 25 years and were attempting to define altered courses of action, tempered by a new sense of restraint, realism, and feasibility. There is consideration of official motivations for seeking new directions, of the factors that inhibit change, and of the nature of the gradualism that accompanied efforts to alter policy within Washington's complex bureaucracy.

The question of why America's postwar foreign policy assumed the

1

character it did immediately following the end of the war provides the basis for the opening chapter of the book. During the short five-year period from 1945 to 1950 America's attitudes toward the postwar world moved rapidly along a continuum from optimism to caution, on to suspicion and distrust, and finally to open hostility. Actually, these American attitudes were not directed toward the world in general, but from the outset, were focused on the threat of communism. This threat, which in the 1950s and early 1960s was seen as emanating from Moscow and pointed toward Europe and the United States, had shifted by the late 1960s and into the 1970s to be a threat from Peking directed against Asia and the United States. The longevity of the single set of perceptions of the world that molded American policy was noted by Sen. J. William Fulbright, and in large part, was attributed to the absence of any "constructive adversary proceedings" within the government.

From Korea to Berlin to Cuba to Vietnam, the Truman Doctrine governed America's response to the Communist world. Tactics changed—from "massive retaliation" to "limited war" and "counterinsurgency"—but these were variations on a classic formulation based on assumptions that few really questioned. Sustained by an inert Congress, the policymakers of the forties, fifties, and early sixties were never compelled to reexamine the premises of the Truman Doctrine, or even to defend them in constructive adversary proceedings. . . . Only in the context of the assumptions of the Truman Doctrine could the Vietnamese war ever have been rationalized as having something to do with American security or American interests.[1]

America's view of the world, and the policies and actions that were developed in accordance with this view, shaped the foreign affairs agencies of the government and gave them a unity of purpose that, as Senator Fulbright suggests, silenced any voices of dissent.

America's military resources, the subject of Chapter 2, were developed as a direct response to the sense of threat posed by communism. Military capabilities, especially nuclear capabilities, quickly came to constitute the primary resource by which the government sought to maintain its security. The discussion of this subject centers on the process by which these capabilities were acquired, the policy implications of this dependence on military capabilities, some characteristics of military thought, and the sources of military influence in policy circles.

In contrast to the nation's awesome military capabilities, consideration is next given to the government's central nonmilitary resource officially responsible for foreign policy, the Department of State. State's responsibilities, capabilities, organization, and operational problems are discussed in order to assess the quality of the resources that are available to the

---

[1] Sen. J. William Fulbright, "In Thrall to Fear," *New Yorker,* January 8, 1972, pp. 41, 53. Published as *The Price of Empire* (New York: Random House Vintage Books, 1972).

President as a basis for political, rather than military, approaches to international problems. Together, State and Defense constitute the government's two basic and complementary foreign policy resources, and for this reason, their strengths and weaknesses and relative influence on policy are considered at length. Other executive agencies that comprise foreign affairs resources are discussed, but emphasis rests with Defense and State.

The central figure in American foreign policy is the President, the subject of Chapter 4. All of the agencies of the so-called foreign affairs bureaucracy constitute supporting units for the President. They advise him, make information available to him, and help him implement his decisions. In the nuclear age, with the President responsible for the security of the most powerful nation in the world, the support provided by the President's executive departments and agencies does not satisfy all of his needs. Thus, in the discussion of the Presidency, considerable attention is devoted to the functions and influence of the President's closest advisers located with him in the White House. The President's methods of being advised constitute, in effect, an information system centered in the White House and modified periodically to meet the particular requirements of individual Presidents. Attention is devoted to the unique aspects of the advisory systems developed by each of the four most recent Presidents, with emphasis on the foreign policy implications of the innovations introduced by President Nixon and his assistant for national security affairs, Henry Kissinger. As an adjunct of the President's advisory system, the Central Intelligence Agency discussed in Chapter 5 functions as the intelligence arm of the President. The CIA, its operations and impact on policy, is considered as the final organizational component of the foreign policy bureaucracy.

In Chapter 6 the Strategic Arms Limitation Talks (SALT) are viewed against the backdrop of the government's diverse disarmament efforts that have occurred since the advent of the atomic age. SALT is analyzed as a foreign policy case study illustrating the interaction of the policies and agencies discussed in the first five chapters. Various levels of intragovernment conflict are depicted and some operating principles of foreign policy making are suggested through an examination of the long series of disarmament machinations that finally, after 25 years, achieved their most significant progress in the form of two arms agreements in the summer of 1972. The analysis of SALT also suggests a strengthened official concern over the security implications of the nuclear arms race as well as the political utility of unlimited military power. These considerations lead to the concluding chapter that considers further indications of policy alterations and new directions in American foreign policy. This examination of change concludes with a number of recommendations for "reforms" in the functions and responsibilities of several agencies and groups that affect America's foreign policy.

There are obvious risks involved in standing back and attempting to generalize about events as recent as those of the last few years. Despite these risks, it can be said that as of early 1973, a sense of pragmatism appears to have begun to affect the outlook of officials responsible for the design of America's foreign policy. It seems that pragmatism, the adherence to the practical, a concept long associated with American values, may be asserting itself in an area of government responsibility in which its impact has not been clearly visible for some years. For Americans, pragmatism, more than idealism or humanitarianism, could constitute a strong and broadly acceptable foundation from which to build toward change. The dawning realization among more and more Americans, both within and outside government circles, that the nation is paying too much for what it is getting reflects a degree of practicality that could begin to move America in a new direction in world affairs.

chapter 1

The Shaping of Policy

A first impression of America's response to international affairs during the 12-month period from mid-1945 to mid-1946 is that an about-face in outlook had taken place within this very short period of time. In mid-1945, following the defeat of Germany, most top American government officials felt satisfied with the accomplishments of their own government and generally optimistic concerning future relations with the Soviet Union, and the world in general. President Truman, for example, one week after assuming the Presidency in April 1945, expressed his faith in the continuation of wartime Allied collaboration following the convergence of British, American, and Russian armies within defeated Germany. The coming together of Western and Soviet forces represented a collaborative effort that had surmounted the "obstacles of distance and of language and of communications," and suggested that the three wartime allies could "live together" and "work together in the common labor of the organization of the world for peace." [1]

A month later the President expressed the belief that confidence "in the good faith and reliability" of the Allies could be reestablished "through frank discussions and the opportunity to know and estimate each other." [2]

The President expressed his faith in getting along specifically with the Russians when, following Presidential adviser Harry Hopkins's talk with

---

[1] Harry S. Truman, *Memoirs* (Garden City, New York: Doubleday, 1955–56), vol. 1, p. 65. (Statement on April 19, 1945).

[2] Ibid., p. 261.

5

Premier Stalin on May 27, 1945, he stated that "the Russians are just as anxious to get along with us as we are to get along with them."[3] Probably the last time the President allowed the emotion of an allied victory to sustain the dream of postwar cooperation with the USSR was immediately following the surrender of Japan when he reflected that the war was won, that he hoped for the rehabilitation of Germany and Japan under the allied occupation, and that "peace and happiness for all countries" had been America's wartime goals.[4] The President pointed out that no nation as powerful as the United States had been "so generous to its enemies and so helpful to its friends," and perhaps the time was at hand when "the teachings of the Sermon on the Mount could be put into effect."[5] The war was over and the President's world view still accommodated his predecessor's optimism toward the future. This mood, however, was to change in a matter of weeks. In the same month that brought the surrender of Japan and the end of the war, there emerged a clear sign of change in President Truman's expressed attitude toward the Soviet Union. Following discussions with Premier Stalin concerning the postwar administration of Berlin, the President indicated that he had come to realize that Stalin was not earnest in his quest for peace. While there was still hope for cooperation, the prospect seemed more remote since the President had come to realize that "force is the only thing the Russians understand."[6] Optimism was replaced, with disquieting speed, by a feeling of deep concern. The source of concern was, in one sense, tied exclusively to the Soviet Union. Beyond this, however, but not unrelated, were the first feelings of anxiety and uncertainty that confronted the United States as it began to sense its position in the world as the most powerful of all nations.

In looking back on the 1945–46 period, it is apparent that it was not a radical change in outlook that took place in the sense of one attitude *replacing* another, but rather the reemergence of a view of the USSR that had been repressed during the wartime alliance. In order to comprehend the feelings of uncertainty and threat that began to shape America's world outlook in 1945, it is useful to look more closely at this period and identify some of the specific factors that provoked a reorientation of foreign policy. These factors provoked such persistent repercussions in policy circles that they continued to shape America's perception of the world for a quarter of a century following the end of World War II. There is another reason for identifying these factors. In order to move beyond the Cold War "frame of mind" and begin to pursue foreign policy alternatives that suggest new directions in international relations, it is important to compre-

---

[3] Donald Brandon, *American Foreign Policy: Beyond Utopianism and Realism* (New York: Appleton-Century-Crofts, 1966), p. 85.

[4] Truman, *Memoirs,* p. 437.

[5] Ibid.

[6] Ibid., pp. 411–12.

hend first the genesis of the Cold War. If one is interested in foreign policy reform it is helpful to know what, at the outset, predisposed the United States to adopt a foreign policy outlook that persisted for 25 years.

The factors that helped build a sense of threat are discussed in the following section. It is suggested that, in addition to the threatening implications of Soviet behavior, America's anxieties were intensified by the limited resources available to the nation to contend with the "enemy." Under such conditions the atomic bomb assumed special importance. In response to a sense of threat, the Truman administration designed the basic components of America's postwar policy, each of which is described.

"First Level" Threats

Several events took place in the months immediately following the defeat of Nazi Germany that acted as catalyst in the reshaping of America's world outlook. While each of these events is significant in itself, considered together they suggested to American policy makers a pattern of aggressive intent that was directed against the non-Communist world. These developments are considered as "first level" events because they constituted an immediate challenge to America's postwar position and shocked the nation into reordering its view of the postwar world. In addition to first level events there were "second level" factors, or more indirect considerations, that contributed to an atmosphere of hostility and an intensification of conflict. First and second level considerations interacted to produce a general sense of threat that caused American officials during the years following the end of the war to conclude that the USSR stood as the central challenge to American security and world peace.

First level events to be considered are the Soviet response to the Yalta agreement; Soviet actions in Iran, Turkey, and Greece; and Soviet demands for war reparations imposed upon Germany.

1. Soviet Response to the Yalta Agreement

The Yalta Agreement, and what came to be regarded as the Soviet betrayal of this agreement, was not only the first but was also the most persistent basis for postwar antagonism between the United States and the Soviet Union. Because it was the initial event to reveal a fissure in the mood of postwar cooperation, Western statesmen came to endow it with a causal significance in the generation of the Cold War.

The Yalta Conference was held February 4–11, 1945, in the former Czarist palace of Livadia overlooking the Black Sea. The participating powers were the United States, Great Britain, and the USSR. At the time of the conference, Soviet forces were about to attack Berlin, with the Red Army already controlling Poland, Hungary, Bulgaria, Rumania, Czechoslovakia, and the eastern portion of Germany. At this time, with the Allied defeat of Germany imminent, American thoughts began to shift to the war against the Japanese in the Pacific. American military advisers to President Roosevelt anticipated a difficult (an estimated one million casualties if American troops invaded the Japanese Islands) and protracted (18 months of war after the defeat of Germany) battle before a Japanese surrender could be expected.[7]

Because of American military predictions concerning the manpower requirements of the final offensive against Japan, there was a strong disposition on the part of American negotiators at Yalta to support diplomatic actions and make negotiating concessions designed to keep Soviet forces committed to the Allied military effort as the focus of the war shifted to the Pacific theater. While Western diplomats were preoccupied with reaching an agreement at Yalta that would insure Soviet assistance in bringing about the earliest possible end of the war, the Soviet Union's primary concern was to achieve a degree of international influence sufficient to assure its own postwar national security. In retrospect, it appears that the USSR, in considering how to rebuild its war-ravaged economy, was convinced that it should first reduce the prospect of a reoccurrence of a military threat to its western border. In terms of Soviet foreign policy perceptions, national security required Soviet dominance over Eastern Europe.

Thus, at Yalta in early 1945, both the United States and the USSR had specific but different motives for keeping alive the wartime mood of cooperation. The USSR, by maintaining a conciliatory attitude and agreeing to support the West in the final military offensive against Japan, hoped to sustain a reasonably flexible and unsuspicious Western attitude toward the presence of Soviet military forces in Eastern Europe. The United States believed that an air of cordiality would dispose Stalin to make Soviet forces available for the war against Japan.

There were five main topic areas discussed at Yalta: (1) The issue of Poland, with the need to decide where to draw Poland's eastern and western borders. There was no settlement of this topic. (2) With regard to Germany and Berlin, three zones of occupation (British, Russian, and American) were agreed on, as was the Allied objective of unconditional surrender. As for war reparations, the USSR proposed that Germany be required to pay, in various forms, $20 billion, half of which was to go to the Soviet Union. The Soviet position was not accepted but was to be a basis for future discussions. (3) The broad outlines of the future United Nations organization were reviewed. (4) A secret and unpublished protocol was drawn up, later to be cleared with China's President Chiang Kai-shek, which granted certain privileges and concessions to the USSR in the Far

---

[7] American military estimates as of November 1944.

East.[8] This protocol was not made public until a year and a half later. (5) The broad approaches to the future treatment of Eastern Europe by the Allies were discussed. Emerging from these discussions, and the source of deep contention between the United States and the USSR in subsequent years, was the Yalta "Declaration on Liberated Europe." This declaration stated that the USSR, the United States, and Great Britain would assure the liberated people of Europe representative and democratic governments, responsive to the will of the people. All three participating powers at Yalta agreed to free elections in Eastern Europe. At the termination of the Yalta Conference, some of the key Western participants were open in voicing their sense of accomplishment and their faith in the prospect of future cooperation among the wartime Allies. The mood of the American delegates as Yalta ended has been described as one of "supreme exaltation." [9] Reflecting and reinforcing this mood was Harry Hopkins, White House adviser to President Roosevelt. After the conference, Hopkins expressed his confidence in the future by stating:

We really believed in our hearts that this was the dawn of the new day we had all been praying for and talking about for so many years. We were absolutely certain that we had won the first great victory of the peace—and, by "we," I mean all of us, the whole civilized human race. The Russians had proved that they could be reasonable and farseeing and there was not any doubt in the minds of the President or any of us that we could live with them and get along with them peacefully for as far into the future as any of us could imagine.[10]

Also sharing this mood of exaltation was Secretary of State Cordell Hull, who stated:

There will no longer be need for spheres of influence, for alliances, balance of power, or any other special arrangements through which, in the unhappy past, the nations strove to safeguard their security or promote their interests.[11]

---

[8] It was agreed to (1) preserve the status of Outer Mongolia (it would remain the Mongolian People's Republic), (2) southern Sakhalin would be returned to the USSR, (3) the port of Darien was to be internationalized, (4) the USSR would annex the Kurile Islands, (5) the USSR would be granted a lease on the Chinese Eastern and Southern Manchurian railways (thus providing an outlet to Darien), and (6) Port Arthur would be leased to the USSR as a naval base. Thus, the Yalta agreement had the effect of restoring the USSR to a position of power in the Far East comparable to that which it had held immediately prior to the Russo-Japanese War of 1904.

[9] Robert E. Sherwood, *Roosevelt and Hopkins: An Intimate History* (New York: Harper and Bros., 1948), p. 869. Documents in the Churchill-Roosevelt wartime correspondence made available in 1972 at the Franklin D. Roosevelt Library, Hyde Park, N. Y., indicated that President Roosevelt adhered to his goal of postwar unity among the wartime allies despite Prime Minister Churchill's efforts to persuade him to limit the role of the Soviet Union in military and political decisions.

[10] Ibid., p. 870.

[11] Quoted by John Spanier, *American Foreign Policy Since World War II* (3d ed; New York: Frederick A. Praeger, 1968), p. 25.

During late 1945 and early 1946, after the surrender of Japan on August 14, 1945, it became clear to the United States that the phrases of the Yalta Agreement having to do with free elections and democratic government in Eastern Europe were interpreted differently by the Russians and the Americans. To Premier Stalin, democratic government meant communist government, since under no other political system was true democracy possible. Elections were free only if they excluded political parties that were opposed to the Communist party, the party of the people. By the end of 1946, Soviet controls became firmly established in Poland, Hungary, Bulgaria, Rumania, and Albania, with Yugoslavia being Communist but under the leadership of Premier Tito. Czechoslovakia, although threatened by Soviet military power, did not acquire a Communist government until early 1948.

The extension of Soviet control into Eastern Europe, viewed by the United States as a clearly aggressive act in direct violation of the Yalta Agreement, was deeply disturbing to the United States. Directly on the heels of the allied defeat of Germany, just at the time when the United States was longing to relax after the sacrifices of a long war and savor its victory, the USSR suddenly loomed as a disruptive, aggressive power. Soviet action in Eastern Europe shattered the illusions that surrounded Yalta and, in addition, suggested further Soviet aggression westward, possibly into Germany, or even beyond. The Western sense of threat was mixed with a certain feeling of resentment: How could the USSR rupture America's satisfying impression that it had been instrumental in restoring the prospect of future peace to all the nations of the world?

One final word concerning the Yalta Agreement. In 1945, America's overriding objective in negotiating with the USSR was to keep the Soviets in the war. In these negotiations, there was little of the wariness and vindictiveness that had come to be associated with prewar American-Soviet relations. Also, the United States had no objection to making the USSR one of the beneficiaries of the breakup of the Japanese empire. Probably, if the availability of the atomic bomb had been anticipated by American negotiators and, as a consequence the imminence of Japan's surrender, the United States would have been less willing to accept Stalin's conditions at Yalta. But this awareness was not a part of United States thinking and thus did not affect American-Soviet relations in February 1945. The Americans left Yalta convinced that they had achieved their objectives.

Looking back through the Cold War years of hostile American-Soviet relations, one is prompted to conclude that America was "betrayed" by the Soviet Union at Yalta. However, a fresh examination of the Yalta proceedings suggests that the USSR had made their interests in Eastern Europe known before the conference began, as they had been explicit in defining their concepts of democracy and free elections. It does not seem, in retrospect, that America was "betrayed," but rather had *allowed* itself to be deluded about the reality of Soviet foreign policy objectives and the future of United States-USSR relations.

2. Soviet Action in Middle East

Soviet actions in response to Yalta would have appeared threatening to the United States under any circumstance, but in conjunction with Soviet action in the Middle East in 1946 the level of threat seemed significantly raised. In addition to attempting to create a belt of communist states along its western border the USSR, during the same 1945–46 period, looked southward with the idea of extending Soviet influence and possibly Soviet control into Iran, Turkey, and Greece. These Soviet efforts are significant, not only because of the actions themselves, but also because America's response to them constituted its first overt stand against the USSR following World War II.

Soviet troops had been stationed in Iran during the war and remained in Iran past the date (March 2, 1946) when they had agreed to leave. To the Iranian government, and to Western leaders, this action appeared to be part of a Soviet effort to extend its influence into northern Iran through the Iranian Communist (Tudeh) party. Objections were voiced by the Iranian, British, and American governments. Firm Western diplomatic opposition to the continued Soviet presence, backed by the implication that force would be used by the West to defend Iran, prompted the USSR to withdraw all of its forces.[12]

Soviet pressure on Turkey for increased Soviet administrative responsibility over the Dardenelles Straits began in June 1945. When the Soviet government urged Turkey to substitute ties with the USSR for its traditional ones with Britain, objections were voiced by England and the United States and, in support of these objections, the U. S. Navy's Sixth Fleet was deployed to the Mediterranean.

It should be noted that while American reactions to Soviet action in Iran and Turkey were military in nature, they were limited to a redeployment of existing forces. American response was administered rapidly and firmly, but with obvious caution and restraint. These actions did not represent the implementation of an overall policy or strategy but, instead, were merely immediate responses to specific events. Whether in response to these actions or not, the USSR almost immediately halted these efforts to extend its influence beyond its southern border.

---

[12] Some years after this event, President Truman indicated that, at the time, he had sent Premier Stalin an ultimatum, informing him that the United States would send troops into Iran if the USSR did not leave and that he (Truman) had ordered preparations of the movement of American land, sea, and air forces. (See John C. Campbell, *Defense of the Middle East: Problems of American Policy* [New York: Frederick A. Praeger, 1960], p. 33.)

With regard to Greece, opposition to the right-wing Greek government, elected in March 1946, had begun in the fall of that year in the form of Communist supported guerrilla warfare. Communist activity was an outgrowth of Communist party resistance to German occupation forces in Greece during the war. When German forces were withdrawn following Germany's defeat, there was a resurgence of Communist activity that was effectively resisted by the Greek government only through the support provided by Great Britain. The continued refusal of the Greek government to confront the internal economic and social problems caused by the war gave impetus to Communist activity in northern Greece. Communist guerrilla forces were aided by supplies coming from the neighboring Communist governments in Albania, Bulgaria, and Yugoslavia.

As the British became less able to continue postwar aid to Greece, the Greek government became unable to mount effective resistance to Communist forces. Aid to resist communism, if it was to come, would have to be provided by the United States. While America was deeply concerned with the possible southward spread of Communism, it was not until March 1947, with the announcement of the Truman Doctrine, that the government made public its decision to act.

3. Soviet War Reparations from Germany

The postwar administration of Germany constituted a continuing source of conflict between the Soviet Union and its Western wartime allies. At Yalta, and again one month after the surrender of Germany, the USSR clearly expressed its conviction that the Allies should extract from the German economy a total of $20 billion (half of which was to go entirely to the USSR) in the form of capital equipment, current production, and manpower resources. At the Potsdam Conference in July 1945, it was made clear that, in addition to this $10 billion, the USSR was to receive 25 percent of the equipment located in the Western zones, only 15 percent of which would be paid for in the form of products from the USSR.[13] By March 1946, Soviet Foreign Minister Molotov demanded the $10 billion in reparations, referring to this amount as having been "guaranteed" at Yalta. By late 1946, due to the rapid shipment of German equipment, products, and manpower to the USSR, only 35 to 40 percent remained of the original industrial capacity within the Soviet zone of Germany.

During the course of these early negotiations with the USSR over the immediate postwar future of Germany, President Truman came to view the Russians as "relentless bargainers, forever pressing for every advantage for themselves."[14] It appeared to the West that the USSR was pursu-

---

[13] The remaining 10 percent of this equipment was to be given outright to the USSR.

[14] Truman, *Memoirs*, p. 411.

ing two objectives in Germany. The first objective was to acquire as much as possible from Germany in the form of war reparations; and second, to so weaken the Soviet zone and perhaps all of Germany, both economically and politically, that it would easily lapse into the Soviet sphere of influence or control. Prospects for such an outcome were strengthened when, in April 1946, the Social Democrats were forced to join the Communists in a single, Communist-controlled political party. The political direction suggested by this move pointed clearly toward the establishment of a one (Communist) party state in the Soviet zone of Germany.

It is possible that if Soviet actions in Eastern Europe, Iran, Turkey, Greece, and Germany had occurred more gradually the United States would have perceived them in a manner that would not have shaken the cooperative mood of immediate postwar East-West relations. But, taken together, all occurring within a one-year period, they represented a pattern of aggressive acts that the United States viewed as seriously threatening.

The character of Soviet actions caused the American government to conclude that cooperation among the wartime allies was over, or was at the least very much weakened. By mid-1946 the Truman administration decided that a policy of firmness was required in all negotiations with the USSR. This implied that American officials believed that if a "policy of firmness and patience" were maintained, Soviet leaders would be struck by the pointlessness of aggression and be moved to adopt a conciliatory, cooperative attitude toward the United States. The illusion of postwar American-Soviet cooperation was thus replaced by another illusion: that through American sternness and reprimand the USSR would be compelled to abandon aggression and adopt a policy of reasonable cooperation. This shift from a faith in Soviet postwar cooperation to a faith in eliciting Soviet reasonableness through firmness became a part of America's foreign policy just as a simple response might occur in the face of a threatening stimulus. It seems that there was little thought given to the question of how much "sternness," in what form, over how long a period of time would be required to force the USSR to behave cooperatively. There also was, at best, only a limited attempt made to appreciate the unique national and ideological motivations and perceptions that lay behind Stalin's postwar actions. American officials simply saw *aggression* and, in response, chose to believe that firmness was the policy that would cause the USSR to see the error of its ways and quickly (it was probably assumed and hoped) "reform."

"Second Level" Factors Contributing to a Sense of Threat

Another perspective from which it is possible to consider the events of 1945–46 is to move beyond the events themselves and glimpse the more general pattern of threat suggested by them. In other words, while the United States was responding to acts of Soviet aggression as they took place, these same events activated, on a deeper level, concerns and anxieties within the United States that were related to more firmly entrenched, broader, and longer term strains in the relationship between America and the Soviet Union. The long history of American-Soviet hostility and the threatening implications of professed Soviet expansionism are two such factors discussed below. Also discussed are four other considerations that intensified tensions and provided a base for conflict. These are the limited basis for American-Soviet cooperation, the bomb, President Truman's personality, and America's self-image. Postwar acts of Soviet aggression quickly came to be assessed by American officials within the context of "second-level" factors and, as a consequence, America's response was more determined, more inflexible, and more defensive than it might otherwise have been.

1. The Long History of United States-Soviet Animosity

One persistent characteristic of American foreign policy since 1917 had been a feeling of distrust and antagonism toward all Bolshevik leaders. This hostility grew from a number of factors, foremost among which were American opposition to Communist ideology, the shocked reaction of Americans to the human suffering imposed upon the Soviet people by a totalitarian regime, the Soviet government's early practice of confiscating American property and mistreating American citizens, the threatening and accusatory tone of official Soviet statements directed against the United States and other non-Communist nations, and Soviet efforts to spread Communist influence to other nations through intervention in their domestic affairs. When, following the defeat of Germany in 1945, the Soviet Union appeared to be reverting to many of these prewar practices, the United States, instead of persisting in an attempt to maintain the atmosphere of wartime cooperation within which a resolution of differences might have been possible, allowed earlier impressions of the Soviet system to reassert themselves. This imposed a premature sense of futility on the possibility of negotiating with the Soviets. Also, set against this backdrop of animosity, the events of 1945–46 appeared as extensions of a Soviet commitment to aggression which the West had overlooked or viewed as a thing of the past as the war drew to an end.

2. The Threatening Implications of Professed Expansionism

If Soviet aggression was alarming to the United States, aggression reinforced by an ideology that appeared to require a continued commitment to expansion was doubly disturbing. War with capitalism, according to Lenin and Stalin, was inevitable. This inevitability, said Stalin, required the USSR to strengthen its security through encouraging the emergence of "friendly" governments on the USSR's western border (in Eastern Europe) and to the south (in the Middle East).

An ideological commitment to the expansion of Communist influence and control suggested economic as well as political dangers. The American business community anticipated the nationalization of the economies that fell under Communist influence. In fact, Stalin let it be known that it was the responsibility of Communists to work to foster revolution in order to accelerate the inevitable demise of the exploitive capitalist system. For the enterprising capitalist whose thoughts in 1945–46 were shifting from wartime production to new opportunities for markets abroad, the USSR, in both theory and practice, presented a disturbing challenge. American industry had been denied access to Eastern European markets and it appeared that economic opportunities in Western Europe stood in jeopardy.

3. The Limited Operational Basis for American-Soviet Cooperation

The cooperation with the USSR that had been experienced by Americans was restricted in time to the shared wartime objective of defeating Germany. There had been no joint long-term planning involving the specification of mutual objectives that might have provided a basis for future agreement. With the ending of the war, the context for cooperation was removed and no shared task or objective was devised as a replacement. Under such circumstances, the two strongest world powers, with a 30-year background of mutual suspicion and hostility, moved toward conflict.

4. The Bomb as a Source of Conflict

At Hiroshima and Nagasaki, the USSR and the rest of the world witnessed the devastating, unprecedented power of America's atomic bomb. This weapon had been and, following Japan's surrender, remained America's powerful secret that was not to be shared with any nation other than Great Britain. The threatening implications of America's atomic monopoly were not lost on the Kremlin leaders. Part of the Soviet reaction to this striking weapons imbalance was to sponsor a crash program to develop their own atomic bomb which they succeeded in doing by 1949. The arms race, which assumed such vast dimensions in subsequent years, began in 1945–46 and injected new suspicions and tensions into American-Soviet relations.

5. The Personality of President Truman

President Truman not only lacked President Roosevelt's determination to avoid a serious conflict with Premier Stalin, but also seemed to derive a sense of personal pride and satisfaction through engagement in conflict. President Truman's writings and speeches suggest that he was able to fulfill some sense of his own responsibility as President if he were able to "lay it on the line with Moscow." [15]

It is interesting to speculate about why President Truman so quickly came to see the USSR as the major single threat to American security. Possibly his lack of experience in the area of foreign affairs and the sud-denness with which he was thrust into a position of tremendous responsibility contributed to this reaction. Also, inexperience disposed the President to depend on his closest foreign policy advisers. These men, among whom the most important were Averell Harriman, James Forrestal, James Byrnes, and Henry Stimson, reinforced and probably encouraged the President's perception of threat. Of the Truman administration, Sen. J. William Fulbright has observed:

> Virtually no one in a position of power was receptive to the hypothesis that Soviet truculence reflected weakness rather than strength. . . . Our own policy was formed without the benefit of constructive adversary proceedings. A few brave individuals, like former Vice President Henry Wallace, offered dissenting counsel—and paid dear for it.[16]

Further, for Harry Truman, following Franklin Roosevelt as President was not an easy task from many points of view. Simply from the desire to quickly acquire a Presidential "style," President Truman's personality caused him to lean toward strong pronouncements against Soviet behavior. Such statements, the President could have assumed, would not appear irresponsible, they would not necessitate in-depth diplomatic interaction for which the government was not prepared. Furthermore, it was difficult at the time for anyone to prove that this was the wrong or ill-conceived approach to adopt in contending with the USSR. If the Soviets remained as aggressive as they seemed to the President and his advisers, then the President would appear to be acting responsibly. If, on the other hand, the USSR turned out to be conciliatory, the President could claim that his "hard line" brought this about.

During the first year of his administration, President Truman, in speaking about relations with the USSR, began saying that "force is the only thing the Russians understand," that he was already "tired of babying the

---

[15] For additional examples of the President's attitude toward the USSR, see Truman, *Memoirs*, pp. 50 and 70–71, and the President's letters to Secretary of State Byrnes, *ibid.*, pp. 551–52. Admiral William Leahy, another Truman adviser, described the President's first high-level meeting with Soviet diplomats Molotov and Gromyko at the White House, April 23, 1945. The President, according to Leahy, used language that was "blunt" and "not at all diplomatic." See William D. Leahy, *I Was There* (New York: McGraw-Hill, 1950), pp. 351–52.

[16] J. William Fulbright, "In Thrall to Fear," *New Yorker*, January 8, 1972, p. 42. Published as *The Price of Empire* (New York, Random House Vintage Books, 1972).

Soviets," and that it was necessary to "face Russia with an iron fist and strong language." These Presidential "insights" suggest impatience, temper, a sense of righteousness, and a tendency to be drawn to simplistic, black and white, evaluations of challenging international situations. To the extent that the President gave vent to his combative disposition, relations between the United States and the Soviet Union became more strained.

6. America's Sense of Self Image

While on the individual level President Truman was drawn to expressing a tough line in exchanges with the Soviet Union, it also seemed appropriate to many United States officials that the world's most powerful nation should begin to act in a manner that reflected its strength and authority. To many Americans it was an indication of weakness to maintain a conciliatory attitude while the Soviet Union was behaving in a manner which appeared clearly aggressive. American officials believed that the eyes of the world were watching and taking measure of the United States and that the appropriate way to behave in order to conform with the requirements of greatness was to stand up to the Russians. Behind America's concern with appearance was a marked sense of uncertainty due to limited experience in matters of international politics. Inexperience and a preoccupation with appearance seemed to dispose America to adopt a manner of outspoken assurance, which further complicated the already strained relations with the USSR.

American officials also felt rebuffed by the USSR. They believed the United States had gone "more than halfway" in an effort to get along with the USSR. In fact, as has been indicated, in early 1945 a number of the highest American officials believed that future relations with the Soviet Union could be characterized by the shared pursuit of common goals. But when the USSR "suddenly" appeared hostile and difficult, this suggested that the Soviet Union had objectives that did not include cooperation with the United States. It seemed almost humiliating for the United States to pursue a conciliatory course of action when the USSR was unresponsive.

The Reciprocal Character of Conflict

For the hostility that characterized the Cold War to develop, it was not sufficient for the United States to feel threatened. The other side of the conflict equation also had to be activated. This occurred as the Soviet Union began to reinvigorate its ideologic and nationalistic perception of the West as an aggressive threat. As with the United States and its assessment of the USSR, the Soviet Union had a set of historical experiences with the West on which to base an updated interpretation of the expansionist inclinations of capitalist society. With regard to the past, there was (1) the limited Allied intervention (including American forces) into western and eastern USSR immediately following the Bolshevik Revolution; (2) the interwar years when the West, especially France, attempted to form a *cordon sanitaire* (a pre-World War II version of post-World War II containment) to keep the West immune from the spread of communism; (3) the failure of Britain and France to join the USSR in an effort to resist the rise of Hitler (This, with the Munich Treaty of 1938, lent credibility to Soviet suspicions that Britain and France, with the tacit support of the United States, would encourage Germany to attack the USSR.) (4) the refusal of the United States to grant diplomatic recognition to the USSR until 1933, 16 years after the establishment of the Bolshevik government; and (5) the West's questionable motives during the war years of 1942 and 1943 for its delay in opening the second front in France, thereby relieving the Soviet forces in their siege against the Germans.

It is possible that, following the defeat of Germany, Soviet leaders noted America's reactions to Soviet efforts to develop spheres of influence west and south of its borders and felt once again the threatening implications of capitalist encirclement.. The circular character of Soviet reactions to America's responses to Soviet actions contributed the early dynamic force to the Cold War. It was not just what the USSR did that set off the Cold War, as is frequently suggested; it was how American officials chose to interpret Soviet actions, and how America acted on its perceptions, that prompted a Soviet response—actions and reactions generating the dynamic abrasiveness of the Cold War.[17]

Although it is not possible to assign a precise date to the beginning of the Cold War, by the time of Prime Minister Winston Churchill's "Iron Curtain" speech in March 1946, at Fulton, Missouri, official United States attitudes toward the Soviet Union had become fairly well defined. The fact that the President shared the speaker's platform with Prime Minister Churchill during the "Iron Curtain" speech suggested agreement with the view that Soviet aggression had created an iron curtain that separated Eastern from Western Europe and that Great Britain and the United States, in the face of a divided Europe, should create a free world "fraternal association," promote French reconciliation with Germany, and support European political integration.[18] Both President Truman and Prime Minister Churchill saw the Soviet Union as the challenge to the

---

[17] For an elaboration and application of the concept of the reciprocal nature of conflict within the context of the Cold War, see the following works by three outstanding contributors to the revisionist interpretation of American foreign policy: D.F. Fleming, *The Cold War and Its Origins*, (2 vols.; New York: Doubleday, 1961); William A. Williams, *The Tragedy of American Diplomacy* (Cleveland: World, 1959); and David Horowitz, *The Free World Colossus*, (New York: Hill and Wang, 1965).

[18] It is probable that President Truman knew beforehand what Prime Minister Churchill intended to say in his Fulton speech. Secretary of State Byrnes had reviewed

prospect for world peace that England and the United States had worked to achieve.

Limited Availability of Resources

It is clear that by early 1946, against the backdrop of threats described above, both President Truman and Prime Minister Churchill perceived a deepening danger to world peace. President Truman and his advisers were unequivocal in their view that Soviet aggression had to be countered. Once this conclusion was reached, however, it was necessary to take stock of the resources that could be used to contend with Soviet aggression. It was immediately apparent that available resources were negligible.

First of all, because of the nation's isolationist background, there was only limited experience from which to draw as America emerged from the war and found itself immediately involved in world affairs. America had always refrained from sustained involvement in international politics. Now, as a consequence, inexperience made it difficult to determine the most appropriate course of action to pursue. In addition to the lack of extended experience in international politics, there existed within the government in 1945 very little institutional support for foreign policy decision making. The Department of State consisted of 3,600 employees, approximately one seventh its present size. The experience of its limited foreign service staff was largely confined to extending assistance and protection to American citizens in their private or business contacts with foreign nationals. The regional research and intelligence functions performed by the State Department during the initial postwar years were severely restricted. For example, one might assume that in 1947, with the President regarding the USSR as the sole threat to international peace, the Department of State would have assembled a depository of information concerning the economic, political, social, and military characteristics of the Soviet Union in order to anticipate probable Soviet courses of action and thus lend foreign policy assistance to the President. Actually, at that time there were only three or four State Department employees who could be termed "Soviet specialists." This number was to increase tenfold by the end of the Kennedy administration.

A second limitation was the lack of military resources. Official pronouncements suggested that the USSR be dealt with "from a position of strength," but in the two years from 1945 to 1947, the United States had allowed its armed forces to decline from a wartime peak of 12 million men to a low of 1.4 million. The fiscal years of 1947 and 1948 were marked by

its contents with the President before the President made the trip with Churchill to Missouri. The President introduced Churchill with, "I know he will say something constructive." See Alfred Steinberg, *The Man from Missouri* (New York; G. P. Putnam, 1962) p. 280, and Robert H. Ferrell (ed), *The American Secretaries of State and Their Diplomacy* (New York: Cooper Square Publishers, 1962), vol. 14, p. 203.

general budget cuts, including cuts in military spending.[19] Military leaders themselves had not yet geared their thinking to the threat already perceived by civilian officials. Most military officers, as the war ended, anticipated with some eagerness a return to the life of the prewar peacetime army, a life in which military decision making was clearly subordinate to the nation's civilian leadership and the military were called upon to participate in policy circles only in the event of a national security crisis. Thus, given the limited capabilities of America's military forces in 1947, and the general disposition of career servicemen to return to the limited and circumscribed mission of prewar years, the postwar military establishment offered little to calm the government's growing anxiety over the Soviet threat.

A third factor that tended to limit the defensive resources available to the government was the postwar domestic orientation that characterized the mood of most of the American people. Following the sacrifices of the war, most Americans were anxious to return to the freedom and comforts of the prewar period. There was a nostalgic longing for the relative ease of the prewar years. Given the mood of the nation in 1947, it would probably have been politically disastrous for the President, in the face of the oncoming 1948 elections, to reinitiate the draft in order to bolster the size of the armed forces. At this time the American people had no appreciation of the implications of standing up to the Russians with force. What this meant in terms of men, money, and equipment was as vague to them as it was to most officials within the government. What was also vague was the nature of the Soviet threat. It was to take the Communist victory in Czechoslovakia and the Soviet blockade of Berlin in 1948, and the outbreak of the Korean War in 1950, to bring the intensity of the Cold War to the consciousness of the American people.

Another deficiency in American resources during the first postwar years was the limited policy direction available to government officials. Prewar foreign policy had been applicable to a different set of perceptions, a different set of obligations, a different way of life, and a different world. The day-to-day demands the government faced following the war made it difficult for officials to focus on the task of establishing longer range policy directions. In addition, as is usually the case in policy planning, efforts to develop useful policies were hampered by the lack of a clear perception of future challenges. Having little experience with or faith in the utility of planning, officials felt confronted with contingencies that seemed too varied to be usefully accommodated by policy.

By the end of 1946, the situation confronted by the United States reduced itself to two basic yet incompatible conditions. One was the grow-

---

[19] Laurence I. Radway, *The Liberal Democracy in World Affairs: Foreign Policy and National Defense* (Atlanta: Scott, Foresman, and Co., 1969), p. 31. For a lucid, concise description of the early postwar period, see Louis J. Halle, *The Cold War as History* (New York: Harper and Row, 1967), especially Chapter 11.

ing preoccupation with an aggressive and powerful USSR, a preoccupation based on a concern for the future of the West and, in particular, the security of the United States. For the United States, this concern represented a new and unprecedented sense of responsibility. In conflict with this preoccupation with a sense of threat was the realization that available resources were extremely limited. There was a striking, and from the United States' point of view, alarming imbalance between perceived national security requirements and available resources. However, despite inexperience, limited trained manpower, lack of clear policy directives, and a largely disinterested population, there was one stunning resource available to the United States. America held a monopoly on the atomic bomb.

The Bomb

America's development of the atomic bomb was probably the most important single event to affect postwar international relations. The bomb immediately exerted a central influence on both the defining and the implementing of American foreign policy. Because of its enormous significance, subsequent chapters will extend the few introductory comments made at this point.

In 1939 American scientists had discussed the military application of atomic energy with United States government officials.[20] The government had also been made aware of the fact that the United States was in competition with Germany to become the first nation to realize the military potential of atomic energy. This led to the establishment of the Manhattan Project, the objectives of which were to produce an atomic bomb that could be carried by aircraft, and to do this before Germany achieved the same goal. Two of the dominant characteristics of the 1939–45 American effort to develop the bomb were, first, the extreme secrecy with which the effort was conducted until the time of the first test of an actual bomb on July 16, 1945; second, the fact that at no time up to 1945 was it suggested by a responsible government official that atomic energy not be used in the war.[21] This question provoked serious debate after 1945, but not before.

On April 25, 1945, President Truman was briefed on the existence of the effort to develop an atomic bomb. He immediately assigned Secretary

---

[20] For an excellent discussion of this subject, see Louis Morton, "The Decision to Use the Atomic Bomb," *Foreign Affairs,* January 1957, pp. 334–53.

[21] For example, Prime Minister Churchill mentioned that one of the appeals of the bomb was to end the war quickly and thus avoid the need for Russian intervention. ". . . There never was a moment's discussion as to whether the atomic bomb should be used or not. To avert a vast, indefinite butchery, to bring the war to an end, to give peace to the world, to lay healing hands upon its tortured peoples by a manifestation of overwhelming power at the cost of a few explosions, seemed, after all our toils and perils, a miracle of deliverance." Winston S. Churchill, *Triumph and Tragedy* (New York: Houghton-Mifflin Co., 1953), p. 639.

of War Henry Stimson to the chairmanship of a committee to study the implications of an atomic weapons capability. On June 1, 1945, President Truman received the results of this study in which the authors unanimously recommended that (1) the bomb should be used against Japan as soon as possible, and (2) it should be dropped on Japan without warning.[22] The President's advisers, by mid-June, generally agreed with these two recommendations. The unified position of the President's advisers was based on the following considerations.

1. Military Considerations

Military considerations were the primary motivation in the development of the atomic bomb and its use against Japan. President Truman, as was true of President Roosevelt, was determined to use whatever resources were available to defeat the Axis powers as rapidly as possible. American military estimates, as mentioned above, had indicated eight months before the bomb was tested that it would require 18 months of combat after the defeat of Germany to bring about the surrender of Japan. In addition, military officials estimated that there would be one million allied casualties as a consequence of the invasion of the Japanese islands. American thinking was also affected by the impression of the inhuman capacity of the Japanese to fight when all odds were against them (Japanese soldiers simply did not surrender). In the light of these considerations, the prospect of having access to a weapon of unprecedented power was particularly appealing since it could be instrumental in terminating the war against Japan in far less time and with a much reduced casualty rate than had been predicted by military officials. Following six years of war, few government officials were expected to question the means by which an end to the fighting might be brought about.

2. Political Considerations

While political considerations played a definite role in the decision to use the bomb, it is difficult to determine the appropriate influence to

---

[22] Secretary Stimson's committee of eight government officials and scientists were assisted by a separate group of scientists, four of whom had assisted in the development of the atomic bomb. President Truman later wrote that the Stimson Committee recommended that the bomb be used against the enemy as soon as possible, that this action be taken without "specific warning," and that it should be used against a target "that would clearly show its devastating strength." The committee did not believe that a preattack "technical demonstration," such as detonation over an uninhabited area, would cause the Japanese to surrender and saw "no acceptable alternative to direct military use." President Truman admitted in *Memoirs* that he personally "regarded the bomb as a military weapon and never had any doubt that it should be used." This view was supported by the President's military advisers and Prime Minister Churchill. (Truman, *Memoirs*, p. 419.)

ascribe to nonmilitary motivations. It has been suggested, for example, that President Truman was eager to defeat Japan before the Soviet Union could fulfill its Yalta pledge to enter the war 90 days after the defeat of Germany, or as it turned out, on the 8th of August.[23] Winning the war in the Pacific without Soviet participation would put the United States in a better negotiating position with regard to territorial concessions to the USSR in Asia. It has also been suggested that, in addition to the bomb's importance in the defeat of Japan, some American officials thought it should be dropped to "make Russia more manageable in Europe."[24] Generally, political considerations related to the bomb have to do with the diplomatic advantage the United States might enjoy over the USSR as a consequence of this unique military capability. If, as President Truman has been quoted as saying, the Soviets only respect force, the atomic bomb could yield some very impressive political advantages for the United States.

Four Elements of Postwar Policy

During the last years of the 1940s American foreign policy assumed some of the basic characteristics that would persist for the following quarter century. Within a five-year period, from 1945 to 1950, there emerged the basic elements of a foreign policy which, nearly 25 years later, remained fundamentally intact.

The year 1947 has special significance as the year when the American public and the world were made aware of three of the basic new elements of American foreign policy, i.e., the Truman Doctrine, the Marshall Plan, and the theory of containment. In April 1949, the signing of the North Atlantic Treaty establishing the North Atlantic Treaty Organization completed the package. All four elements of American foreign policy were conceived and designed in an effort to enable the United States to deal more effectively with the Soviet Union. Attention is drawn to this point because it indicates that, immediately following the war, the United States

---

[23] Norman Cousins and Thomas K. Finletter, "A Beginning for Sanity," *Saturday Review,* June 15, 1946, pp. 5–9, 38–40. This thesis is supported by Secretary Forrestal's quoting Secretary Byrnes statement on July 28, 1945, that he was anxious to defeat Japan before the Russians could attack.

[24] Morton, "Decision to Use Atomic Bomb," p. 347. Morton states, ". . . some responsible officials feared the political consequences of Soviet intervention and hoped that ultimately it would prove unnecessary. This feeling may unconsciously have made the atom bomb solution more attractive than it might otherwise have been. Some officials may have believed, too, that the bomb could be used as a powerful deterrent in Soviet expansion in Europe, where the Red tide had successively engulfed Rumania, Bulgaria, Jugoslavia, Czechoslovakia, and Hungary. In an interview with three of the top scientists in the Manhattan Project early in June [1945], Mr. Byrnes did not, according to Leo Szilard, argue that the bomb was needed to defeat Japan, but rather that it should be dropped to 'make Russia more manageable in Europe.'"

became locked into a way of viewing the world that had the USSR as its continuing central preoccupation.

1. The Truman Doctrine [25]

Following strong United States pronouncements against Soviet action in Turkey and Iran, Soviet pressure subsided. However, Soviet support for Communist insurrectionist activity in Greece continued and the United States began to believe that, in this instance, the USSR was pursuing a different, less direct approach toward achieving expanded influence in the Middle East. If Greece were to fall to communism, the United States theory ran, Turkey and Iran would soon fall to Soviet control and, "inevitably" the entire eastern Mediterranean would be sealed behind Communist lines. In addition, the fall of Greece would establish two Communist nations (Greece and Yugoslavia) to the east of Italy, which could lend strong support to the Italian Communist party, the largest in Western Europe. If Italy were to become a Communist nation, France, with the second largest Communist party in Western Europe, could, it was theorized, easily follow. Communism in Greece was thus viewed as a threat to the security of Western Europe. Consistent with this line of reasoning, if Western Europe were threatened, the survival of the United States would be in danger.

On March 12, 1947, President Truman appeared before a joint session of Congress. In terms of the evolving postwar character of American foreign policy, this Presidential speech was of considerable importance because, for America, it constituted a radical departure from past practices and because it established what was to become a consistent method whereby America attempted to contend with communism in the world. President Truman, after describing Communist efforts to gain political influence in Greece, said that the United States must help free people to maintain their political institutions when these institutions were threatened by aggressive attempts to eradicate freedom and impose totalitarianism.[26] Communism in Greece, since it undermined the basis for international peace, caused the security of the United States to be threatened.[27] This being the case, President Truman continued, it must be the policy of the United States to support free people, anywhere and at any time, to help them resist subjugation by armed minorities within their

---

[25] See Appendix A for the complete transcript of the Truman Doctrine.

[26] One month before delivering this speech, President Truman received a note from the British government informing him that drastic economic conditions in England made it necessary for Great Britain to withdraw all support from Greece by the end of March 1947.

[27] It is interesting to note that in 1947 the rationale for a way of viewing the Communist threat was developed that persisted through more than two decades and reappeared, fundamentally intact, in the guise of the "Domino Theory," the theoretical justification for American involvement in Vietnam. See further discussion of this point in Chapter 7.

countries or by external aggressors. The United States must help make it possible for free people to determine their own future in their own way. The President stated that American assistance should be primarily financial to promote economic stability and free political processes. Finally, the President requested that Congress appropriate $400 million for economic aid and military supplies for Greece and Turkey. The President stressed the fact that he did not want to intervene in Greece with American troops, but he urged that American civilian and military personnel be dispatched to assist with economic reconstruction and military training.

The importance of the Truman Doctrine to American foreign policy must not be minimized. First, it constituted an expansionist action on the part of the United States. America had never before proclaimed that it had a national interest in domestic developments within Middle East nations. Second, the Truman Doctrine supported an interventionist position. It stated that the United States, to promote its own national security, *should* intervene in the internal affairs of Greece. Proclaiming the legitimacy of intervention was a striking deviation from the constraints imposed by the Monroe Doctrine. Third, it initiated the beginning of economic and military aid to nations resisting Communist aggression. It suggested to the world that the United States was willing to use its resources to help build or maintain within another nation a form of government that America found acceptable. Fourth, by stressing the view that American security was threatened by political developments in Greece, it initiated the practice of attempting to "scare the hell out of the country," meaning the American people, to gain Congressional support for foreign policy actions.[28] Beginning with the Truman Doctrine, the threat of communism was the device that served this purpose. Fifth, the Truman Doctrine represented a unilateral action taken by the United States in an attempt to promote international stability. This approach to the maintenance of international order was conceived, announced, and implemented outside the United Nations, the international organization for world peace to which the United States had pledged its support but which, by this unilateral act, the President chose to ignore. As became almost immediately evident, the Truman Doctrine did not stand as the single instance in which the United States acted outside of the United Nations in response to perceived threats to its own and free-world security. Sixth, the Truman Doctrine set forth themes justifying American foreign involvement that have been used by American officials from 1947 to the present. It is a striking aspect of the Truman Doctrine that its justifications for American intervention in foreign areas were repeated by Presidents from Truman

---

[28] It was reported that Sen. Arthur Vandenburg (Republican, Michigan) told President Truman that he would have to "scare the hell out of the country" in order to get Congress to provide aid to Greece and Turkey. As it turned out, following Truman's speech, it took only two months for Congress to perceive the threatening implications of Communist aggression and to appropriate funds.

through the most recent administrations of Presidents Johnson and Nixon. Figure 1, *A Quarter Century of Policy Consistency*, indicates the persistence of the thematic justification for America's intervention in foreign areas.

2. The Marshall Plan

On June 5, 1947, at the commencement exercises at Harvard University, Secretary of State George Marshall announced America's willingness

FIGURE 1

A Quarter Century of Policy Consistency

(all quotations from the *United States Department of State Bulletin*)

Recurring Justification for American Foreign Involvement	President Truman	President Johnson	President Nixon
To resist Communist aggression	"The very existence of the Greek state is threatened by the terrorist activities of several thousand armed men, led by Communists." (March 23, 1947)— Text of Truman Doctrine	"We have been engaged in a struggle in Southeast Asia to stop the onrushing tide of Communist aggression." (April 8, 1968)	America has sacrificed for "the right of 18 million people in a faraway land to avoid the imposition of Communist rule against their will." (May 11, 1970)
To create a chance for democracy	"Greece must have assistance if it is to become a self-supporting and self-respecting democracy" and "We must assist free peoples to work out their own destinies in their own way." (March 23, 1947)	"The people of South Vietnam will be given the chance to work out their own destiny in their own way." (July 25, 1966)	"We seek the opportunity for the South Vietnamese people to determine their own political future without outside interference" and to "seek their own destiny." (March 9, 1970)
In response to request for assistance	"The United States has received from the Greek Government an urgent appeal for financial and economic assistance." (March 23, 1947)	"A friendly nation (South Vietnam) has asked us for help against the Communist aggression." (January 25, 1965)	"In response to the request of the Government of South Vietnam, President Eisenhower sent economic and military equipment." "Cambodia has sent out a call to the United States . . . for assistance." (November 24, 1969, and May 18, 1970)

FIGURE 1—(Continued)

Recurring Justification for American Foreign Involvement	President Truman	President Johnson	President Nixon
To provide economic and military aid for security	"Our help should be primarily through economic and financial aid which is essential to economic stability and orderly political processes" and "One of the primary objectives of the foreign policy of the United States is the creation of conditions in which we and other nations will be able to work out a way of life free from coercion." (March 23, 1947)	The $350 million planned for Vietnam is "indispensable to military success, economic stability, and continued political progress. (March 6, 1967) [The United States' goal in South Vietnam is to make it] "possible for them to choose their own destinies without coercion." (January 30, 1967) "We will use our strength to block aggression when our security is threatened." (December 25, 1967)	"There is no goal to which this nation is more dedicated . . . than to build a new structure of peace where every nation can be free and independent with no fear of foreign domination." (October 26, 1970)
To preserve peace and freedom throughout the world	"The free peoples of the world look to us for support in maintaining their freedoms. If we falter in our leadership, we may endanger the peace of the world— and we shall certainly endanger the welfare of our own Nation" and "No other nation is willing and able to provide the necessary support." (March 23, 1947)	"Since World War II, America has been found wherever freedom was under attack or wherever world peace was threatened . . . because at one time no other nation could do it." (August 31, 1964)	"We were left in 1945 as the one nation with sufficient strength to contain the new threats of aggression" and "Any hope the world has for the survival of peace and freedom will be determined by whether the American people have the moral stamina and the courage to meet the challenge of free-world leadership." (October 6, 1969, and November 24, 1969)

to contribute significantly to the rebuilding of war-ravaged Europe.[29] England's industrial sources of income had been brought to a near standstill by the war, and thus there was no way for Britain to pay for imports

[29] Undersecretary of State Dean Acheson briefed the British on the contents of the Marshall Plan on June 4. The plan was immediately supported by British and French Foreign Ministers Bevin and Bidault.

of food and raw materials. Germany and France were economically depressed, both economies having been severely damaged by the war. Desperate economic needs were widespread throughout Europe, and yet there were no resources to pay for the materials and equipment required. Under the Marshall Plan, European nations were invited to specify their economic requirements for recovery. A list of requirements would be presented to the United States with a plan for utilizing American economic aid in order to resolve national economic problems. The Organization for European Economic Cooperation (OEEC) represented the Marshall Plan participants collectively and helped in drawing up plans for the effective utilization of American economic assistance to meet regional needs.[30]

There were aspects of the Marshall Plan to which attention should be drawn because of a similarity to aspects of the Truman Doctrine. First, the central motivating factor once again for the genesis of the Marshall Plan was the USSR. The United States believed that the security of Europe, i.e., the ability of Europe to resist Communism, was dependent on its rapid economic recovery. American officials saw a depressed, dislocated European economy as a vacuum into which an aggressive Soviet Union could force its influence. The Marshall Plan was to provide a means for countering Soviet efforts to extend still further their influence in Europe. Also, the security of a foreign area, this time Europe, was again equated with the security of the United States. Just as the Truman Doctrine broke with the Monroe Doctrine, so did the Marshall Plan. Finally, as the Truman Doctrine professed to support the maintenance of representative (Western) political institutions in Greece, the Marshall Plan was designed to promote economic integration and cooperation among the nations of Europe. It was hoped that America's past domestic economic experience could be a model for Europe's future development. Through economic integration, political integration might develop, and cooperation, rather than violent international conflict, could begin to characterize the future relations among European nations. Perhaps, some Americans theorized, European nations might ultimately establish a set of political relationships that resembled America's federal system.[31]

In order to establish the OEEC, a conference of European nations (France, Great Britain, the USSR) and the United States convened in

---

[30] The successor to the OEEC was the 23-nation Organization for Economic Cooperation and Development (OECD) with responsibilities for international monetary and trade cooperation.

[31] The idea of promoting economic unity in Europe through the Marshall Plan was expressed by William L. Clayton, Undersecretary of State for Economic Affairs, "Europe cannot recover from this war and again become independent if her economy continues to be divided into many small watertight compartments as it is today." Quoted by Max Beloff, *The United States and the Unity of Europe* (Vintage Books, 1963) p. 28.

Paris on June 27, 1947. The USSR was invited to participate because the United States believed that the Western European nations would not have agreed to join the Marshall Plan if, by excluding the USSR, overt acknowledgment were given to the existence of an East-West split. Soviet Foreign Minister Molotov came to the Paris meeting, only to withdraw on July 2.[32] Three considerations seem to have caused the USSR to decide against participation: (1) it did not wish to make statistical data available to the West concerning Soviet economic conditions, (2) the USSR believed that through participation in the American-supported Marshall Plan it would thereby extend to the United States some degree of influence over Soviet economic planning, and (3) the USSR did not believe it was in its own national interest to participate in a program that was established to strengthen the economic stability of Western European capitalist states.

President Truman signed the Economic Cooperation Act on April 3, 1948. The OEEC (formed on April 16) requested from Congress $22 billion to be administered by the OEEC for European economic recovery over a period of four years. Congress reduced this amount and appropriated $17 billion to be spent over four years, from late 1948 to 1952.[33] As it turned out, $12.5 billion was spent during this period, with Great Britain, Ireland, Sweden, and Portugal indicating by mid-1951 that they no longer required economic assistance through the OEEC.

3. The Theory of Containment [34]

Without a conceptual context, the various elements that comprise a foreign policy achieve no clear operational relationship. The theoretical basis for American foreign policy in the late '40s was the theory of containment. Drawn by Ambassador George F. Kennan from his official and scholarly exposure to the Soviet Union, this theory provided the rationale and objectives for the Truman Doctrine, the Marshall Plan, and two years later the North Atlantic Treaty Organization.[35] It lent to these programs their long-range perspective and gave to United States officials a set of

---

[32] Foreign Minister Molotov, at a June 27 meeting in Paris, stated that the USSR could not participate in the OEEC because such a program would be a violation of national sovereignty. An awkward situation arose when Czechoslovakia, after it accepted a July 4, 1947 invitation to participate, was then forced by the USSR to withdraw.

[33] The 16 participating European nations were Great Britain, France, Austria, Belgium, Denmark, Greece, Iceland, Ireland, Italy, Luxembourg, Netherlands, Norway, Portugal, Sweden, Switzerland, and Turkey.

[34] See Appendix B for the complete text of George F. Kennan, "The Sources of Soviet Conduct" *Foreign Affairs*, July 1947, pp. 566–82.

[35] Professor William A. Williams suggests that President Truman's vigorous assertion of America's worldwide opposition to communism represented the incorporation of Kennan's containment thesis into the Truman Doctrine speech of March 12, 1947.

precepts to view the relationship of the Soviet Union and the Western world.

The theory of containment was first made public in an article entitled "The Sources of Soviet Conduct," the first third of which was devoted to a discussion of the 30-year historical background of the USSR.[36] Ambassador Kennan began his article with the identification of four key assumptions underlying Communist thought: (1) man's character is determined by the economic process by which goods are produced and exchanged, (2) capitalism exploits the working class, (3) capitalism contains the seeds of its own destruction and will disappear through the revolutionary transfer of power to the workers, and (4) capitalism's final desperate gasp will assume the form of imperialism which, in turn, will generate war and other revolutions. The need for revolution, Kennan stated, is stressed by Communist ideologists, stressed to such an extent that there is no attention given to the systematic development of a socialist program for the postrevolutionary period, except for the "nationalization of industry and the expropriation of large private capital holdings . . ."

Kennan pointed out that since 1917 the Bolshevik regime had worked to secure itself against antagonistic forces at home and abroad, the external threat being the antagonistic system of capitalism. This line of thought, Kennan stated, assumed particular relevance to Soviet and American foreign policies, since it led to the concept of capitalist encirclement, the persistent fear of capitalist intervention, and the requirement for constant police vigilance to thwart agents of capitalist aggression. Thus, in 1947, Kennan saw the structure of Stalinist Russia as committed to warding off the forces of aggressive capitalism surrounding the USSR. Kennan made two interesting observations related to the Soviet view of themselves under siege. First, he believed that the official Soviet perception of the capitalist menace provided a useful justification of the oppressive domestic dictatorial system. Second, he noted the cause and effect relationship between Soviet officials' seeing all non-Communist governments as enemies and the development of antagonistic attitudes toward the USSR on the part of non-Communist nations, especially the United States. This antagonistic view toward the West provoked a set of responses from Western nations that substantiated the original Soviet pronouncements.

Next, Kennan described two conditions that were basic to the 1947 Soviet outlook. These were "innate antagonisms between capitalism and socialism," and the Kremlin's privileged status of infallibility. Being infallible, the USSR could resort to numerous and varied tactics in its effort to bring down capitalism, with all of these tactical maneuvers supported by unquestioning adherents of the party line. At this point in his essay

---

[36] Kennan, "The Sources of Soviet Conduct."

Kennan expressed his containment thesis, i.e., "the main element of any United States policy toward the Soviet Union must be that of a long-term, patient but firm and vigilant containment of Russian expansive tendencies."

Attention should be drawn to two observations set forth by Kennan. First, he referred to the Soviet sense of time, or disregard for time, on at least four occasions in his article. The Soviets were in no hurry, they had no timetable, no feeling that their objectives must be achieved by some specific date. Since they believed that they would inevitably triumph over capitalism, they could afford to wait. The commitment of the USSR to the patient and persistent pursuit of its expansionist objectives must be countered by the United States, Kennan suggested, with innovative, long-range policies, backed by the appropriate application of human and material resources. United States policy must not be sporadic, reactive, fluctuating, or based on "the momentary whims of democratic opinion."

Kennan's second observation was more of a warning and was related to the Kremlin's concern for international prestige. Because of this it was possible that the United States might, through "tactless and threatening gestures," force the USSR into a position from which Soviet officials would find it difficult to back down. Kennan advised that ". . . demands on Russian policy should be put forward in such a manner as to leave the way open for a compliance not too detrimental to Russian prestige." [37]

If United States policy remained sensitive to shifting and persistent Soviet maneuvers and took corresponding actions to contain Soviet aggression, what then? Was this to be the continuing, permanent shape of American foreign policy for decades into the future? Kennan said no. As a result of being contained, tensions between the dictatorship of the proletariat and the workers would become more intense and would force the Soviet leadership to make social, political, and economic concessions. Stresses created by the war, severe shortages of consumer goods, rigid government controls, and demands imposed on all segments of the labor force for increased production had already given rise to a sense of despair which would impair the USSR's ability to achieve a strong, balanced economy. In fact, Kennan suggested that Soviet society, rather than a capitalist society, contained the seeds of its own destruction.

Containment implied more than merely keeping the USSR from extending its political control. The policy of containment was viewed by Kennan as having a positive dimension. By making information available to Soviet citizens concerning American life, values, and standard of living,

---

[37] In the time since Kennan wrote these words, the United States has been engaged in four military confrontations with Communist forces (Berlin, Korea, Cuba, and Vietnam). Of these four crises, it was probably during the 1962 Cuban missile crisis that the most literal application of this advice was made. See the discussion of decision-making options in Ellie Abel, *The Missile Crisis* (New York: Bantam Books, 1966).

the people of the USSR would be able to appreciate the vitality and appeal of America. This awareness would not only challenge Soviet statements concerning the pending demise of capitalism, but would also make the capitalistic world appear more promising and attractive than its Communist competitor. Beyond this, the containment of communism would create such frustrations within Soviet society that the Soviet political system would be forced to modify its arbitrary police controls and make some concessions to popular demands.

Given the USSR's commitment to the eventual triumph of communism in the world, Kennan believed that American interests required that communism be contained. However, he never indicated *how* to contain communism or what the specific consequences of containment would be. Finally, a minor observation. It seems ironic that Kennan, in the last sentence of his essay, stated that Providence had given the American people the challenge of the Kremlin which required them to accept "the responsibilities of the moral and political leadership *that history plainly intended them to bear*" (emphasis added). This statement had an odd ring to it. It embodies a deterministic point of view that resembled the tone of inevitability permeating the political theory that Kennan urged America to contain.[38]

W. Averell Harriman, Ambassador to the Soviet Union from 1943–46 and close adviser to President Truman, supported Kennan's view of the USSR and shared his conviction that the Soviet Union had to be regarded as a rival power in the postwar world. Kennan's containment thesis was based on a conviction that the United States must "regard the Soviet Union as a rival, not a partner in the political arena," and that the United States could not expect "to enjoy political intimacy with the Soviet regime." [39] Ambassador Harriman, reflecting Kennan's point of view, consistently advised President Truman that in relations with the USSR, there could be no appeal to common purposes. He also advised the President that "certain elements around Stalin misinterpreted our generosity and our desire to cooperate as an indication of softness," and said that in order to disabuse them of this impression the President should "stand firm." [40] The President and Ambassador Harriman shared points of view that neatly accommodated the theory of containment. Secretary of State James Byrnes was slightly less convinced of the diplomatic intransigence of the

---

[38] For some of Ambassador Kennan's "second thoughts" concerning the containment doctrine, see discussion in Chapter 7.

[39] Walter Lippman, *The Cold War: A Study in U.S. Foreign Policy* (New York: Harper and Bros., 1947), p. 60. Lippman discussed Kennan's disbelief in the possibility of a settlement of the issues raised by the Cold War. Lippman suggested that rather than containment, diplomacy could function in its traditional capacity of conducting relations among rival powers which did not enjoy political intimacy or respond to common purposes.

[40] Truman, *Memoirs*, p. 70.

USSR. He advocated a "policy of firmness and patience," believing that this would cause Soviet leaders to see the pointlessness of their rigidity and agree to compromise. Relatively minor shades of difference in opinion concerning how to deal with the USSR were evident in the thinking of Truman, Harriman, and Byrnes, but there was enough consistency of thought among them to have led Kennan to anticipate a warm responsiveness to his theory of containment.

The clearest alternative to the theory of containment expressed from within the government at this time was voiced by Secretary of Commerce Henry A. Wallace. Wallace, it has already been suggested, was practically alone among top-rank American political figures in seriously questioning the President's "get tough with Russia" policy. During the summer of 1946 Secretary Wallace began to suggest meetings with Soviet officials to develop specific plans for improving American-Soviet relations. On September 12, 1946, Wallace delivered a speech at Madison Square Garden in New York in which he stated that the United States had no legitimate concern in the political affairs of Eastern Europe, just as the USSR had no legitimate concern with the political affairs of Latin America, Western Europe, and the United States. United States officials, Wallace advised, should stop listening to those who advised that the United States and the USSR could not get along.[41]

The Wallace position and the support he was able to elicit within the nation had no significant impact on the acceptance of the theory of containment within the Truman administration. By 1948, it was generally believed in Washington that the Soviet Union was committed to the pursuit of supremacy in international politics. If this was to be prevented and if a reasonably equitable balance of power was to be maintained in East-West relations, it was up to the United States to see that it was done. Some students of American foreign policy have suggested that the theory of containment embodied some striking reversals of traditional American policies in that isolationism was exchanged for extensive international involvement.[42] However, a different interpretation seems feasible. America's immediate postwar response to the challenge of international involvement remained affected by the nation's isolationist background. This isolationist heritage continued to impress itself on the thinking of American officials. The theory of containment, the Truman Doctrine, and the Marshall Plan suggest that America had not yet made a full, long-term commitment to international politics and was reluctant to do so. American officials seem to have believed that if communism were contained for

---

[41] This speech was cleared by the President but the President's response following its delivery in New York led to Wallace's resignation and his determination to try for the Presidency in 1948.

[42] See, for example, Michael H. Armacost, *The Foreign Relations of the United States* (Belmont, Calif.: Dickenson Publishing Co., 1969), p. 57.

several years, its aggressive character would soften. European nations, with short-term assistance from the United States, could become economically stable and more politically unified. The American hope was that these actions, rather than leading to sustained government involvement abroad, would create conditions that would permit the expansion of American business but allow the government to revert to a more passive international role.

4. The North Atlantic Treaty Organization

If the Marshall Plan was to be effective in containing communism, it required a protective outer shell strong enough to ward off Communist expansion while the economic rebuilding it envisioned could begin to take effect. The conviction that economic recovery required military security grew stronger in American minds as the bitterness between the United States and the Soviet Union came to be expressed with greater sharpness following the commencement of Marshall Plan aid to Europe. Communist activity appeared to increase in France and Italy, the Communist party assumed political control in Czechoslovakia in early 1948, a Communist blockade of West Berlin was imposed in 1948 and 1949, all against the backdrop of Moscow's strident anti-American propaganda.

These events strengthened America's feeling of need for a peacetime military alliance to protect the nations of Europe against Communist aggression. The formal expression of this requirement was the North Atlantic Treaty, signed by the United States in April 1949, with eleven other nations: Canada, Great Britain, France, Italy, the Netherlands, Belgium, Luxembourg, Portugal, Iceland, Denmark, and Norway. With this treaty linking the United States militarily with the nations of Western Europe, the North Atlantic Treaty Organization was created.[43] The membership later expanded to 15 when Greece, Turkey, and West Germany joined.

The heart of the North Atlantic Treaty was Article Five, which stated:

The Parties agree that an armed attack against one or more of them in Europe or North America shall be considered an attack against them all and consequently they agree that, if such an armed attack occurs, each of them . . . will assist the Party or Parties so attacked by taking forthwith, individually and in concert with the other Parties, such action as it deems necessary, including the use of armed force, to restore and maintain the security of the North Atlantic area.

Thus, with America's signing the first peacetime military alliance in its history, Europe became America's first line of defense against the growing

---

[43] In early 1948, France, Great Britain, and the Benelux nations had signed the Brussels Treaty, a joint defense agreement with a Consultative Council and structure for the development of a common defense for Western Europe. The Brussels Treaty provided the basis for what one year later, with American support, was developed into NATO.

threat of communism. Here again was a reflection of the belief that Soviet aggression could be contained if America, operating from a position of strength, demonstrated its determination to stand firm, and if provoked, its willingness to fight. NATO, in effect, represented the basis for the American effort to contain communism by military means.[44] The creation of NATO was also a consistent extension of the expansionist implications of the Truman Doctrine and Marshall Plan in that it committed American forces to military action outside the United States in defense of Western Europe. Following the signing of the NATO treaty, plans for a military assistance program were developed, and after the Senate ratified the treaty in July 1949, President Truman requested nearly $1.5 billion to be sent to treaty members in the form of military aid during the first year of NATO operations.

From 1949 on, America's defense strategy presupposed collaboration and mutual support among the military forces of the United States and the European members of NATO. Although NATO forces were drawn from the combined military establishments of America and Western Europe, they were still numerically inferior to the ground forces available to the Soviet Union. Because of limited military resources, the NATO strategy designed for the defense of Europe was based on the concept that the restricted ground forces available to the West would stand as a "trip wire." Enemy forces moving against Europe would, by activating this trip wire, indicate the seriousness of their aggressive intent. NATO ground forces would defend Europe as long as possible while NATO's atomic weapons capability, provided and controlled by the United States, would be directed against tactical targets in the field and also be employed in a strategic capacity against the source of aggression.

The NATO strategy, the defensive capability of which was necessarily dependent on America's atomic weapons stockpile, offered some reassurance to the European powers as long as the United States possessed a monopoly on atomic weapons. But after 1949, as the USSR began to build its own store of atomic weapons, serious questions began to enter the minds of European statesmen. Would America use its atomic capability to defend Europe against a Soviet attack? Would the United States risk involvement in an atomic war for the sake of European security? The deeper question European nations asked themselves was whether they wanted to be defended by America's atomic weapons at the cost of being incinerated in the process. All of these doubts provided the basis for strains within the NATO alliance during the years following 1949.

---

[44] Ambassador Kennan has suggested that the United States may have made a mistake by including Turkey and Greece (admitted to NATO in 1952) in NATO because this strengthened the Soviet impression of American-sponsored "aggressive encirclement." But, as Kennan indicated, "certain circles within our government" wanted military bases in these two nations and thus their admission was not seriously questioned. See George Kennan, *Memoirs* (Boston: Little, Brown, and Co., 1967), p. 411.

America's Burden

Financially and militarily the United States was disposed to shoulder a burden that it regarded as mandatory if democracy was to be preserved. It is a testimony to the intensity of the sense of threat felt by the President, his advisers, and the Congress that while America's economic resources had never been extensively utilized by the federal government for domestic purposes, they began at this time to be committed, with little official hesitancy or trepidation, for economic and military programs in the war against communism.

In the short space of three years the mood of America had shifted from optimism, self-confidence, and a vision of international cooperation to a feeling of anxious uncertainty, intensified by a deep sense of threat. This shift in mood and the clarity with which a bipolar confrontation was perceived was concisely described by former Secretary of State Dean Acheson:

Many times . . . I have remarked upon our misconceptions of the state of the world around us, both in anticipating postwar conditions and in recognizing what they actually were when we came face to face with them. . . . Only slowly did it dawn upon us that the whole world structure and order that we had inherited from the nineteenth century was gone and that the struggle to replace it would be directed from two bitterly opposed and ideologically irreconcilable power centers.[45]

---

[45] Dean Acheson, *Present at the Creation* (New York: W. W. Norton, 1969), pp. 725–26.

chapter 2

The Developing Military Capability

America, by the end of the 1940s was beset by a sense of threat. Its immediate response was to develop a military capability to contend with this threat. During the 1950s and '60s, in the course of attempting to develop the ability to defend the free world against communism, the military, the managers of America's military resources, came to exercise increasingly greater influence among foreign policy decision-makers. How this came about and some of the characteristics of this influence are the central topics of this chapter. The first question to consider is why the military did not exercise influence in policy circles immediately following the war. This situation changed after American officials came to attach such importance to the atomic bomb and related military capabilities. Because it changed, and because of the extent of the influence of military opinion on policy that resulted from this change, the discussion then considers the subject of military attitudes—how military officers viewed their profession and how they believed national security could be assured in a threatening international environment. Next, the defense organization is described as it was developed to achieve basically two objectives: provide a means of producing the military capabilities that the nation's civilian leadership believed were necessary and, while fulfilling this objective, maintain America's traditional civilian control over the military. Finally, some of the factors are considered that have contributed a military emphasis to American foreign policy during the past quarter century.

It is difficult from the vantage point of today to look back at the

1945–50 period and appreciate the character of America's military organization at that time. Not only was it smaller and less affluent, as has
already been pointed out, but its aspirations stood in striking contrast to
those associated with the military as the Cold War years unfolded. With
the surrender of Japan in August 1945, top American military officials
anticipated a great reduction in both the size and responsibilities of the
armed forces and a return to the less rigorous life of peacetime. Thus, in
late 1945, the military establishment could accurately be described as
"docile and relatively starved." [1]

As America began to move into the era of the Cold War, military capabilities did not correspond, in the eyes of civilian officials, with the task
that it was America's responsibility to shoulder. America had committed
itself to the support of democratic principles in the face of aggressive
communism. It had made explicit its commitment by means of the Truman
Doctrine, the policy of containment, and by its determination to stand in
defense of Europe through extending military and economic assistance.
However, while American officials were expressing their determination to
resist communism, they also began to look around and take stock of the
military resources on hand with which to back up their statements. Not
only was it difficult to find the basic military resources, such as arms and
men, that might be used to contain communism, but the military did not
behave in a manner that suggested they had even "gotten the word"
concerning the nature of the challenge confronting America. There was
an almost complete absence of a spirited, cocky military disposition to
match that which characterized many of the President's statements.

Postwar Military Passivity

Following World War II, the orientation of the military was toward a
return to the life of the 1930s.[2] In striking contrast, the orientation of the
civilian leadership, as described in the preceding chapter, was to take on
the mission of containing communism. As suggested by Richard J. Barnet:

Indeed, there is considerable evidence that the civilian managers, particularly
at the beginning of the postwar period, have been far readier than the military
to commit American forces to actual combat. Apprenticed to the military in
World War II, the top civilian national security elite absorbed the basic military
outlook but not the soldier's professional caution. Perhaps because they lacked
combat experience, they underestimated the difficulties and risks in using military power. In 1946 the Joint Chiefs of Staff cooled the State Department's
enthusiasm for sending an ultimatum to Yugoslavia for shooting down an

---

[1] Gabriel Kolko, *The Roots of American Foreign Policy* (Boston: Beacon Press,
1969), p. 27.
[2] A novel that conveys a sense of prewar peacetime army life, the motives of army
personnel, and the tasks and concerns which consume their energy, is James Jones's
From Here to Eternity (New York: Charles Scribner's Sons, 1950).

American plane. In the earliest days of the Cold War it was the State Department that kept urging a big military buildup to furnish support for our political position, while the Defense Department set more modest goals for itself.[3]

There are several reasons for the inhibitions that affected top military officials in the immediate postwar years and caused them to refrain from more active participation in the design or implementation of a foreign policy that would contain communism. First, there was no tradition in America for the active participation of the military in the process of formulating foreign policy. The armed forces had always been regarded as a resource to be employed at the discretion of the civilian leadership. The precedent of civilian leadership had, through decades of experience, been clearly established in American political life. "In the vast preponderance of cases," Professor Cecil Crabb points out, "military officers trained in the American constitutional and philosophical tradition remain fully conscious that their role in policy determination is important but always *subordinate;* they accept the principle of civilian control over the military as one of the cornerstones of the democratic system." [4]

Second, the military, immediately following the war, had no resources with which to wield political influence. The most impressive war machine ever constructed was being depleted at a rate that suggested a reversion to the familiar American pattern of military impotence in time of peace. Defense expenditures dropped from $81 billion in 1945, the last year of the war, to $11.8 billion (the postwar low) in 1948. The defense budget grew to $12.9 billion in 1949 (possibly affected by the Communist takeover in Czechoslovakia) and reached $13 billion in 1950.[5] With the outbreak of the Korean War in June 1950, the defense budget soared to $44 billion. With a budget of approximately $12 billion during the immediate postwar years (approximately one third of the entire federal budget), there was no possibility of expanding the military establishment in terms of either equipment or personnel, military manpower having dropped from 12 million in 1945, immediately prior to the defeat of Germany, to 1.4 million in 1947.

A third reason for the minimal political influence exercised by the military immediately after the war was the fact that in peacetime, American policy makers tended to draw a clear distinction between military and nonmilitary approaches to international problems. The American tradition in the formulation and implementation of foreign policy had been for the President to confront international problems with what resources he and his Department of State could bring together. If the problems were not resolved through diplomatic channels and if it was concluded that national security was immediately threatened, the President and the Ameri-

---

[3] Richard J. Barnet, *The Economy of Death* (New York: Atheneum, 1969), p. 83.

[4] Cecil Crabb, *American Foreign Policy in the Nuclear Age* (Evanston, Illinois: Row and Peterson, 1960), p. 76.

[5] Fiscal year 1950 ended only three days after the outbreak of the Korean War.

can people would resign themselves to the need to leave temporarily their peacetime occupations and rechannel their energies into the concentrated, all-out task of activating and expanding the nation's limited peacetime military resources. Absent was a continuously ongoing and clearly inter-related application of political and military capabilities to international problems by the President. In both world wars, the requirement for American military involvement was viewed by Americans as the consequence of the failure of political means to resolve international problems. When American leaders became convinced that a growing threat to their national security could not be resolved through political (nonmilitary) channels, military force was used. When political interaction ended, full military action took over. Military force, however, was used in a non-political manner. That is, America used its power to eradicate as quickly as possible that which it regarded as threatening. Once this was accomplished, military involvement ceased and was replaced by limited diplomatic interaction. It was almost as if, with the two world wars, American leaders saw a kind of cancer of international proportions that would poison American life if rapid action were not taken. A surgical act, employing military power under emergency conditions, was required to eradicate this cancer. Once the infectious growth was removed, the world's ills would be cured and American military power could be reduced to its limited prewar status and international involvement would again be based on "necessary" political interaction.

The three reasons described for the limited influence of the military in policy circles were, in a basic sense, tied to the isolationist experience of American foreign policy. There was simply no need to maintain a large permanent military establishment since it was not anticipated that postwar American foreign policy would call for such a capability any more than pre-World War II foreign policy had required it. For example, at the end of the war in Europe in 1945, General George Marshall remarked that "the rate of demobilization has been determined by transportation facilities. . . . It has no relationship whatsoever to the size of the Army in the future."[6] In other words, American demobilization and the character of the future peacetime army was in no way determined by the anticipated requirements for American political *and* military interaction in international affairs.

However, with the emergence of the Cold War immediately following the conclusion of World War II, the corresponding development of increased political influence by the military was directly attributable to the *civilian* decision that, to contain communism and preserve democracy, a greatly expanded military capability was mandatory.

---

[6] General George C. Marshall, Army Chief of Staff, to Joint Session of Congress, *U.S. Defense Policies Since World War II* (House Document 85:1, Number 100), p. 5. Quoted by Paul Y. Hammond, *The Cold War Years* (New York: Harcourt, Brace, and World, 1969), p. 10.

Official civilian perceptions of national security requirements changed rapidly following World War II. In fact, it was the very suddenness with which the government came to see its security in jeopardy that affected the direction American foreign policy was about to take. The Truman Doctrine, NATO, and the theory of containment, three components of America's postwar foreign policy, established requirements that could be satisfied only by the creation of an impressive military force. After all, without a striking military capability, the officially pronounced commitment to defend Europe, as well as Greece and Turkey, against enemy aggression, and the determination to contain the USSR would have appeared to other nations as no more than words. Beyond this, an impressive military force was required to contend effectively with the expansionist Soviet state, a nation that, it was believed, was sensitive only to a show of force. America saw communism as a threat to its political, economic, and moral values. The geographic locus of communism was the USSR, an aggressive, interventionist power, committed to the ultimate attainment of world influence. Furthermore, American officials were convinced that it was impossible to negotiate with the Russians. What was the point of negotiations, American officials asked themselves, if international agreements would not be honored? Diplomatic integrity and keeping one's word represented values alien to Communists and shared only by the democracies. If, by the late 1940s, the President and his advisers had concluded that it was only military force that was capable of deterring the USSR from further aggression, there was no responsible alternative but to develop rapidly a military capability that would elicit the respect of the Soviet Union.

The Bomb and Policy Considerations

America possessed one unprecedented, awesome military capability—its monopoly on the atomic bomb. If Soviet officials respected force, it was America's possession of the bomb that should provoke respect of the most profound dimensions—especially after the fate of Hiroshima and Nagasaki. It is possible to appreciate the deep impact that the bomb itself, as well as its broader military and political implications, must have had on American and Soviet statesmen by noting what two of these weapons did to two Japanese cities.

Each atomic bomb dropped on Japan was 1,000 times more powerful than any single weapon that had been developed up to that time. Figure 2 details the casualties in Hiroshima and Nagasaki as a result of the American attack. For comparative purposes, it is a striking fact that a single conventional (nonatomic) one-ton high explosive bomb, if dropped on Hiroshima, would have caused casualties up to 100 persons, as opposed to the 144,000 casualties that resulted from the single 20-kiloton atomic bomb dropped on Hiroshima.

FIGURE 2
Casualties at Hiroshima and Nagasaki *

Zone	Population	Density (per square mile)	Killed	Injured
Hiroshima:				
0 to 0.6 mile	31,200	25,800	26,700	3,000
0.6 to 1.6 miles	144,800	22,700	39,600	53,000
1.6 to 3.1 miles	80,300	3,500	1,700	20,000
Totals	256,300	8,400	68,000	76,000
Total casualties	144,000			
Nagasaki:				
0 to 0.6 mile	30,900	25,500	27,200	1,900
0.6 to 1.6 miles	27,700	4,400	9,500	8,100
1.6 to 3.1 miles	115,200	5,100	1,300	11,000
Totals	173,800	5,700	38,000	21,000
Total casualties	59,000			

* Samuel Glasstone (ed.), *The Effect of Nuclear Weapons* (U.S. Atomic Energy Commission, 1962), p. 550. The population estimates apply only to civilians in the target areas and do not include an unknown number of military personnel. Reference to the three zones in column 1 indicates varying distances from ground zero. The 20-kiloton atomic weapons dropped on Hiroshima and Nagasaki were detonated at approximately 2,000 feet altitude and thus there were negligible fallout effects. In Hiroshima, 81 percent of the buildings in the city proper were destroyed.

There is no doubt that world leaders were immediately aware of the unprecedented power of the atomic bomb. In retrospect it appears obvious and logical that the President and his advisers would link the possession of the bomb with the means of containing communism. In America's hands only rested the most powerful military weapon in the world. To the President and his advisers there were additional attributes of the bomb. First, the bomb suggested a means of resolving the conflict in official circles between the demand for maximum national security and the reluctance to spend large sums of federal money to rebuild and support an impressive military force. A large military force was expensive, and in addition, had never been a fixed part of American peacetime life. Nuclear weapons were relatively inexpensive and, although not an adequate substitute per se for the demobilized armed forces, they did constitute an impressive military capability. Thus, from the standpoint of economy and public opposition to the continued maintenance of armed forces at wartime levels, nuclear weapons held a special appeal. General Maxwell D. Taylor, writing about the cost of ground forces and the attractiveness of defense through a nuclear weapons capability, said:

Neither the Truman administration nor the American people were prepared to foot such a bill, particularly that part of the program which would have been a tacit admission of lack of foresight. Under such circumstances, it is not surprising that the idea of relying on nuclear weapons and strategic bombing for national defense had great appeal. Such a military program appeared to offer us a way out of fighting dirty, costly wars with Communist masses on the ground.[7]

If the bomb could, in the long run, save money and avoid the reinstitution of the military draft, it would automatically appear to offer domestic political advantages for any President in his quest for broad national acceptance.

The bomb had other political advantages. It lent national status and distinction to the United States. It seemed to symbolize the new physical and technological superiority of the United States, and in this context, American officials began to consider the possible diplomatic advantages associated with an atomic bomb monopoly. It was appealing to think that diplomatic advantages might be enjoyed without the protracted face-to-face interaction that was usually a prerequisite for diplomatic effectiveness. Possession of the bomb would allow the United States to sit back and exercise its influence in diplomatic circles while, at the same time, avoiding lengthy and often tedious conference participation. For a nation still deeply affected by its isolationist background, the bomb was an attractive acquisition. The impact of the bomb on official thought was clearly set forth by Gar Alperovitz:

> . . . it is abundantly clear that the atomic bomb profoundly influenced the way American policy makers viewed political problems. Or, as Admiral Leahy has neatly summarized the point, "One factor that was to change a lot of ideas, including my own, was the atomic bomb. . . ." The change caused by the new weapon was quite specific. It did not produce American opposition to Soviet policies in Eastern Europe and Manchuria. Rather, since a consensus had already been reached on the need to take a firm stand against the Soviet Union in both areas, the atomic bomb *confirmed* American leaders in their judgement that they had sufficient power to affect developments in the border regions of the Soviet Union. There is both truth and precision in Truman's statement to Stimson that the weapon "gave him an entirely new feeling of confidence."[8]

To fulfill the deterring intentions of the Truman Doctrine and NATO, it was necessary to make their tangible military basis vividly apparent to the Soviet Union. In other words, to the theory of containment it was necessary to add the actual ability to contain. In response to this need, a call was issued to the military requiring them to gear up to support the foreign policy commitments already established by the President. Moving into the Cold War sometimes resembled the process of preparing to go to war in the traditional sense in that the military was required to develop rapidly the capability to support specific civilian policy decisions that had to do with restraining the "enemy" in the cause of national security. The

---

[7] Maxwell Taylor, *An Uncertain Trumpet* (New York: Harper and Row, 1960), p. 13.

[8] Gar Alperovitz, *Atomic Diplomacy: Hiroshima and Potsdam* (New York: Simon and Schuster, 1965), p. 227.

atomic bomb, mainly because of the reasons discussed, quickly became the core of the effort to revitalize the nation's military capability. It was around the bomb that military manpower, equipment, and research were organized. The obsession with this revolutionary military capability laid claim to official thought and money and, during most of the 1950s, precluded serious consideration of a more diversified military force.

The government's turning to the military at this time was an extremely significant development. The military had always constituted a resource that could be turned to and rapidly built up at times when America felt threatened. However, something different and more demanding was being required of the military at this time. Military capabilities were to be developed and maintained to assure the effectiveness of President Truman's Cold War policies. It was believed that the effectiveness of the President's policies could be achieved by making the nation's military capabilities sufficiently visible to deter any potential aggressor. Here were the rudimentary outlines of the strategy of deterrence, a subject of extreme importance to be discussed below. Deterrence provided the conceptual setting that brought military skills into policy circles. Since, from the beginning, the military came to constitute the most important resource that the civilian leadership depended on during all the Cold War years, it is important to specify some of the characteristics of the military outlook, or the way in which the military generally viewed the world.

The Military Turn of Mind

The central thesis of the military approach to problem resolution in international affairs was the achievement of dominance through the application of force. Once a level of dominance was established, any problem could be resolved since any situation could be forced to conform to demands of the dominant power. The American military mind tended to see nations as being in a constant condition of conflict, or at least competing for increased political influence. War represented a form of competition at a highly intensified level of interaction. The mission of the military, in the competitive international setting, was to utilize the instruments of violence—men and arms—to minimize their nation's insecurity. To the military mind, international life was constantly threatening because of the persistent competitive quest for power. One way to make the world less threatening was to use force to compel other nations to comply with some standard of behavior. In this characteristically military point of view, force represented the appropriate means to correct an unacceptable (therefore "wrong") international situation.

Consider, for example, the Truman Doctrine and NATO. The United States saw Communist influence emanating from Moscow and directed toward the non-Communist areas of the Middle East and Western Europe.

If the Soviet Union were to take over these regions, the United States would be isolated and left vulnerable to a subsequent aggressive thrust from the USSR. This perceived threat required that American military force be mobilized to contain communism. To the military mind, the ability to contain communism would be strengthened only marginally by an exploration of the existing and anticipated economic, political, and social resources available to the Soviet leadership that would actually enable the USSR to carry out such an ambitious aggressive undertaking. There was an impatience with such "abstract" considerations since they did not appear to have a *direct* bearing on the immediate task of achieving dominance through the application of force. The military mind could acclimate itself much more readily to the more simple, less qualified assumption that the USSR was committed to aggression, it had specific military resources at hand to carry out aggression, and this aggression would occur in Europe and the Middle East. Such a clear-cut view of a military confrontation called for the countering of enemy forces with superior American forces in order to contain communism. Thus, a very complex problem (the probable courses of action to be pursued by the USSR and the appropriate American response to these actions) was reduced to terms that made it an exclusively military problem, a problem that could be resolved through the application of force.[9]

The offensive utility of any military organization was its ability to bomb an enemy, attack a bridge, or mount an offensive against enemy forces. For the military man to perform this type of task efficiently, it had to be perceived in simple terms, i.e., in terms that allowed the problem to be resolved by physically eliminating it. His efficiency was increased to the extent that he could think in these relatively simplistic terms. Consistent with this observation, Professor Cecil Crabb has suggested that, "Above all, military leaders are too often tempted to reduce complex diplomatic issues to contests of power and force and, in the process, to gloss over political, economic, cultural, and ideological dimensions of foreign policy." [10] The military mind was trained to view problems in a particular way. In order to dispose the officer to accept the intellectual constraints associated with seeing the world in this "particular way," his total life was routinized to the extent possible. Emphasis was placed on values such as tradition, order, discipline, unity, and esprit.[11] Stress was also placed on the hierarchical chain of command relationship that existed in any military organization, i.e., directives of the superior officer being implemented without question by the subordinate officer.

There were two important aspects of the "particular way" in which the

---

[9] For an illustration of the military approach to conflict resolution, see the hypothetical military briefing described at the end of Chapter 3.

[10] Crabb, *American Foreign Policy,* p. 77.

[11] Samuel P. Huntington, *The Soldier and the State* (Cambridge, Massachusetts: Belknap Press of Harvard University Press, 1957), chapter 3.

military tended to see the world of international affairs. The first had to do with the disposition of the military to intensify the character of the threat. In addition to distorting reality through simplication, reality was also altered by enlarging the dimensions of what appeared threatening. The military strategist believed there were fewer risks involved if one presumed the "worst case" and then acquired the military capability to contend effectively with this presumed worst case. This line of thought provided a justification for an enlargement and strengthening of military resources to negate a presumed threat and, as a consequence, offered maximum assurances of actually eliminating it. The second aspect of the military view of international affairs was that threats to national security were usually based on an assessment of enemy capability rather than enemy intentions. For example, with regard to the Soviet Union, the military strategist was prone to indicate what aggressive action the USSR was capable of undertaking, rather than attempting to ascertain, through an analysis of intentions, what it was probable the USSR would do. Some of the characteristics of the military mind were succinctly summarized by Professor Samuel P. Huntington:

The military ethic emphasizes the permanence, irrationality, weakness, and evil in human nature. It stresses the supremacy of society over the individual and the importance of order, hierarchy, and division of function. It stresses the continuity and value of history. It accepts the nation state as the highest form of political organization and recognizes the continuing likelihood of wars among nation states. It emphasizes the importance of power in international relations and warns of the dangers to state security. It holds that the security of the state depends upon the creation and maintenance of strong military forces. It urges the limitation of state action to the direct interests of the state, the restriction of extensive commitments, and the undesirability of bellicose or adventurous policies. It holds that war is the instrument of politics, that the military are the servants of the statesmen, and that civilian control is essential to military professionalism. It exalts obedience as the highest virtue of military men.[12]

Professor Huntington mentioned that "civilian control is essential to military professionalism." Although this subject will be discussed more fully later on, a word is appropriate at this point. It was traditional in American political life for the executive and legislative branches of the government to make all policy decisions affecting domestic and foreign affairs. The Constitution and actual practice provided a basis for the persistence of civilian leadership. In foreign affairs, policy was determined by civilian officials who created the broad policy and legislative guidelines within which the defense establishment worked. Military officers implemented foreign policy decisions through the deployment of forces to overseas positions, through providing aid and training to the armed forces

---

[12] Ibid., p. 79.

of other nations, and through the development of strategic and tactical military capabilities. During the postwar years, as military capabilities came to play a more central role in the implementation of American foreign policy, some in America came to fear the possible alteration in the civilian-military relationship. This led the President and Congress to pass a series of laws designed to strengthen civilian control over the military. Despite impressions to the contrary, civilian control of American foreign policy has continued uninterrupted through American history up to the present time. To the extent that the military appeared to have achieved dominance, it was the decision of civilian officials to expand the utilization of military capabilities that created this impression.

To lend further definition to the military turn of mind it is helpful to compare military and civilian attitudes so that differences in orientation can be appreciated. This contrast also makes it possible to appreciate a basic source of conflict in the civilian-military working relationship. Briefly described below is the military and civilian orientation toward career, day-to-day situations, and the product of professional effort.

1. Career Attractions and Attitudes

For the military, the structured, organized, planned existence within the established system held a definite appeal. Within the system the career objective was to rise in rank. The generally accepted method for achieving success, i.e., rank, in the military was to undertake nothing that might involve risk, nothing that might offend or separate one from the system, nothing that would "make waves." Thus, the military attitude was one of caution, reflecting the belief that it was right to be skeptical of innovation since, after all, old ways were best. All of these attitudes were reinforced by the realization that promotion in rank and related material advantages came largely as a result of the passing of time in grade.

For the civilian, career attractions were not based solely on the availability of a clearly structured setting.[13] The fact that the civilian world accommodated the individual's preference for options, and the fact that rewards were frequently associated with some risk-taking and were related to quality of performance constituted attractive components of the nonmilitary life. For civilians, it was advantageous to demonstrate some imagination. There remained a *tradition* of respect for creative innovation. In the competitive civilian situation, management was responsive to new approaches to business problems so far as they contributed to profit.

---

[13] The discussion of contrasting military and civilian attitudes does not ignore the fact that the characteristics ascribed to the military also exist among some civilians in large industrial enterprises and other departments of the government. However, in a relative sense, the military attitudes described have a more general and consistent application to the military than to civilians.

2. Day-to-Day Situations

For the military, a prevalent disposition was to get through each assignment with the "least sweat." The military advised each other not to become too involved and not to make long-term commitments since both could leave one vulnerable to criticism. But then, since military assignments were usually for a period for only three years, it was difficult to become too involved. Of these three years, it usually took one year to learn the new job and the final year was devoted to tapering off in preparation to moving on.[14]

For the civilian, it was necessary early in one's working years to become engaged in building a career that would stretch over a 40- or 45-year period. The civilian wanted to "get involved." His success was usually related to how involved he became. The civilian may choose to move frequently from job to job but when assuming a new position his inclination to become involved in order to succeed was not dampened by the knowledge that he would be automatically reassigned in three years.

3. The Product of Effort

For the military, the chief goal was the quick payoff. Having a relatively short term of assignment to any task, and yet being conscious of having to prove his worth by "showing something" to a superior (or to Congress, in the case of the General-grade officers), the officer usually thought in terms of short-term productivity. He wanted something that did not require much time to produce and the utility of which could be

---

[14] Professor Oscar Grusky, in his study of a military organization as compared to a large industrial organization, found significant differences between military officers and business executives in the length of time spent in the organization. Almost one half of the air force officers had been at the base one year or less, while only slightly more than 2 percent of the business managers had been with the firm for a comparable period of time. Also, almost nine out of ten business executives had at least five years of service with the corporation, while only about one officer in 20 stationed at the military installation had a similar length of service. "All too frequently, the first year of a three-year tour of duty is spent familiarizing oneself with idiosyncrasies of the base, the second in implementing a number of relatively limited rule changes, the third in setting the base in order in anticipation of departure." See Oscar Grusky, "The Effects of Succession: A Comparative Study of Military and Business Organization," in Morris Janowitz (ed.), *The New Military: Changing Patterns of Organization* (New York: Russell Sage Foundation, 1964), pp. 89–96.

Professor Adam Yarmolinsky made an interesting comment concerning the tour of duty assignment as it applied to Vietnam. "The military went into Vietnam on a business-as-usual basis. Vietnam command assignments for career officers were (and still are) averaging less than a year in order to permit as many officers as possible to have their turn at command, rather than two years, so that commanders could apply what they had learned in the first year. The duration of assignments is measured by what they can do for a man's career, in helping him to get his tickets punched, rather than by what he can do in the assignment." Adam Yarmolinsky, "The Impact of Vietnam on the Military Establishment," *The Yale Review*, Summer 1972, p. 489.

easily demonstrated, such as engineering hardware (a new visual aid device, for example) or a piece of equipment (a new offensive weapon for jungle warfare).

For the civilian, with a longer range point of view toward his job, greater attention had to be devoted to long-term requirements and planning. He was usually disposed to specify production objectives that supported long-range objectives. Before producing a piece of equipment, it was important to know how this product would contribute to the overall corporate interest. In common jargon, the civilian's interests were tied to "the big picture."

The contrasts between military and civilian attitudes are significant for two basic reasons. They created difficulties in the military-civilian working relationship, a relationship brought about by the demands of America's foreign policy. Second, since military "tendencies" might not always best serve the cause of national security, there was an intrinsic basis for conflict in the military-civilian relationship. Military efforts to be on the safe side with regard to America's national security frequently prompted military analysts to overestimate a threat. This estimate generated a level of military capabilities that the enemy could understandably view as provocative. Their predisposition to adhere to traditional, prenuclear military practices and strategic concepts and to view innovation with skepticism could cause the military to approach conflict situations in a manner that was inappropriate for the nuclear age. The military attitude toward seeking quick results through the application of force suggested an interventionist disposition that the civilian leadership had a responsibility to restrain.

Department of Defense Organization

It is not possible, within the context of the American political system, to design and establish as law a defense organization that will absolutely assure the perpetuation of civilian dominance over the military. It is possible, however, to create an organizational structure that will strengthen the *probability* that this traditional relationship will persist. Since World War II, and especially since the passage of the National Security Act of 1947, one of the central objectives that has shaped the organizational design of the "defense establishment" has been the continuation of the tradition of civilian control.[15] In addition to organization, the continuation of civilian leadership in military affairs is dependent on (1) Presidential determination to keep defense operations under civilian control, (2) firm

---

[15] The defense establishment is comprised of government organizations concerned with maintaining national security. Those that exercise a significant influence on American foreign policy are the Department of Defense, the Department of State (discussed in Chapter 3), the National Security Council, and the Central Intelligence Agency (discussed in Chapters 4 and 5).

commitment on the part of the civilian leadership within the Defense Department to maintain their traditional position of dominance, and (3) acceptance by the military of their administrative subordination to civilian officials.

Beginning in 1947, a series of legislative acts and amendments to these acts were passed intended to bring into existence a more effective military organization and, at the same time, preserve civilian leadership. The difficulty of this process, both the strengthening of the military arm of the government and the intention not to strengthen it too much, made it necessary to move cautiously toward a more centralized and unified defense establishment.

The National Security Act of 1947 established the Department of Defense over which was placed a Secretary of Defense who reported directly to the President. The Secretary of Defense, with support drawn from his Office of the Secretary of Defense (OSD), was to manage the Department of Defense made up of three military departments, the army, navy, and newly created air force. Each service department was headed by a civilian secretary directly subordinate to the Secretary of Defense. Under each civilian secretary was the operative senior military commander for each service, who served as a member of the Joint Chiefs of Staff.[16]

The Joint Chiefs of Staff (JCS), established by the 1947 act, consisted of a chairman, chosen from one of the military services, and the senior military commanders of the army, navy, air force, and marines. The JCS had the dual function of serving as the "principal military advisers to the President, the National Security Council, and the Secretary of Defense," and, in addition, constituting "the immediate military staff of the Secretary of Defense." Thus, in addition to serving the Secretary of Defense, the Joint Chiefs were granted direct access to the President that did not require the approval of the Secretary of Defense. The functions of the JCS, in addition to advising the President and advising, briefing, and providing a staff for the Secretary of Defense, were (1) to insure coordination in overall national defense planning, (2) to prepare strategic and logistic military operational plans, and (3) to provide "strategic direction" for military commanders in the field.[17]

---

[16] For example, John W. Warner was (as of February 1973) the civilian Secretary of the Department of the Navy. Administratively subordinate to Secretary Warner was navy Admiral Elmo R. Zumwalt, Jr., who was both Chief of Naval Operations and the navy member of the Joint Chiefs of Staff.

[17] The task of coordinating overall defense planning was complicated by the reservation that the JCS were to avoid creating, in effect, a totally unified system of military command. One of the concerns of Congress in passing the 1947 National Security Act was that a degree of military unification would be achieved that would endow the JCS with power comparable to that exercised by the German General Staff before and during World War II.

The function of providing strategic direction involved the responsibility for determining the appropriate allocation of military resources in support of the foreign policy determined by the President. The Joint Chiefs were thus responsible for the task of recommending to the President what specific portions of the nation's military resources should be applied to the fulfillment of foreign policy goals. To assist the Joint Chiefs in the performance of their tasks, the 1947 National Security Act provided for a Joint Staff that consisted of approximately 450 officers.

To summarize the significant provisions of the 1947 National Security Act, four points may be noted:

1. The Act created the position of Secretary of Defense, a civilian official, who represented the new Department of Defense in meetings of the President's cabinet and the newly established National Security Council.

2. The Secretary of Defense headed the Department of Defense which housed the three military services.

3. The Joint Chiefs of Staff were established to advise and support the Secretary of Defense and the National Security Council, to promote coordinated interaction among the army, navy, and air force, and to organize military support for the implementation of foreign policy.

4. The Secretary of Defense and the Joint Chiefs of Staff were the President's key advisers in the area of national security affairs.

In 1949 the position of the Secretary of Defense was strengthened by an amendment to the 1947 National Security Act. First, the secretary was provided three assistant secretaries as well as more staff assistance in the Office of the Secretary of Defense. Second, the secretary was given more authority over the Department of Defense budget through the creation of the position of comptroller. The comptroller was to also function as the secretary's budget adviser. Providing the secretary with increased control over the military budget, and as a consequence, weakening the influence of the individual military services, was an important development in strengthening the secretary's power within the department.[18]

The Defense Reorganization Act of 1958 further strengthened the position of the Secretary of Defense as the central figure in the management of defense matters.[19] First, with this act, the secretary came to exercise real direction and control over the three military services. This was made possible through the delegation to the secretary of authority to

---

[18] The 1949 amendment also created the position of Chairman of the Joint Chiefs of Staff. In 1953, President Eisenhower's Reorganization Plan Number 6 further strengthened the position of the defense secretary by providing him with six additional assistant secretaries.

[19] See Burton M. Sapin, *The Making of United States Foreign Policy* (New York: Frederick A. Praeger, 1966) chapter 6, for a lucid and concise description of the significance of the 1958 Defense Reorganization Act.

transfer, abolish, reassign, and consolidate military functions among the services. Also, the secretary was authorized to assign responsibility for the development and operational use of new weapons to one or more of the military services. Thus, through this act, the secretary was given direct control over defense research, the power to determine the rate at which the products of military research would be made operational, and the responsibility to decide to which of the military services authorization would be delegated for the management of new weapons systems.

Second, the dominance of the secretary within the Defense Department was reinforced by further expanding (beyond the provisions of the 1949 amendment) the size of the Office of the Secretary of Defense, the secretary's own support organization. Over 2,000 personnel (primarily civilian), including nine Assistant Secretaries of Defense, were attached to OSD. It was from this administrative base that Secretary of Defense Robert McNamara drew the authority and support that enabled him to exercise the leadership potential that came to be built into the secretary's position during his years in the Pentagon.

Third, the 1958 act increased the power of the Joint Chiefs of Staff. By this act the Joint Chiefs were given operational control over the military commanders of the unified and specified forces in the field.[20] The exercise of this authority, facilitated by the creation of a supporting Joint Staff, enabled the Joint Chiefs to offer greater support to the Defense Secretary since a clearer definition had been given to the command relationship between the Joint Chiefs and field commanders. With the 1958 act, the Joint Chiefs, the Joint Staff, and the three military service staffs had the authority to assure the translation of policy directives into military operations. Further, with the strengthened OSD, the Defense Secretary was provided with a resource to be used for the generation of policy recommendations.

The effect of these three changes, beyond making the secretary clearly the dominant figure in the Pentagon, was to (1) move further in the direction of centralizing in civilian hands the power and responsibility for the application to foreign policy goals of military capabilities, (2) strengthen the postwar trend toward increased functional integration

---

[20] Unified Commands were those in which units of all the services in particular geographic areas were under the command of one officer, usually representing the service of predominant interest in that area. For example, the Unified Command in the Pacific area (CINCPAC) was headed by a navy admiral, and the one in Europe (CINCEUR) was commanded by an air force general. Strike Command (STRICOM), created in 1961, was composed of units from the air force, navy, and army, and was designed for quick reaction in limited war situations.

Specified Commands were units within one of the military services that were deemed important enough to be under the operational control of the JCS. One example of a Specified Command was the Strategic Air Command (SAC), a part of the air force.

among the military services, and (3) reinforce the practice of having a civilian adviser to the President in the field of military affairs.

One further point concerning the 1958 act. With regard to the trend toward increased functional integration among the military services, the act provided for "the carrying out of any supply or service activity common to more than one military department by a single agency or such other organizational entities as he [the Secretary] deems appropriate." In line with this grant of authority, six Defense Department agencies were established to "carry out . . . service activity common to more than one military department." Four of these integrated agencies, each directly responsible to the Joint Chiefs, were concerned with matters of military intelligence, intelligence communications, military communications, and management and research related to nuclear weapons. The two other agencies, both responsible to the Secretary of Defense, were concerned with supply and fiscal advisory services pertaining to defense contracts.[21] Figure 3, *Organization of the Department of Defense,* indicates the hierarchical relationship of the various units comprising the Department of Defense. The creation and continued operation of the integrated Defense agencies reflected the post-1958 effort to minimize interservice and functional duplication in the interest on achieving greater overall Defense efficiency.

An indication of the Defense Department's more active and sustained involvement in foreign policy matters was the creation in May 1961 of an Assistant Secretary of Defense for International Security Affairs (ISA). The Assistant Secretary for ISA, designated as the "principal staff assistant to the secretary" in the field of international security, headed the Office of International Security Affairs, which was located in the Pentagon and consisted of a staff of approximately 250, over half of whom were civilian. The functions of ISA were the following:

(1) To provide a central organization within the Defense Department for the determination of departmental policy positions in the area of foreign affairs. Through the coordinated consideration of the military *and political* aspects of foreign policy, it was intended that a defense position be developed that reflected more than purely military considerations. For example, two important areas of concern to policy makers within which political and military considerations constantly interacted and to which ISA assigned staff personnel were those of foreign military aid and arms control and disarmament.

(2) To provide a focal point in the Pentagon from which to issue state-

---

[21] These six agencies, each established under authority granted by the 1958 act and each directed by a military officer, were (in the order used above): (1) Defense Intelligence Agency, (2) National Security Agency, (3) Defense Communications Agency, (4) Defense Atomic Support Agency, (5) Defense Supply Agency, and (6) Defense Contract Audit Agency.

FIGURE 3
Organization of the Department of Defense *

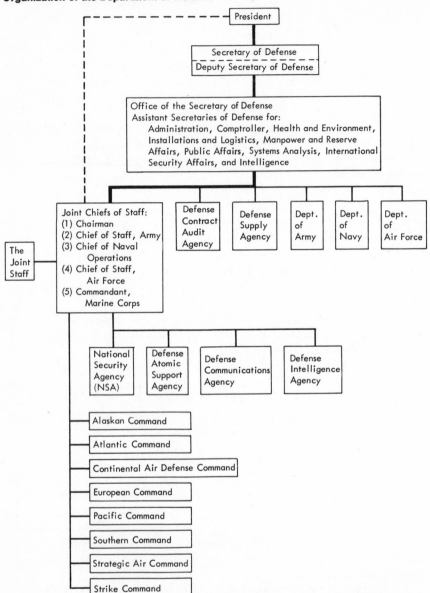

* Adapted from *United States Government Organization Manual, 1971–1972,* (Washington, D.C.:
U.S. Government Printing Office, 1971), p. 616.

ments defining the department's position on foreign policy problems and thereby provide overall guidance for other Pentagon offices. In theory, all Pentagon views were to be considered by ISA in order to arrive at a departmental position.

(3) To provide a contact point within the Pentagon through which improved interaction with the Department of State could be conducted. In other words, ISA was to provide a channel through which State Department personnel could carry on an exchange of views with the Joint Chiefs and members of the OSD Staff.

(4) Finally, to provide the secretary with a source of foreign policy advice to complement the professional military opinion made available to the secretary through the Joint Chiefs of Staff.

Factors Strengthening Military Influence

The point has been stressed that in both a traditional and organizational sense there has been consistent adherence to the principle of civilian dominance over the military in matters of foreign policy. It has also been stated that the military themselves, following the war, were psychologically disposed to be, at most, implementers rather than formulators of foreign policy. Why then, it may be asked, does the military *appear* to be dominant, so omnipresent, in these matters? Why does American foreign policy seem to be deeply committed to the use of military power for the resolution of conflict? What, during the last quarter century, has accounted for an apparent growth of military influence sufficient to provoke American students, academicians, Congressmen, citizen groups, newspaper editors, and veterans to express alarm.

Many considerations are relevant to these questions. However, four important factors contributed to the military emphasis in American foreign policy: (1) a military response continued to constitute the reflex reaction to a sense of threat, (2) the Department of Defense exercised great influence through the administration of money and defense-related employment, (3) the concentration on a nuclear weapons capability carried the military into policy circles, just as (4) the strategy of deterrence, the key concept of national security, kept the military involved with policy. A brief discussion of each of these factors, especially that of nuclear deterrence, will help clarify their significance.

1. A Reflex Reaction to Threat

In a certain sense, certainly in a traditional sense, a military response could seem to be the logical, natural, and thus generally acceptable reaction to a feeling of threat. As has been stressed, America felt deeply threatened in the 1946–49 period and almost automatically did what nations were conditioned to do through centuries of experience—turn to its military resources for defense. The government publicized the character of the threat, revised and made more efficient its defense organization, and embarked on a concentrated effort to develop military strength that could restrain Soviet aggression. This national security effort quickly focused on the task of building a modern military capability of strategic proportions. The vigor, broadly supported determination, and financial investment that was associated with this effort resulted in bringing the military into the position of representing the central resource of America's security.

2. Money and Defense-Related Employment

America was rich enough to build the most powerful military organization in the world. Spending for defense began to increase with America's involvement in the Korean War and grew steadily to the point of consuming over fifty percent of all federal expenditures during the 1950s and over 40 percent during the 1960s. Figure 4, *National Defense Expenditures,* indicates federal expenditures for national defense as a percentage of total federal spending from fiscal year 1942 through fiscal year 1972.

FIGURE 4
National Defense Expenditures *
(as per cent of federal spending)

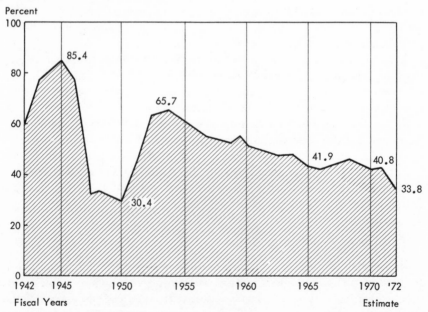

* Adapted from *National Journal,* February 6, 1971, p. 288.

The power to spend gave the Department of Defense a source of influence greater than that enjoyed by any federal agency. Having more money and personnel than any other government organization, the Department of Defense could establish an elaborate network of contractural relationships with private industry for the production of military equipment in support of the mission to contain communism.[22] As America's economy became increasingly keyed to defense production, the products of the military-industrial association were managed by the Defense Department, a responsibility that lent increased prestige, authority, and political leverage to the military.

For example, by the beginning of the 1960s, U. S. Congressmen had become increasingly outspoken in expressing an interest in maintaining a steady growth in the number of defense industries and installations located in their states. At that time (1961), it was estimated that 282 of the 437 members of the House of Representatives had within his or her congressional district one or more of the 738 installations of the armed forces, the Atomic Energy Commission, and the National Aeronautics and Space Administration.[23] By 1962, the states of Kansas, Washington, New Mexico, California, and Connecticut had 20 to 30 percent of all their manufacturing employment in the defense area.[24] Many Congressmen operated on the assumption that it was their responsibility to see that the economic welfare of their state was maintained or improved through efforts to draw more defense activity to the areas they represented. When, for some reason, a Congressman believed that a fair share of defense-sponsored activity had not been allocated to his district, he exhibited few inhibitions in expressing his complaints. Senator Ken Hechler of West Virginia spoke to this effect in 1959:

. . . I am getting pretty hot under the collar about the way my state of West Virginia is shortchanged in Army, Navy, and Air Force installations. . . . I am going to stand up on my hind legs and roar until West Virginia gets the fair treatment she deserves.[25]

The influence and power of the military increased steadily and Congressmen came to associate the nation's economic health (and their own political careers) with the continued expansion of defense production.

---

[22] In 1972, one million government civilians were full-time employees of the Department of Defense. There were 2.4 million men and women in the United States armed forces. Additional Defense Department "employees" were the two to three million people on the payrolls of defense contractors, plus others (such as bankers, lawyers, accountants, and public relations men) who worked for defense contractors.

[23] *Congressional Quarterly*, March 24, 1961, p. 464.

[24] U.S. Arms Control and Disarmament Agency, *Economic Impacts of Disarmament* (Washington, D.C.: January 1962), p. 4. The national average for manufacturing employment in defense industry was 7.3 percent.

[25] *Congressional Record*, June 1, 1959, p. 9486.

3. Quest for Nuclear Supremacy

America, with a four-year monopoly on the atomic bomb, had access to greater military power than any nation on earth. Anxious to influence the course of world events in a manner that would assure national security, it explored the potentialities of nuclear weaponry and developed them rapidly on an elaborate scale. Feeling threatened and being rich were the two prerequisites that propelled the United States toward the massive undertaking of developing increasingly more sophisticated nuclear weapons systems. Once again, it was the military that became the central element in the program to acquire a nuclear deterrent. In a sense, it was understandable that American decision-makers would use the resource with which they, among all the nations of the world, were uniquely endowed. What was more difficult to comprehend, and a problem that will be considered, was the *degree* of dependence that America came to place on the bomb. It was this degree of dependence that brought the military managers of this weapon into foreign policy circles.

4. Strategy of Nuclear Deterrence

A significant factor that brought the military to the forefront of foreign policy planning and implementation was the extent to which the strategy of nuclear deterrence came to pervade the broad sweep of foreign policy operations. Deterrence, as the vehicle that brought and continues to contribute unprecedented influence to the military, is of such importance that this subject will be developed somewhat more fully than was the case with the preceding three points.

Professor Thomas Schelling, in the preface to his book *Arms and Influence,* pointed to the fact that it was easier to destroy than to create.[26] He described this power to destroy or hurt as constituting the basis for a strong bargaining position. Criminal gangs used it, as did some political organizations to coerce votes. A bargaining position that was derived from the physical harm one nation *could* do to another was dependent on strategies of terrorism, retaliation, and reprisal—and also deterrence. With the development and stockpiling of nuclear weapons by the United States, there was a revolution in the relation of the military to foreign policy, a change that was traceable to the revolution in explosive power.

The bargaining power that the United States acquired with the acquisition of nuclear weapons was made to sound more impressive, and thus acceptable, by referring to it as the policy of deterrence. Deterrence seemed very close to containment, a policy position that enjoyed broad

---

[26] Thomas C. Schelling, *Arms and Influence* (New Haven: Yale University Press, 1966), pp. v–vi.

acceptance within the government. The strategy of deterrence may be defined as a means of preventing war by threatening to inflict upon an aggressor damage calculated to exceed his anticipated postattack advantages.[27] As deterrence came to represent the heart of America's national security policy, executive agencies such as the Defense Department, the Atomic Energy Commission, and the State Department, through its foreign policy statements (threats), assumed responsibility for the development, maintenance, and political utilization of the nation's military capability, all making a concerted effort to have their actions lend deterrence credibility.

Although deterrence as an element of national policy or diplomacy was not a new concept in international relations, it assumed a distinct and unique significance with the advent of nuclear weapons. When war was restricted to the use of nonnuclear or conventional weapons, it was possible for belligerent powers engaged in war to determine when their survival, or system of national values, was in jeopardy and then cease to fight. The rate at which the devastating effects of nonnuclear warfare increased was sufficiently gradual so that when a saturation point had been reached, a halt to the war could be called. In other words, the amount of combat devastation could be generally controlled through mutual decisions by the combatants. A general nuclear war would be different. The devastating blast, thermal, and radiation effects of nuclear war probably would not be inflicted on a target nation in small, gradual increments. The first strike would probably be designed to obliterate the target nation's retaliatory strength and thus would involve the employment of a large number of weapons. The target nation, alerted by its warning system, would have released its strategic nuclear force or would employ its second-strike reserve to attack the enemy. The mutual devastation that would follow such an exchange would make the traditional concepts of winning or losing in combat completely irrelevant as a means of assessing the relative status of the combatants at the termination of a nuclear war.

This change in the concept of "winning" in combat brought a new and distinct meaning to the policy of deterrence. Prenuclear weapons undoubtedly had a deterrent capability, but these same forces could also be used with the intention of winning a war. Damage to all warring powers could be expected but it was not considered probable that the weapons

---

[27] Deterrence, as a national strategy, has been defined by many writers concerned with military science and foreign policy. The definition given above embodies the important aspects of most of these definitions. One concise definition, given by air force General Curtis LeMay, described deterrence as the capacity to inflict a level of damage that an enemy would consider unacceptable. *United States Senate Study of Air Power,* (Hearings before the Subcommittee on the Air Force, Committee of the Armed Services, 84th Congress, 1956), p. 220.

themselves would cause a level of destruction that would obliterate the broad political and social characteristics of a nation. A war that involved the exchange of nuclear weapons could result in such destruction. The increased certainty that great destruction would be inevitable as a consequence of a general nuclear exchange made it necessary to alter strategic thinking with regard to how nuclear forces could best be used to serve the interests of national security. In fact, following August 1949, when the USSR broke America's monopoly on atomic weapons three years ahead of American intelligence estimates, it became critically important to reassess all of the nation's strategic concepts.[28] Following 1949, America began to think of nuclear weapons not as a means of defeating a potential enemy in combat but instead as a means of deterring an enemy attack.

For a military commander, the deterrent role of nuclear weapons represented a changed situation. The commander had traditionally been responsible for making decisions concerning the application of force. The application of force was a means of "winning" in combat. Nuclear deterrence, however, was concerned with the potential, as opposed to the actual, application of force. If nuclear weapons were ever employed in battle, deterrence would have failed. The deterrent policy, therefore, did not accommodate the military concept of winning in battle. Considerations concerning the development and maintenance of national security by means of deterrence thus involved what has been termed the "skillful non-use of military forces." [29] The security advantages to be derived from the nonuse of weapons were based largely on the ability to convince a potential enemy that (1) there existed a military force capable of inflicting an unacceptable level of damage, even under postattack conditions, and (2) there existed a commitment to employ this nuclear power under certain circumstances. When the strategy of deterrence is considered in the sense of the "skillful non-use of military forces" it becomes more than a military policy and assumes the proportions of a national policy calling for the intelligent utilization of civilian as well as military resources.[30]

Two implications emerged from the requirements of an effective policy of deterrence. First, decisions concerning defense were related to matters of foreign policy exactly as political decisions were related to the formulation of military policy. Second, it was necessary that the combined skills of diplomacy and military science be developed and applied to complement each other in support of national policy. The indivisibility of the

---

[28] Four years later, on August 21, 1953, the USSR detonated its first hydrogen bomb, just ten months after the United States successfully tested its first hydrogen bomb.

[29] Thomas C. Schelling, *The Strategy of Conflict* (Cambridge, Massachusetts: Harvard University Press, 1960), p. 9.

[30] Albert Wohlstetter has described some of the requirements of a deterrent policy, in addition to that of a weapons capability. See Albert Wohlstetter, "The Delicate Balance of Terror," *Foreign Affairs*, January 1959, pp. 21–34.

civil and military aspects of national defense problems came to be one of the significant characteristics of the nuclear era.

Deterrence Through Massive Retaliation

America's thinking about military requirements for national security was deeply affected by the Korean War, when American forces fought to defend the South Korean government against the North Korean attack launched on June 24, 1950. The Korean War experience gave rise to a number of reassessments within policy circles concerning the matching of the nation's military strengths with the requirement to contain communism. Involvement in future "Koreas" could seriously erode America's military capabilities since Communist forces could always outnumber America's and thus impair America's ability to meet its first defensive responsibility, the protection of Western Europe against a Soviet advance. American officials began to think that the nation's technological advances could be the basis for the development of a military capability that could offset the local ground force advantages enjoyed by the USSR and its Communist satellites. America had the technical and economic resources to develop a strategic force, in the form of the Strategic Air Command (SAC), and through SAC it could attack communism, not in local wars where American forces would be at a constant disadvantage, but at the source of aggression.

Following the election of President Eisenhower in 1952 and during the eight years of his administration, a number of doctrines of deterrence were proposed but the one to which the Korean experience seemed to contribute most directly and the one to which the strongest official support was given was that of massive retaliation. This doctrine and its vigorous espousal was primarily associated with the President's Secretary of State, John Foster Dulles. In considering Secretary Dulles's statement of massive retaliation, given its first public presentation on January 12, 1954, it should be recalled that at that time the main instruments of deterrence that had been developed for the contingencies of an attack against the United States and Western Europe were SAC and NATO. In the mid-'50s the policy of deterrence was not supported by a military strength that could secure the areas of the Middle East, Southeast Asia, and the Far East (other "Koreas") against enemy attack, and the doctrine of massive retaliation was set forth as a means of rectifying this perceived defense inadequacy. Secretary Dulles stated that local defense in various areas of the non-Western world was important, "but there is no local defense which alone will contain the mighty land power of the Communist world. Local defense must be reinforced by the further deterrent of massive retaliatory power." [31] Secretary Dulles went on to state that the President and his

---

[31] *New York Times,* January 13, 1954, p.2.

advisers, represented by the National Security Council, had made the basic decision "to depend primarily upon a great capacity to retaliate instantly by means and at places of our own choosing." [32]

With the enunciation of this doctrine Secretary Dulles clearly indicated that the United States would be in a position to determine how and where to counter enemy action rather than have the enemy determine the conditions of combat. The United States would also be able to cope effectively with the enemy without American ground forces having to engage enemy forces in geographically remote areas of the world.[33] During the months and years following the statement of massive retaliation, Secretary Dulles gradually introduced policy pronouncements that modified the doctrine. In March 1954, he announced that the deterrent aspect of massive retaliation was not intended to mean that "if there is a communist attack somewhere in Asia, atom or hydrogen bombs will necessarily be dropped on the great industries of China or Russia." [34] Several years later, in October 1957, Secretary Dulles stated that in the future it might be feasible to place less reliance on deterrence of vast retaliatory power.[35]

By 1957 it appeared that while the doctrine of massive retaliation had undergone certain significant modifications, it still constituted the *mode* of operation by which the policy of deterrence was to be supported. In other words, although this doctrine was modified, America's military capabilities remained largely dependent on nuclear weapons to meet even those military contingencies that were less than general war and that did not demand an attack directed against the Soviet or Chinese mainland.

During the last years of the Eisenhower administration and the first years of the Kennedy administration, the concept of retaliating massively was still relevant to the national policy of deterrence, but to it was added the possibility of using nuclear weapons for limited wars. This additional dependence on nuclear weapons was reemphasized at the end of the first year of the Kennedy administration when Deputy Secretary of Defense Roswell Gilpatric stated that a nuclear retaliatory capability of "lethal

---

[32] Ibid.

[33] On March 13, 1954, Vice President Nixon gave his interpretation of Secretary Dulles's doctrine. This interpretation is interesting in that it provided a simple explanation of massive retaliation, and perhaps because of its simplicity, it provided an interpretation that gained broad general acceptance. Vice President Nixon stated:

"Rather than let the Communists nibble us to death all over the world in little wars we would rely in the future primarily on our massive mobile retaliatory power which we could use at our discretion against the major source of aggression at times and places that we choose.

"We adjusted our armed strength to meet the requirements of this new concept and, what was just as important, we let the world and we let the Communists know what we intended to do." *New York Times*, March 14, 1954, p. 44.

[34] *New York Times*, March 17, 1954, p. 4.

[35] John Foster Dulles "Challenge and Response in United States Policy," *Foreign Affairs*, October 1957, p. 31.

power" was considered mandatory for both general and limited war.[36] According to Deputy Secretary Gilpatric, the United States would employ nuclear weapons in a limited war "if our interest should so require." [37]

During the 1960s, under the impetus of President Kennedy and Secretary of Defense Robert McNamara, an effort was sponsored within the Defense Department to develop a more diversified military capability that would enable the United States to engage in limited wars and employ only conventional (nonnuclear) weapons to deter Communist aggression.[38] However, during the 1960s, as United States forces continued to suffer heavy casualties in the Vietnam war, a persistent concern existed in both public and official quarters that, in order to assure "victory," it would be necessary for the United States to introduce into combat low-yield tactical nuclear weapons. During early 1968 a number of official actions and statements suggested that combat conditions required the use of nuclear weapons.[39] Credibility was given to this possibility because, from the standpoint of increasing domestic opposition to America's deepening involvement in the war, it had become politically infeasible for the President to assign additional American ground combat forces to Vietnam. Therefore, it appeared to some that the time could have arrived when the President would decide to draw from America's impressive stockpile of nuclear weapons.

Security: An Elusive Objective

A number of the factors that have strengthened the policy influence of the military have been discussed. Taken together, the sense of threat, de-

---

[36] *New York Times,* October 22, 1961, p. 1.

[37] Ibid.

[38] For a discussion of the need to strengthen America's nonnuclear power and the nuclear strategy of counterforce (America's "principal military objectives . . . should be the destruction of the enemy's military forces, not of his civilian population," thereby ". . . giving a possible opponent the strongest imaginable incentive to refrain from striking our own cities."), see address given by Secretary Robert McNamara, "Defense Arrangements of the North Atlantic Community," at commencement exercises at the University of Michigan, June 16, 1962. Speech reprinted in *Department of State Bulletin,* July 9, 1962, pp. 64–69.

[39] Rumors concerning the possibility of using nuclear weapons in Vietnam arose in early February 1968, when several nuclear physicists were sent to Vietnam by the Department of Defense. The rumor began to circulate that the reason for this trip was to assess the feasibility of introducing tactical nuclear weapons in the Vietnam war. The plausibility of the rumor was strengthened by the fact that 5,000 United States marines entrenched at Khe Sanh were threatened by an estimated 20,000 to 50,000 North Vietnamese troops. This issue was intensified when Senator Eugene McCarthy, with reference to the use of tactical nuclear weapons in Vietnam, said, "If they haven't been considered by the Pentagon in some sort of program planning, I would be very much surprised." General Earle Wheeler, then Chairman of the Joint Chiefs of Staff, added to the atmosphere of uncertainty by indicating that he did not *think* nuclear weapons would be required to defend Khe Sanh.

fense spending, dependence on the bomb, and defense through deterrence possessed a logical consistency and a mutually reinforcing effect that buoyed up the military and sustained them in their position of unprecedented visibility and greatly expanded policy influence. As more money was spent to develop more sophisticated weapons that were employed to enhance deterrence, America's behavior and statements assumed a more aggressive and threatening quality. This phenomenon had the effect of provoking the USSR into strengthening its military capabilities, which in turn caused a new level of anxiety within the United States that prompted further expenditures of money for arms. The central military character of what came to be called the arms race had such an intimate relationship with so many diverse aspects of American life that the military themselves came to be associated not only with official policy circles but with the much broader areas of private industry and the research programs within the nation's colleges and universities.

During the last half of the 1960s and into the 1970s basic questions were asked by increasing numbers of government officials and private citizens concerning the emphasis given to military capabilities as the means for implementing American foreign policy. The economic burden of the arms race and the cost, in dollars and human lives, of the Vietnam war caused a growing number of Americans to question the appropriateness of the imbalance between military and nonmilitary spending. There seemed to be no end to the requests for funds by the military for the development of more advance weaponry. Each weapons acquisition by the United States or the Soviet Union was eventually matched by the other nuclear superpower, and this catching up process was used to justify further spending for arms superiority. But adequate security never seemed to be achieved. Furthermore, serious doubts affected policy makers concerning the practical utility of military power. The nuclear powers were self-deterred from initiating a general war, and for the United States, the Vietnam war caused many to question the national advantage of ever again being drawn into a limited war in the more remote areas of Asia or Africa. With the 1970s the impressive power of the American military establishment remained unimpaired, but the disposition of the civilian leadership to turn to the military for policy implementation became considerably more restrained.

chapter 3

The State Department:
A Nonmilitary Resource

America responded to the threat of communism by developing a military capability of spectacular proportions. So great was the nation's reliance on this capability that it almost seemed to be the only resource available to serve the cause of national security. However, this was not the case. The government maintained a number of nonmilitary resources to help promote the nation's security, the most significant of which was the Department of State, the subject of this chapter. In the discussion that follows, four other nonmilitary resources of the government, the Agency for International Development, the Arms Control and Disarmament Agency, the United States Information Agency, and the Peace Corps, are considered, but each is discussed as an agency allied with and in support of the State Department.

The main reason for considering the State Department at some length is to gain an appreciation of the status of the principal resource available to the government that could provide an alternative to the military response to threat. The impressive development of the nation's military capabilities gives rise to the question of whether there was complementary development of America's nonmilitary resources and, if not, why not?

Another reason for studying the State Department has to do with the amount of criticism that for some years has been directed against the department. For example, it has been suggested that if one were to ask a cross section of informed Washington observers which government agency most needed reform, a substantial number of respondents would nominate the Department of State.[1] One reason for such criticism is that an increasing number of Americans have become sensitive to the direct relationship between their personal welfare (in terms of national security as well as private commercial interests) and their government's diplomatic negotiations and official commitments in foreign areas. To those whose interests are involved, the State Department seldom seems to perform with complete adequacy. Another source of criticism springs from a constant sense of international crisis and accompanying anxieties. The persistence of crisis is frequently blamed on State Department deficiencies.

A more basic criticism of the Department of State has also been expressed. To a number of students of America's foreign policy it appears that the State Department remains locked into a pre-World War II mold with perceptions and skills that do not correspond with the requirements of America's role in the nuclear era. One of the objectives of reviewing some of the characteristics of the department and describing some of its problems is to arrive at some conclusions concerning the validity of these criticisms.

The discussion of the State Department begins with a consideration of the functions of the Secretary of State—providing support to the President in the area of foreign affairs and managing the State Department's internal operations. To assist the secretary in the performance of these functions are a number of support activities operating within the department. The most important of these support activities are described, as are the operations of the four agencies allied with State mentioned above. Next, five of the department's basic problems are set forth and then considered from the standpoint of why they have persisted so long. Finally, State is looked at in contrast to the Defense Department in an effort to illustrate how State's approach to problem resolution differs from that of the military and, in addition, to suggest why nonmilitary influence in foreign policy circles appears to be second to that exercised by the President's military advisers.

The Department of State has two basic functions. One is the responsibility for representing, in a diplomatic capacity, the interests of America and its citizens in relations with other nations. The other function is to advise the President concerning all aspects of foreign affairs. To perform these functions, there are at present 24,000 State Department employees working in Washington and at the 117 U. S. embassies and 149 other overseas posts around the world, on an annual departmental budget of approximately $400 million, the smallest total budget of any cabinet-level department. Of the 24,000 employees of the State Department, 8,500 are

---

[1] Keith C. Clark and Laurence J. Legere (eds.), *The President and the Management of National Security* (New York: Frederick A. Praeger, 1969), p. 115.

foreign service and staff officers, 5,500 are civil servants, and the remaining 10,000 are foreign nationals, paid by the U. S. government, working in various American missions abroad.

Functions of the Secretary

1. Advising the President

The first function of the Secretary of State is to act as the President's principal adviser on foreign affairs. Once the President has reached a decision concerning foreign policy, based at least in part on the advice offered by the Secretary of State, the secretary must then help determine how the decision is to be implemented.

Although the Secretary of State is formally designated as the President's principal foreign affairs adviser, the manner in which the advisory role has been carried out has varied considerably under different postwar Presidents. In terms of the Secretary of State actually conforming to the role of the President's key foreign affairs adviser, and in terms of a compatible operational relationship between President and secretary, President Truman and Secretary Acheson complemented each other very neatly. President Truman believed that the Secretary of State should act as the "direct representative of the President for all foreign ambassadors," and that he was also in charge of American ambassadors abroad.[2] The President warned that the Secretary of State should never consider himself "the man in the White House," and the President should not try to act as the Secretary of State.[3]

Secretary Acheson expressed his view of the complementary role of the Secretary as follows:

[Truman] looked principally to the Department of State in determining foreign policy and—except where force was necessary—exclusively in executing it. . . . The Secretary saw his own role as Chief of Staff to the President in foreign affairs, directing and controlling the Department, keeping the President abreast of incipient situations that might call for decisions or action, acting as principal assistant in making the decisions and assuring action upon them.[4]

Subsequent Presidents, together with their Secretaries of State, could generally agree with the stated Truman-Acheson interpretation of their working relationship, but few were able to function in conformity with these somewhat idealized descriptions. Under President Eisenhower Sec-

---

[2] Harry S. Truman, *Memoirs* (Garden City, New York: Doubleday, 1955–56), vol. 1, pp. 330 and 547.

[3] Ibid.

[4] Dean Acheson, *Present at the Creation* (New York: W. W. Norton, 1969), pp. 734–35.

retary of State John Foster Dulles was delegated broad authority over foreign policy. Secretary Dulles rarely accepted advice from subordinates, worked out problems directly with foreign statesmen, and followed a general practice of informing the President, frequently after the fact, of actions he as secretary had already initiated. President Eisenhower's practice of "leaving it to Foster" reflected the President's implicit faith in his secretary's decision-making ability as well as the President's disposition to delegate his authority in the area of foreign affairs. Both Presidents Truman and Eisenhower, although they had specific foreign policy objectives they wished to achieve, were disposed to rely on the more experienced talents of their Secretaries of State.[5] In contrast to this situation, President Kennedy, in a manner similar to that of President Franklin Roosevelt, was drawn to the practice of being his own Secretary of State, personally handling matters in the field of foreign affairs, building his own staff of advisers, and using his Secretary of State primarily to run the State Department. Presidents Roosevelt and Kennedy were more anxious to practice first-hand the intricacies of international diplomacy and thus sought Secretaries of State with skills that were primarily designed to support the implementation of their policies: Secretary of State Cordell Hull through his close relations with Congress, and Secretary of State Dean Rusk with his tested administrative abilities, respectively. President Johnson, forced by the Vietnam war to make more and more critical decisions in the area of foreign affairs, relied on Secretary Rusk for policy advice much more consistently than had President Kennedy. President Johnson also depended on members of his White House advisory staff for support, a practice that contributed to a tendency to bypass the State Department. President Nixon has moved even further in this direction by working out foreign policy problems through his White House Special Assistant for National Security Affairs, Dr. Henry Kissinger. While President Nixon has solicited advisory input from the Secretary of State, he has used the resources of the State Department primarily to help implement decisions arrived at within the White House.[6]

These observations illustrate an important point. The character of the President's relationship with his Secretary of State is defined by each President. The Secretary and the Department of State exist to support the

---

[5] The Truman-Acheson relationship seemed to work effectively, but the President sometimes expressed irritation with tendencies on the part of career personnel in the State Department. "The difficulty with many career officials in the government is that they regard themselves as the men who really make policy and run the government. They look upon the elected officials as just temporary occupants. . . . The President of the United States, and not the second or third echelon in the State Department, is responsible for making foreign policy. . . ." Truman, *Memoirs*, vol 2, pp. 164–65.

[6] The trend toward the increased role of White House advisory groups in assisting the President in foreign policy decision making is discussed further in the following chapter.

President and it is the President's prerogative to determine how that support can be most usefully rendered.

2. Managing State's Internal Operations

To implement Presidential foreign policy decisions, the secretary's second basic duty is to direct and manage the operations of the State Department. This responsibility is closely tied to the secretary's advisory task since any advice given by the secretary to the President, if it is responsibly and constructively conceived, must be based on a precise assessment of the implementation capabilities of the Department. It would be irresponsible of the secretary to advise the President to pursue a course of action for which the State Department lacked the required supporting resources. Looking at the interrelationship of the secretary's two basic duties from a somewhat different standpoint, the more effective the secretary is in strengthening and extending the role of his department, the more options for action the secretary can, in his advisory role, present the President for consideration.

One consequence of the varying conceptions of foreign policy roles held by different Presidents has been the diverse attributes represented by the different Secretaries of State. The scope of this diversity is suggested by the strong assertiveness reflected by Secretary Dulles, in contrast with the more retiring, subordinate role assumed by Secretary Rusk. However, despite the varying skills and roles exhibited by different Secretaries of State, the personnel of the State Department itself constitute a continuing and constantly available resource for foreign affairs advice, information, and administrative support. Presidential requirements vary from one administration to another and Secretaries of State change as each new President attempts to satisfy his unique foreign policy demands. State's 24,000 personnel constitute the resource that continues to support the fulfillment of departmental responsibilities year after year, administration after administration. This suggests a three-sided relationship within which there is occasional conflict of interest. Each President has certain convictions concerning foreign policy objectives and the best means for realizing these objectives. On the other hand, the career employees within the department, most of whom have worked for State longer than any single President has been in office, have developed over the years an adherence to views and methods of operation that Presidents find difficult to alter. The Secretary of State, standing between the President and the personnel of his department, attempts to bridge any gap that may exist and bring his department into the position of being able to offer strong Presidential support.

In support of his two basic functions, the Secretary of State has undertaken a number of additional related tasks. First, when sensitive international negotiations arise, to help implement Presidential policy decisions as well as gather useful information for subsequent input to the President, the secretary participates in discussions as the ranking American diplomat. Second, again serving Presidential policy and departmental interests, the secretary interacts with Congress by testifying before Congressional committees, contacting individual Congressmen, inviting Congressmen to participate as members of international delegations, and submitting reports and studies to Congress describing anticipated or on-going Presidential programs in the international area. Third, in an effort to build popular support for Presidential programs or decisions, the secretary presents statements of policy to the press and the public. Fourth, as has been mentioned above, implementation of Presidential policy requires the secretary to interact with other executive departments and agencies to organize concerted support for Presidential programs within the executive branch. Finally, the secretary supports the President and departmental interests as a participant in cabinet meetings and as a member of the National Security Council.[7]

Support for the Secretary

1. Administrative Support

Within the Department of State, the Secretary of State is provided support and assistance in the fulfillment of his diverse responsibilities by the Office of the Secretary. Within this office are the Undersecretary of State, the secretary's second-in-command who serves as acting Secretary of State when the secretary is away from Washington; the Undersecretary for Political Affairs, the third ranking officer in the department; the Deputy Undersecretary for Economic Affairs; the Deputy Undersecretary for Management; and one or two Ambassadors-at-Large who serve the President in critical situations abroad, working to resolve conflicts and lessen international tensions.[8]

In recent years there have been two tendencies on the part of Presidents who profess a concern with the Secretary of State's ability to cope with the broad demands of his job. One tendency practiced (but never openly espoused) by Presidents Kennedy, Johnson, and Nixon, was to have selected members of the White House staff perform some of the foreign policy advisory tasks that had traditionally been the responsibility of the Secretary of State and his department. This development is discussed more

---

[7] Recent secretaries have sometimes sensed a conflict of interest in their efforts to support, on one level, the President and, on another level, the departmental concerns of their own personnel. More will be mentioned in Chapter 4 concerning this sense of conflict that becomes most pronounced at meetings of the President's cabinet and NSC.

[8] Shortly before World War II, the office staff directly serving Secretary Hull consisted of approximately two dozen aides. During the following 30 years, this staff grew to 15 times its prewar size.

fully in Chapter 4. The other tendency, manifested by Presidents Kennedy and Johnson, was to issue directives and establish supporting administrative units designed to strengthen the ability of the secretary and his department to exercise more effective coordinating authority over government agencies that also have responsibilities in the area of foreign affairs.[9] One such effort to strengthen the secretary's ability to coordinate interagency programs was made by President Johnson on March 2, 1968, when he provided the secretary's first deputy, the Undersecretary of State, with a small substantive staff over which the Undersecretary was made "Executive Chairman." This staff, called the Senior Interdepartmental Group (SIG), was to provide staff support for all of State's top officials within the Office of the Secretary of State. SIG membership included six other regular members: the Deputy Secretary of Defense, the Administrator of AID, the Chairman of the JCS, the Director of USIA, the Director of CIA, and the Special Assistant to the President for National Security Affairs. The agencies represented by SIG's membership suggest its function: to integrate on-going overseas programs sponsored by various government agencies. To assist SIG in its mission, Interdepartmental Regional Groups (IRGs) were established, each composed of the same departmental representation as was SIG but at the next lower administrative level.

The potential effectiveness of the SIG and IRG structure was never fully realized and these groups were abandoned by President Nixon. This ineffectiveness was due in part to the reluctance of the Secretary of State to delegate sufficient authority in his undersecretary. Second, the SIG was never used for any of the major policy issues with which the Johnson administration was concerned.[10] Because of its marginal utility within the State Department, President Nixon transferred the basic SIG/IRG structure to the White House where he believed its function of providing improved coordination among the executive agencies involved in foreign affairs would have a more appropriate base.

2. Regional Support

Support for the secretary below the administrative level of the Office of the Secretary is organized along two lines—in terms of regional, or

---

[9] Other federal agencies obviously involved in the management of foreign programs include the Department of Defense and the Central Intelligence Agency. However, agencies such as the Departments of Treasury, Agriculture, Labor, and Commerce also conduct programs that extend to foreign countries.

[10] John F. Campbell writes that SIG, during its three-year existence, "deliberated upon such third order problems as the size of the U.S. military-aid program to the Congo, the question of Export-Import Bank credits for a harbor improvement project on the island of Antigua, and the feasibility of an American proposal to the North Atlantic Council concerning a reorganization of NATO headquarters military staffs. Even on these lesser issues, it was unusual for a firm decision to be reached, transmitted to the Secretary of State and the President, and acted upon." John C. Campbell, *The Foreign Affairs Fudge Factory* (New York: Basic Books, 1971), p. 88.

geographic, responsibilities, and in terms of functional responsibilities. (See Figure 5, *Organization of the Department of State*.) The department contains five regional bureaus plus the Bureau of International Organization Affairs which is concerned with United Nations matters.[11]

FIGURE 5

Organization of the Department of State *

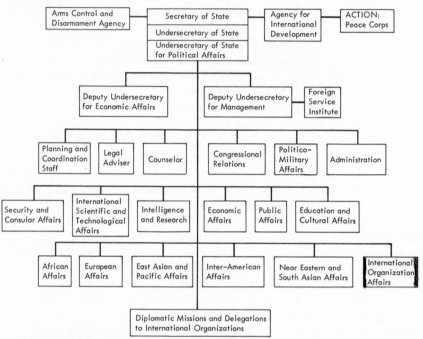

* Adapted from *United States Government Organization Manual, 1971–1972* (Washington, D.C.: U.S. Government Printing Office, 1971), p. 614.

The regional bureaus, the administrative core of the State Department, are staffed largely by career foreign service officers and dominate the day-to-day operations of the department. Each of State's five regional bureaus is made up of country "desks" to which analysts are assigned who study and report on the internal affairs of specific nations administratively within the geographic jurisdiction of their bureau.[12] For example, the regional Bureau of European Affairs, headed by an assistant secretary,

---

[11] The five regional bureaus in the State Department, each headed by an Assistant Secretary of State, were (1) African Affairs, (2) European Affairs, (3) East Asian and Pacific Affairs, (4) Inter-American Affairs, and (5) Near Eastern and South Asian Affairs.

[12] As of mid-1972, the term country "office" replaced that of country "desk." There are a total of approximately 45 country offices distributed among State's five regional bureaus.

includes six country offices, each office headed by a director.[13] Within each office there are a varying number of country "desks." The same administrative breakdown applies to the other four regional bureaus.

3. Functional Support

The functional bureaus of the State Department oversee areas of departmental responsibility that cut across geographic regions. The Bureau of Intelligence and Research, for example, is concerned with the collection and analysis of intelligence data that pertain to all geographic regions. The Bureau of Economic Affairs is responsible for the preparation of economic reports concerning economic issues related to all geographic areas. The most recent addition to the functional bureaus is the Bureau of Politico-Military Affairs which is concerned with the relationship between military and political problems.[14]

4. Overseas Coordination Support

Within each of State's regional bureaus there are a number of country directors, one for each country or group of several countries within the administrative jurisdiction of the bureau.[15] The function of each country director is to maintain coordination within his country among the various on-going programs sponsored by agencies of the United States government with responsibilities abroad. All communications and issues affecting relations between the United States and a specific country are coordinated by the country director stationed at the State Department in Washington. Thus, a strong, assertive country director, with the cooperation of an effective American ambassador in his country of responsibility, is capable of exercising a major impact on policy in the course of conducting routine, day-to-day exchanges between his country desk in Washington and the related embassy staff abroad. The country director, as the centralized Washington contact point for the conduct of American affairs in a specific

---

[13] In the European Affairs Bureau there are directors for (1) Canada; (2) Central Europe (Germany, Austria, Switzerland); (3) Eastern Europe (Bulgaria, Czechoslovakia, Hungary, Poland, Rumania, Yugoslavia); (4) Northern Europe (United Kingdom, Ireland, Finland, Scandinavia, Iceland, Malta, Bermuda); (5) USSR; and (6) Western Europe (Italy, France, Benelux). There are also Offices of Regional Political-Military Affairs (NATO, etc.) and Regional Political-Economic Affairs (OECD, EEC, Euratom, etc.). There are country "desks" for specific countries such as the USSR, Poland, Germany, etc.

[14] See Figure 5, *Organization of the Department of State* for a complete list of the various functional bureaus. With regard to the Politico-Military Bureau, just as the Pentagon's Office of International Security Affairs was the DOD's "little State Department," the Politico-Military Bureau was State's "little DOD."

[15] Each country director is administratively one step higher and more senior than the desk officers under him.

country, can influence policy through actions such as recommending foreign aid levels, initiating exchange programs, and delegating tasks to embassy personnel.[16] Through the country desk the country director receives copies of almost all field reports from the country or countries for which he is responsible. These consist of State-generated messages as well as messages prepared by the other agencies that comprise the country mission in the nation for which the country director is responsible. When action by the United States is required, the country director is normally the initiator and acts through communications with the ambassador.

In foreign areas, the key person authorized to coordinate government operations is the ambassador. This authority has been delegated to him by the Secretary of State and made the ambassador responsible for the direction, coordination, and supervision of interdepartmental (civilian and military) activities sponsored by the government overseas.[17] Efforts to strengthen the coordinating authority of the ambassador had been attempted earlier by President Truman who, in 1951, supported the concept of the country team headed by the ambassador (Chief of Mission), and by President Kennedy, whose 1961 circular letter authorized United States ambassadors abroad to supervise the activities of all civilian representatives of the government in the country to which they were assigned.

In most countries, especially within the larger embassies, country teams are organized in an effort to facilitate the coordinating tasks of the ambassador. The country teams are organized directly under the ambassador, each country team being essentially a committee consisting of the heads of all the government agencies attached to a specific embassy. In addition to State's foreign service personnel, the country team usually includes employees of the Agency for International Development, Peace Corps, United States Information Agency, Central Intelligence Agency, and often a Military Assistance Advisory Group (MAAG).

The country team concept, designed to integrate the diverse programs of numerous government agencies all operating out of one embassy, and giving to the ambassador, as Chief of Mission, the authority to direct all government activities within a single embassy, is a reform effort aimed at a very real problem. At the present time there are over 40 U. S. government agencies conducting overseas programs. This involves a total of 23,000 federal employees assigned to American embassies, of whom only 5,000 are attached to the State Department.[18] In the American embassy in London, for example, 44 U. S. government agencies are represented and only 15 percent of the total personnel attached to the embassy are State

---

[16] The actual influence of the country director is diminished somewhat by a number of complicating circumstances within and outside the State Department. These circumstances are discussed at the conclusion of this chapter.

[17] Excluded from this grant of authority are military forces operating in the field.

[18] This figure does not include U.S. military forces assigned overseas.

Department employees.[19] The organization and principal functions carried out at the larger American embassy are illustrated in Figure 6, *Functions of a Diplomatic Mission.*

FIGURE 6
Functions of a Diplomatic Mission *

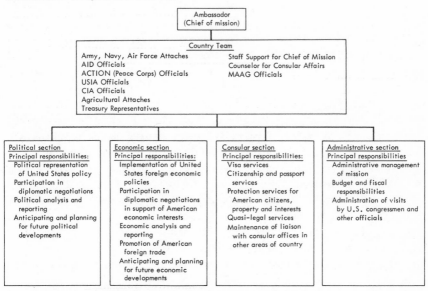

* Adapted from Sheldon Appleton, *United States Foreign Policy,* (Boston: Little, Brown and Co., 1968), Chart A, "Basic Organization of a Diplomatic Mission," p. 139.

State's Allied Agencies

There are four federal agencies administratively associated with the State Department to which only passing reference has been made so far: the Agency for International Development, the United States Arms Control and Disarmament Agency, the United States Information Agency, and the Peace Corps. Since the functions of each of these agencies are clearly

---

[19] The country team concept, with the ambassador's powers of authority being strengthened, suggests a constructive reform effort. However, during the decade since President Kennedy's letter, it has remained difficult for State to actually "take charge." Other agency officials frequently operated from the embassy to which they were assigned with larger budgets than were available to the ambassador. In addition, they had access through their own reporting channels to their individual agency headquarters in Washington. Robert Kennedy observed in 1967 that in some countries the authority of the ambassador was exceeded by the AID administrator, in some other countries the dominant American official was the CIA representative, while in many Latin American nations it was the chief of America's military mission whose authority exceeded that of the ambassador. Robert Kennedy, *Thirteen Days* (New York: Signet Books, 1967), pp. 114–15.

in the area of foreign affairs, a brief description of the responsibilities of each is provided at this point.

1. Agency for International Development

The Agency for International Development (AID) was established by Congress in 1961 to administer nonmilitary United States foreign assistance. From the outset of the agency's life, one of the guiding principles in the American aid program was to extend economic and technical assistance to the less developed nations to bring these countries to a level of self-sufficiency. Prior to the existence of the Agency for International Development, the United States had extended economic assistance to other nations for purposes of development, but development in a somewhat different sense. From the end of World War II until the early 1950s American aid was largely applied to the reconstruction of Europe. Then, during the 1950s, aid was used to contain communism and was directed to nations such as South Korea, Taiwan, Iran, Turkey, and Greece. With the 1960s, the fostering of economic development became the central purpose of technical aid and economic assistance extended by the United States. In the sense that foreign aid involved the extension of capital (in the form of loans and grants), commodities, and expertise from the United States to other countries, it represented, in the words of Professor Samuel Huntington, "a foreign counterpart of federal grants-in-aid to the states." [20]

To reinforce the possibility of economic development, funds were used to educate and develop human resources within developing areas through technical cooperation. An effort was made with all aid programs to adapt the terms of the aid and the form of technological implementation to the needs and potentialities of each receiving nation. More recently, AID has attempted to increase the participation of American private industries in programs designed to develop physical and human resources of the less developed nations.

In an organizational sense, AID is formally a part of the State Department and its administrator is directly responsible to the Secretary of State. Despite this administrative relationship, AID enjoys a significant degree of operational autonomy, although it is required that all AID operations and policies be initially cleared by the secretary.[21] AID programs are

---

[20] Samuel P. Huntington, "Foreign Aid—For What and For Whom?," *Foreign Policy*, Winter 1970–71, p. 163.

Within AID, the Office of Program and Policy Coordination assumes the responsibility for (1) translating AID funds into specific country programs, and (2) planning long-range assistance programs aimed at systematic assistance intended to yield economic independence.

[21] Once the State Department approves the granting of aid to a nation, then AID exercises its administrative independence by determining the form (grants, loans, technical personnel) of aid, the programs to be initiated or supported in the host nation (agriculture, mining, textiles, etc.), and the scheduling of assistance (time and amounts).

administered by the appropriate AID regional bureau, but once again, all overseas AID missions operating in the field are required to do so with the knowledge and approval of State's country director.[22] As members of the American country team operating under the American ambassador, AID personnel report to Washington headquarters through the ambassador.

In the early 1970s there were approximately 14,000 to 15,000 personnel employed by AID, 25 percent of whom worked in Washington. One half of the agency's total personnel was made up of foreign nationals working for AID within their own countries. As of early 1970, there were slightly over 5,000 American AID personnel working in over 80 countries.[23] AID's annual budget since 1965 has fluctuated near the $2 billion level.[24] The main limiting factor on AID appropriations, which have been less than one half of 1 percent of the total GNP, has been the suspicion and hostility of Congress.[25] Widespread disapproval, or at best skepticism, was expressed by a coalition of liberal and conservative Congressmen and extended to every aspect of the nation's foreign aid program: the program's concept, purpose, effectiveness, quality of AID personnel, administration of funds, and finally, the responsiveness, or lack thereof, expressed by recipient nations. To many Congressmen it appeared that America was a victim of poor business judgement when it was spending $2 billion a year in foreign aid and was deriving only a negligible return from its investment. The number of problems facing AID, especially those related to the difficulty of recruiting skilled technicians, and the reservations, based on

---

[22] AID has four regional bureaus: East Asia; Near East and South Asia (combined); Latin America; and Africa.

[23] This meant that there were several hundred more Americans working abroad for AID than for the Department of State. Twenty to 30 percent of AID's employees were assigned to Vietnam as part of the Vietnamization program.

[24] The following table indicates the AID program for fiscal year 1972 by functional categories (in millions of dollars):

Agriculture	376.5
Community and urban development/housing	42.8
Education	186.6
Health	103.4
Industry	590.5
Labor	12.1
Population/family planning	74.5
Public administration	29.6
Public safety	25.1
Transportation	60.8
Program support and miscellaneous	253.3
Other	130.5
Total	1,876.7

U.S. Department of State, *U.S. Foreign Policy, 1969–70* (Washington, D.C.: U.S. Government Printing Office, 1971), p. 222.

[25] The organizational source of Congressional suspicion of AID was the House Appropriations Subcommittee on Foreign Operations. The individual source of suspicion was Representative Otto Passman, Chairman of the House Subcommittee on Foreign Operations.

feelings of nationalism and a desire for neutralism, of leaders of many of the developing nations of Asia and Africa toward the presence of American AID administrators within their countries, provoked questions in Congress as to the appropriateness of the nation's present aid program. Some of the implications of these views and recommended changes for the future administration of foreign aid are discussed in Chapter 7.

2. Arms Control and Disarmament Agency

A second agency enjoying a semiautonomous status in its relationship with the State Department is the United States Arms Control and Disarmament Agency (ACDA), an agency proposed by President Kennedy and created by Congress September 26, 1961.[26] It was intended that this new agency would provide a permanent center for disarmament planning. It was also intended that it would provide a basic capability and continuously operating resource so that disarmament could begin to enjoy serious consideration as a major aspect of national security policy rather than as a topic for periodic diplomatic gatherings, always subject to haphazard handling. The stated objectives of ACDA were: (1) to conduct, support, and coordinate research for arms control and disarmament policy formulation; (2) to coordinate and disseminate public information concerning arms control and disarmament; (3) to prepare for and manage United States participation in international arms control and disarmament negotiation; and (4) to prepare for and direct American participation in any arms control or disarmament agreements of which the United States is a participant.[27]

Since the establishment of ACDA in 1961, the scope and effectiveness of its activities have been limited by the fact that nuclear arms constitute

---

[26] This bill brought into being for the first time a disarmament agency that was established by Congressional action, with authority and functions prescribed by law. The fact that ACDA was created by an act of Congress, rather than by executive order, was of some significance in itself. It was intended that legislative sanction would tend to give the agency more prestige and support than if it had been created by executive order. It was also hoped that it would be a means of keeping Congress informed concerning disarmament planning and negotiations. (Sen. Hubert Humphrey had complained that with past disarmament efforts, such as those sponsored by Harold Stassen, President Eisenhower's Special Assistant for Disarmament, there had been a reluctance on the part of executive aides, on the grounds of "executive privilege," to keep Congressional committees informed regarding disarmament.) Hopefully, this new legislative link between ACDA and Congress could alter the attitude of skepticism or opposition toward disarmament held by most Congressmen.

[27] Public Law 87-297, 87th Congress, 1st Session, September 26, 1961, Section 2. The term "arms control" does not necessarily imply a reduction or elimination of arms, as suggested by the concept of disarmament. Arms control efforts are designed to prevent a war that might occur through accident or inadvertence. Agreements such as the Non-Proliferation Treaty, the Hot Line Agreement, the Limited Test Ban Treaty, as well as unilateral actions restricting the actual combat use of nuclear weapons, are compatible with the concept of arms control. See related discussion in Chapter 6.

the basis and the substance of the United States' strategy of deterrence, the nation's basic means of containing communism. In a still broader sense, the general orientation of America's foreign policy described in Chapter 1 suggests that the impact on policy exercised by ACDA was destined to be minimal, and perhaps the strongest justification for establishing the agency was to strengthen the public image of the United States as a nation seriously committed to the cause of peace through disarmament. Since deterrence was the sanctioned national defense policy, it was able to shape, in large part, various governmental attitudes toward the alternative policy of disarmament. Or, to state this point somewhat differently, both disarmament and deterrence share a vital and fundamental interest, namely, that of preventing war through the proper management of nuclear weapons. However, while disarmament and deterrence have a common goal, they represent alternative methods. The conflicting aspect of this relationship has provided the basis for the development within the government of diverse attitudes toward disarmament.[28]

In a policy atmosphere that equated greater national security with greater stockpiles of arms, it was necessary to provide ACDA with sufficient authority to initiate and coordinate disarmament activities and also to have its voice heard in competition with advisory input that emanated from the Defense Department. Anticipating this problem, the 1961 legislation creating ACDA specified that the Director of the Arms Control Agency be the "principal adviser to the Secretary of State and the President on arms control and disarmament matters."[29] In other words, in order to assure that ACDA's director had an open and direct channel to the President, disarmament recommendations were to be submitted to both the President and the Secretary of State. (See Figure 7, *Organizational Relationship Among the Director, ACDA; the President; and the Secretary of State.*)

The approximately two hundred employees of ACDA, operating on an annual budget of nearly $10 million, have been instrumental in bringing to fruition such significant arms control agreements as the Limited Test Ban Treaty, the Hot Line between Moscow and Washington, the Non-Proliferation Treaty, and the agreements to prohibit nations from placing weapons in space or on the ocean's floor.[30]

3. United States Information Agency

The third State-related agency to be discussed is the United States Information Agency (USIA). As the United States became increasingly

---

[28] These diverse attitudes are discussed in more detail in Chapter 6.

[29] Public Law 87-297, Section 22.

[30] The participation of ACDA in the Strategic Arms Limitation Talks is discussed in some detail in Chapter 6.

FIGURE 7

**Organizational Relationship Among the Director, ACDA;
the President; and the Secretary of State**

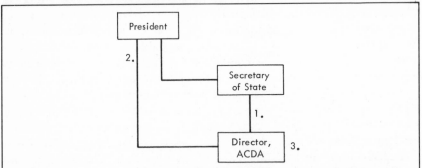

1. The Director of the Arms Control and Disarmament Agency, directly subordinate to the Secretary of State in directing work of Agency and in conducting disarmament negotiations.
2. The director, directly subordinate to the President in coordinating disarmament activity among government agencies and in directing disarmament research.
3. The director, reports to both the President and the Secretary of State concerning disarmament policy recommendations and advice.

involved in international affairs during the postwar years, and as it sought to persuade the leaders and people of other nations to support its political and economic values, the need for an American propaganda agency became clearly apparent. By the end of the Truman administration the United States had accumulated enough experience in interacting with the Soviet Union to appreciate the fact that an American propaganda agency was a competitive requirement in the effort to contend effectively with the varied international "selling" techniques employed by the USSR. Thus, on August 1, 1953, the United States Information Agency, headed by a director appointed by the President, was established as an "independent" agency with the legislative directive to "promote a better understanding between the people of the United States and the people of other countries." In practice, the State Department exercises policy guidance over all USIA activities designed to convey the official depiction of the United States to other nations. USIA activities are organized in terms of five categories of propaganda media: (1) Press and Publications Service; (2) Motion Picture Service; (3) Information Center Service; (4) Broadcasting Service; and (5) Television Service.[31]

The five media services are used by USIA personnel to support the agency's activities of: (1) promoting the flow of information about the United States to the world; (2) presenting American government policies

---

[31] The Voice of America (VOA) reached 28 nations through almost 800 broadcast hours per week. The annual cost of VOA was $34 million. It was estimated that VOA reached five to ten million listeners in Communist nations. The daily worldwide USIA audience has been estimated to be 25 million people.

and programs to the world; (3) supporting the implementation of American foreign policy; (4) furthering goodwill and public understanding between the United States and the people of other nations; (5) providing counsel and advice to American government officials concerning public relations; and (6) countering propaganda inimical to the interests of the United States, wherever and whenever it appeared.[32] USIA supports these various areas of activity through its 9,000 employees (one half of whom are foreign nationals) who work in the United States and at some 250 USIA overseas posts established in over 100 nations. The annual USIA budget in the 1970s has been slightly less than $200 million, less than half of 1 percent of the nation's defense budget and 10 percent of the annual foreign aid expenditures.

USIA has confronted a number of problems in an effort to carry out the activities listed above. For one thing, the Congressional skepticism or disapproval that was directed at AID and ACDA was also extended to USIA. Propaganda was a concept to which many Americans attached negative connotations, particularly international propaganda in peacetime. To many Congressmen, USIA was tainted with the unsavory implications of a propaganda agency and this impression tended to inhibit Congressional funding. Congressmen often found the idea of overtly funding a propaganda organization (such as USIA) to be an affront to the image of straightforward openness with which most Americans wish to be identified.

A second problem had to do with the intangible nature of USIA's accomplishments. It was difficult for government officials to know whether funds the government was investing in its propaganda program were "paying off." In other words, did the USIA really change anyone's mind? Former USIA director Edward R. Murrow observed that, "No computer clicks, no cash register rings when a man changes his mind or opts for freedom."[33] The absence of a measurable achievement limited Congressional appropriations. It is ironic in a sense that many Congressmen seem to have been brought to the point of extending token support to USIA largely because the Communist "enemy" has presumably enjoyed political advantages through its 50 years' use of propaganda themes and techniques.

A third problem is related to the rapid changes in the leadership of the agency. Since 1953 there have been seven directors of USIA, each a political appointee and each with his own objectives and his own ideas as to how these objectives should be realized. None of the directors has been a professional information specialist but, instead, was drawn from backgrounds in law, broadcasting, administration, journalism, or diplomacy.

---

[32] Edward L. Bernays and Burnet Hershey (eds.), *The Case for Reappraisal of U.S. Overseas Policies and Programs* (New York: Frederick A. Praeger, 1970), pp. 8–9.

[33] Quoted by Cecil Crabb, *American Foreign Policy in the Nuclear Age* (Evanston, Illinois: Row and Peterson, 1960), p. 353.

Finally, because USIA's mission enjoyed only minimal sympathy or support within the government, its resources and programs were seldom coordinated with the plans and operations of the other federal agencies engaged in overseas activities. One point of view concerning the agency's activities, and one that was supported by a number of observers of USIA, was expressed by Professor Edward Bernays,

> . . . The Agency's activities are mainly holding operations, a don't-rock-the-boat policy, instead of an imaginative, professional, contemporary social-science oriented operation, fulfilling the promise of its important mission. The Agency goes through the motions of spending its appropriations, happy if no Congressman raises a public ruckus by questioning its actions. . . .[34]

4. Peace Corps

The fourth and final State-related agency to be considered is the Peace Corps. This agency, also under the policy direction of the Department of State, was established in early 1961.[35] The purpose of the Peace Corps was to help developing nations meet their need for trained manpower by making available to interested nations American men and women who were trained to work in the various occupational fields that matched the needs of the requesting nation. Peace Corps volunteers served with no salary for two years, working and living in the local community where they were sent by the director in their assigned country.

As with America's propaganda efforts, the attempt by the United States to develop a program that was based on Americans living and working with the people of developing nations paralleled a long-term program designed by the Soviet Union. The Soviet effort to extend influence to the developing nations had been a part of Soviet foreign policy from the time the Bolsheviks first achieved political ascendancy in the USSR. The three basic themes of the Soviet program developed by Lenin and subsequently amplified by Stalin and Khrushchev were: (1) freedom for the underdeveloped nations from colonial (capitalist) rule and exploitation; (2) national self-determination for all developing nations; and (3) the establishment of an alliance between the proletarian forces of the advanced industrialized nations and the revolutionary forces of the developing nations. The Peace Corps and AID represented the agencies that had the task of competing with a nation that, first, had a well-developed ideological justification for involvement in the developing nations; second, had over 50 years experience with the national problems and sensitivities of the developing nations; and third, had a political system that Soviet officials

---

[34] Bernays and Hershey, *Case for Reappraisal*, p. 9.

[35] As of July 1, 1971, administrative change made the Peace Corps and Vista (Volunteers in Service to America) both part of a new organization named ACTION, headed by the Director of the Peace Corps.

attempted to "sell" as a model for the developing nations, a system advertised as yielding a modern industrialized economy within a generation, in contrast to the many decades required by the American system.[36]

In early 1972 there were approximately 7,400 Peace Corps volunteers on active assignment in 57 countries, with some 900 additional volunteers in training. This level of volunteers was slightly more than half the number of volunteers that worked in the Peace Corps during the peak years in the middle 1960s.[37] In the 1970s an effort was made to make available to developing nations volunteers who possessed more specialized occupational skills.[38] During 1971, almost 50 percent of the volunteers were agricultural specialists, skilled tradesmen (such as machinists and carpenters), or professionals (such as architects, engineers, businessmen, and city administrators). The shift in requests for volunteers away from the liberal arts generalist and toward the volunteer with specialized skills is reflected in Figure 8, *Requests for Peace Corps Volunteers by Skill Area.* To attract larger number of skilled and professional volunteers the Peace Corps in 1969 began to accept families and, within two years, over 100 families were assigned to overseas posts.

During the past ten years some officials within developing nations have reacted adversely to what they regarded as Western intervention in the form of Peace Corps volunteers. This led to the withdrawal in 1970, for example, of Peace Corps personnel from Libya, Somalia, Ceylon, and Guyana. On the other hand, in the 1970s the Peace Corps reentered Guinea, from which it had been requested to withdraw in 1968; volunteers entered Mali for the first time, and new programs were initiated in Malta, the Congo, and Mauritius. As part of an effort to increase the rate of acceptance and to lengthen the term of duty of volunteers in overseas posts, the Peace Corps has stressed the need to increase cooperative programs between the United States and the host country. This effort was strengthened through the practice of hiring host country nationals to comprise up to one half of the overseas administrative staff and of spon-

---

[36] One advantage from which the USSR benefited in its approach to the developing nations was its attitude toward time. Believing that the triumph of communism and the demise of capitalism were inevitable, Soviet officials frequently exhibited less urgency in their efforts to gain political influence than has been exhibited by their official counterparts in the United States. Congress, in making funds available to the Peace Corps and AID, was most strongly motivated by tangible evidence of a dollar being well spent. Since progress in moving an agrarian, illiterate population toward modernization does take time, tangible "proof" of progress was difficult to set before Congress. This fact, combined with Congress' adherence to the concept that "time is money," has resulted in only modest financial support being granted for America's nonmilitary programs in the developing nations.

[37] The peak year for Peace Corps personnel was 1966, with 12,313 volunteers drawn from 42,246 applications. The budget was $113 million. One reason for such strong interest in the Peace Corps at this time was that draft deferments were granted for Peace Corps service. Draft deferments were not granted during the 1970s.

[38] *U.S. Foreign Policy, 1969–70*, p. 304.

FIGURE 8

Requests for Peace Corps Volunteers by Skill Area *

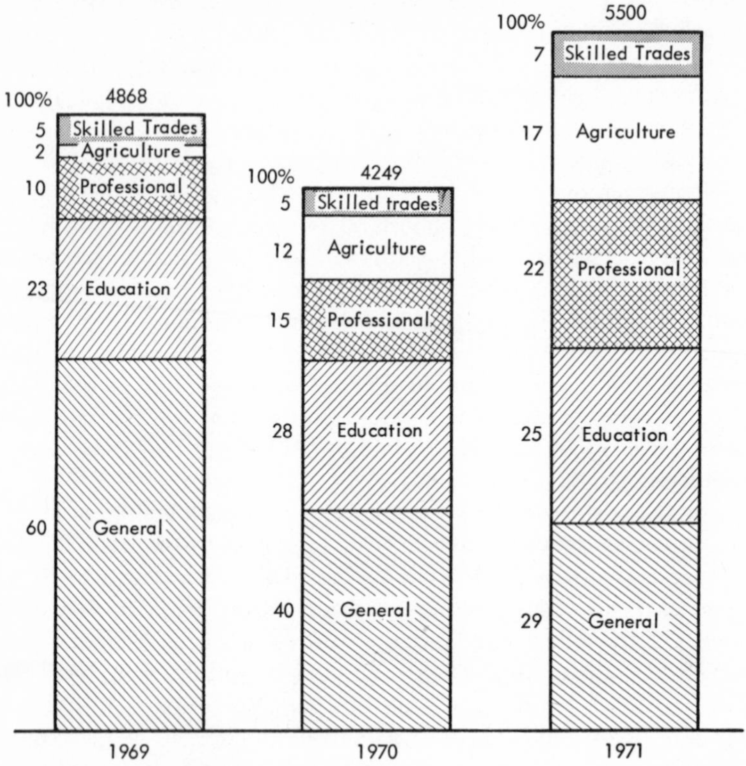

* Adapted from *United States Foreign Policy, 1969–1970*, p. 305.

soring more in-country training for volunteers. The long-range objective was that the "recruitment, selection, placement, and evaluation of Peace Corps volunteers and their projects can be done on a joint basis with the host country." [39]

As of early 1972 the scope of the future Peace Corps activity was in doubt. Its budget had been cut annually since 1968 and in fiscal year 1972 the corps was required to operate on a budget of approximately $75 million. As was also true of AID, the Peace Corps budget was attacked annually by Louisiana Representative Otto Passman, Chairman of the House Foreign Operations Subcommittee of the Appropriations Committee. Congressman Passman was quoted as stating: "If I had to meet my Maker in three minutes and the last decision the Good Lord would let me

---

[39] Ibid., p. 307.

make . . . it would be to abolish the Peace Corps. That is my feeling. I might as well put it in the record." [40]

Some of State's Problems

During the years since World War II, as the size and responsibilities of the Department of State have grown, a number of problems have persisted within the department, problems that for 25 years have continued to block the department's ability to realize its full potential as a resource from which the President can draw support for his foreign policy commitments. An appreciation of some of the major long-term problems that have weakened the effectiveness of the department contributes to an understanding of the department itself. For example, insight into the character of the State Department is gained by recognizing the fact that the departmental weaknesses discussed below have persisted for over two decades despite broad recognition of their existence and repeated efforts both within and outside the department to rectify these deficiencies. In considering the departmental weaknesses, it is useful to think of them in relation to the President's responsibilities in the area of foreign affairs. As has already been noted, the President turns to the State Department when seeking foreign policy advisory and administrative support. The adequacy of the support he receives determines the extent to which he can actually use the department and the extent to which nonmilitary approaches to problem solving can influence Presidential decision-making. If the President concludes that the department is of questionable or limited utility, there are several consequences that necessarily follow. First, a limitation is placed on the scope and depth of the President's relationship with his Secretary of State. Second, the President will seek advisory alternatives to State, alternatives such as the Department of Defense or the President's White House advisers. Third, this condition of being bypassed by the President will deprive State of its legitimate advisory function and immediately generate morale problems that intensify existing departmental difficulties.

Some of the problems that have plagued the State Department for the last quarter century are related to (1) the acquisition and retention of qualified personnel, (2) the operating procedures adhered to by the department, (3) the role of policy planning, (4) the department's relatively low domestic status, both within and outside government circles, and (5) the character and quality of the Presidential-secretarial relationship. The State Department was not unique in having these basic problems plague its operations and diminish its effectiveness. No executive department was immune from such difficulties. What was perhaps unique with regard to

---

[40] Editorial, "The Peace Corps," *Boston Globe,* January 8, 1972.

the State Department was, first and most important, the relation between the persistance of these problems and the security of the nation. American diplomacy and foreign policy, because of these problems, was heavily burdened in its effort to achieve maximum diplomatic effectiveness in the cause of national security. Potential capabilities were prevented from developing fully to match actual responsibilities. Second, with regard to departmental personnel, State's recurring problems prevented the department's unusually rich (in education and career motivation) human resources from becoming broadly developed and applied to the diverse and challenging problems of diplomacy in the nuclear era. Third, and perhaps most perplexing, the department has expended time and resources on repeated efforts to reform and reorganize its own operation. Each postwar President sponsored a reorganization of the department. Although improvement was evident over the years, the striking persistence of a set of basic problems lent to State a certain dubious distinction.

1. Personnel

Several conditions of employment within the Department of State have had a detrimental effect on all 24,000 employees of the department. First, Presidents have followed the practice of appointing friends and supporters to diplomatic posts as a reward for political services rendered. This form of "recognition" was extended to economically successful individuals brought from positions outside the government to head a diplomatic mission or to assume the ambassadorship in a country where it was usually difficult to view the working and living conditions as corresponding to those of a "hardship" post. As Professor Arnold Whitridge has pointed out, ". . . It is depressing to note that as of now only eleven out of the 27 embassies in Europe are headed by career men. The remaining sixteen have gone to friends of the President." [41] This practice has meant that a career State Department foreign service officer, an individual who may have devoted over 20 years to the slow process of rising, level by level, through positions of increasing responsibility within the service, could suddenly be superseded by an "outsider" who, usually because of a financial contribution to the President's political party, was rewarded by an ambassadorial appointment. The practice of Presidential appointments within the foreign service carried with it the obvious disadvantage of contributing to poor morale within the State Department. Another disadvantage, in addition to the usual diplomatic inexperience of such Presidential appointees, was the fact that political appointees tended to have little interest in working toward long-term improvement of departmental practices or policy plan-

---

[41] Arnold Whitridge, "Friendship and Our U.S. Envoys," *New York Times,* July 24, 1971, p. 25.

ning. Why should a political appointee bother becoming involved in the problems of long-range reform if, because of his nongovernment background in business or law, he was generally unfamiliar with the intricacies of State's complex problems and, furthermore, he was not to be associated with diplomacy for long anyway?

Before the existence of a professional career diplomatic service, the practice of "paying off" political debts with an embassy, a consulate, or a diplomatic assignment was understandable. When it occurred in the 1970s, it reflected a limited appreciation of the relationship between skilled, professional diplomacy and American national security. President Kennedy made a serious effort to reduce the number of ambassadorial positions open to political appointees. By 1962, 68 percent of all ambassadorial posts were occupied by officers drawn from the career service, as opposed to only 40 percent from the career service in 1955.[42] At the present time slightly more than 70 percent of all ambassadorial positions are filled by career foreign service personnel.[43]

A second personnel problem was pay. State Department salary scales are not sufficiently high to attract and retain the diverse professional skills required by modern diplomacy. This problem became most evident as the need for highly specialized technical and professional skills were sought in support of foreign assistance programs in areas of Asia and Africa. The State Department found it difficult to compete with nongovernment agencies that offered considerably higher salaries. The ultimate in financial recognition, enjoyed by less than 10 percent of the department's foregin service officers, was, in 1972, less than $36,000 a year. The average foreign service officer, after 20 years of career service, earned approximately $20,000 a year. Low pay scales contributed to a moral problem and also encouraged attitudes of caution and defensiveness, a condition about which more will be mentioned.

A third factor that made it difficult for State to attract and retain specialists was a working environment that many professional personnel (linguists, country specialists, scientists, agronomists, engineers, executives, and economists) did not regard as conducive to their maximum professional development. It was the generalist, the individual who knew a little about the many substantive and administrative requirements of the State Department, who fared best under conditions that involved geographic mobility at the rate of changed assignments every two or three years. Such short tours of duty made it extremely difficult for foreign service officers either to broaden their professional competence through continuous in-

---

[42] Arthur M. Schlesinger, *A Thousand Days* (Boston: Houghton Mifflin, 1965), pp. 429–30.

[43] See discussion of this subject in, Ellis O. Briggs, "The Staffing and Operations of Our Diplomatic Missions," in Henry M. Jackson (ed.), *The Secretary of State and the Ambassador* (New York: Frederick A. Praeger, 1964), p. 151.

volvement with regional problems or to enjoy the personal satisfaction of applying their special skills to a task with the knowledge that they would be around to see the constructive effects of their efforts. The specialist usually found geographic mobility and relatively low pay personally frustrating and professionally unrewarding. For the last ten years, Presidents have been sensitive to the conflict between the growing need for specialists and the perpetuation of conditions that deterred the professionally competent from employment with the State Department. The unresponsiveness of the State Department to President Kennedy's concern over the lack of professional specialization was described by Professor Schlesinger:

A friend of Kennedy's on a trip to Morocco came upon a young officer who loved the country and had learned the Berber languages but was about to be transferred to the Caribbean. When this was reported to the President, he said wearily that he had sent the Department a memorandum six months ago saying that it was better to let officers build up expertise than to rotate them mechanically every two years.[44]

As a consequence of these working conditions, it is the generalist who has tended to be attracted to the State Department, who has been most readily accepted by other career officers, and who has been rewarded by promotion within the organization. State's recruitment and promotion programs did not suggest that regional expertise and specialization were highly valued qualities. Former Secretary of State Acheson pointed out that the foreign service officer, encouraged by training and experience to become a generalist, sought to avoid making quantitative assessments of economic or military capabilities.[45] Professor Schlesinger observed that during the Kennedy administration State Department efficiency reports did not assess an officer's "Knowledge of Country and Area" and younger officers were concerned by the fact that the higher their specialized qualifications for assignment to a specific country, the lower their rating would be under the heading of "General Usefulness." [46]

Finally, with regard to the matter of promotion within the career service, rewards tended to be associated with seniority, with ability seeming to be a secondary consideration. It was generally difficult for career officers to be promoted to positions of major responsibility during their most vigorous and productive years (35 to 45 years of age). Such key positions were awarded to older men with "correct" career records. Once again, this practice favored the generalist rather than the specialist.

---

[44] Schlesinger, *Thousand Days*, p. 412.
[45] Dean Acheson, "Eclipse of the State Department," *Foreign Affairs*, July 1971, p. 605.
[46] Schlesinger, *Thousand Days*, p. 409.

2. Operating Procedures

The operating procedures by which State did its job weakened State's effectiveness during the entire postwar period. One of the most striking aspects of this situation was the fact that despite long acquaintance with procedural deficiencies on the part of students of diplomacy both within and outside the department, despite numerous efforts undertaken in an attempt to rectify deficiencies, and in spite of varying recommendations for change, State's operating practices remained largely intact over the past quarter century.[47]

The first problem hampering State Department operations was the assiduous adherence to long-standing procedural routines. This practice fostered a generally conservative, cautious (and thus slow-moving) atmosphere within the department. The pervasiveness of traditional caution perpetuated a tendency for foreign service officers to adhere to the guiding operational maxim of "don't rock the boat." This atmophere discouraged risk-taking in the preparation or processing of information from overseas posts. While order was maintained, and while the obvious dangers of impressionistic reporting were avoided, the objectivity of reports coming into Washington from overseas was distorted by a studied effort to avoid statements that might reflect adversely on other State Department personnel, might leave the reporter vulnerable to criticism, or might conflict with the position of one's immediate superior. One analysis of State Department operations included the observation that the Department "contains the norms that inhibit open confrontation of difficult issues and penalize people who take risks." [48] This study went on to identify four norms of departmental behavior: (1) a reluctance to confront others openly, even on substantive issues; (2) a tendency to hide emotions, be cautious about trusting others, and avoid openness in discussing interpersonal or substantive problems potentially embarrassing to superiors or peers; (3) an inclination to mistrust those who were aggressive and competitive; and (4) a tendency to withdraw from such conflicts when raised.[49]

---

[47] Professor Schlesinger reported that President Kennedy "well understood the difficulty of converting a tradition-ridden bureaucracy into a mechanism for swift information and decision [but] . . . it was a constant puzzle . . . that the State Department remained so formless and impenetrable. He would say, 'Damn it, Bundy and I get more done in one day in the White House than they do in six months in the State Department.' " Schlesinger, *Thousand Days*, p. 406.

[48] Chris Argyris, *Some Causes of Organizational Ineffectiveness Within the Department of State* (Washington, D.C.: U.S. Government Printing Office, January 1967), reported in *New York Times*, January 27, 1967, p. 16.

[49] Ibid., p. 16. One of the events that strengthened the cautious inclinations of State Department personnel was the action by Sen. Joseph McCarthy, beginning in February 1950, of charging the department with harboring hundreds of "card-carrying Communists." The department was so intimidated by this charge, and Secretary of State

With rewards (promotion) seeming to be associated with *not* being completely open or candid, it was understandable that a preoccupation with the career implications of a report took precedence over the quest for objectivity. A former ambassador observed that,

Men with a spark and independence of expression are at times held down, whereas caution is rewarded. . . . I have seen men's careers set back and in fact busted because they held the right views at the wrong time, or for reporting accurately facts which were not popular at the time.[50]

Thus, while the State Department drew into its ranks carefully selected, well-educated, highly motivated young men and women, the "system" diminished them.

In addition to the adverse effects of cautiousness on diplomatic reporting, there were also problems involving the lack of effective coordination of information within the department. Important reports sometimes failed to reach proper top level administrators. There were indications of much useless or irrelevant information being filtered upward for review by top level administrators, information that could have been responsibly processed at lower administrative echelons. Higher officials became so encumbered with paper that they had little time to devote to broader policy matters or to the consideration of possible future trends.[51] The volume of reports passing between Washington and diplomatic posts abroad was so great that embassy officers found themselves tied to their desks by seemingly endless requirements to produce and process reports.

Time-consuming delays frequently blocked the efficient flow of information. It has been reported that instructions to an ambassador could require up to 27 departmental signatures before they were cleared and dispatched to the field.[52] One new State Department official reported that, through diligence and prodding, he was able to put a moderately important cable through to an embassy in Southeast Asia in one week's time.[53] Theodore

---

Dulles was so anxious to make the McCarthy charges groundless, that during 1953 most high ranking foreign service officers were dismissed, resigned, or were placed in politically insensitive positions. The repercussions of this experience echoed for years within the department, passing on to new personnel the sense of old anxieties. See discussion by Hans J. Morgenthau, "John Foster Dulles," in Norman A. Graebner (ed.), *An Uncertain Tradition* (New York: McGraw-Hill, 1961), pp. 297–302.

[50] Briggs, "Staffing and Operations of Diplomatic Missions," pp. 134–35.

[51] The longevity of the paper processing problem in the State Department is underscored by the fact that Stanley Griffis made the following statement as long ago as 1948 while Ambassador to Poland: "Of the tons of reports on every subject that are rushed with great haste, and at great cost by airplane, I doubt if fifty per cent serves any useful purpose or contributes anything to the Department's knowledge." Quoted by Robert H. Ferrell in Samuel F. Bemis (ed.), *American Secretaries of State and Their Diplomacy* (New York: Cooper Square Publishers, 1963–66), vol. 15, p. 47.

[52] *New York Times,* January 18, 1971.

[53] Ibid.

Sorenson wrote that President Kennedy believed that State "spoke with too many voices and too little vigor."

He felt that it too often seemed to have a built-in inertia, which deadened initiative and that its tendency toward excessive delay obscured determination. . . . It was never clear to the President (and this continued to be true, even after the personnel changes) who was in charge, who was clearly delegated to do what, and why his own policy line seemed consistently to be altered or evaded.[54]

One clue as to why time-consuming delays hampered message processing was provided by Secretary Rusk who suggested that it was one of the department's operating principles to be sure than no link in the processing chain was inadvertently given a "left-out" feeling. Such an operating principle suggested an elaborate information processing system.[55]

3. Policy Planning

In May 1947, Secretary of State George Marshall established the Policy Planning Staff (PPS), as a part of the State Department, with Ambassador George Kennan as its head. This small group, originally eight men and a permanent secretary, had the task of defining in some detail America's policy toward the other nations of the world. The PPS was to support the secretary in efforts to examine and integrate State's programs, not from a regional or functional orientation, but from a global as well as a long-range point of view. The PPS function was to attempt to anticipate future contingencies and to prepare a set of possible responses to these anticipated events. It was intended that the planning process enable the United States to act more frequently in the capacity of initiator in foreign affairs and reduce the number of instances when the nation was confronted with unanticipated events and then compelled to respond as quickly and adequately as possible. It was assumed that an explicit statement of policy could provide a point of reference to which day-to-day responses and initiatives could be related. Ambassador Kennan recounted that, in becoming head of the Policy Planning Staff, he was simply advised that the new group should "avoid trivia." [56] Secretary Acheson had some additional observations to make concerning the PPS function:

---

[54] Theodore Sorenson, *Kennedy* (New York: Harper and Row, 1965), p. 287.

[55] Secretary Rusk recounted to Sen. Henry M. Jackson's National Security Subcommittee that he often read in the morning telegrams specific questions to which he knew the specific answer, but each telegram would nonetheless have to go "on its appointed course into the Bureau, and through the office and down to the desk. If it doesn't go down there, somebody feels that he is being deprived of his participation in a matter of his responsibility. Then it goes from the action officer back up through the Department to me *a week or ten days later* and if it isn't the answer that I knew had to be the answer, then I [have to] change it." Schlesinger, *Thousand Days*, p. 412. (Emphasis added.)

[56] George F. Kennan, *Memoirs, 1925–50* (Boston: Little, Brown and Co., 1967), p. 326.

The General [Marshall] conceived the function of this group as being to look ahead, not into the distant future, but beyond the vision of the operating officers caught in the smoke and crises of current battle; far enough ahead to see the emerging form of things to come and outline what should be done to meet or anticipate them. In doing this the staff should also do something else—constantly reappraise what was being done.[57]

The rationale behind creating the Policy Planning Staff was that, since the regional and functional bureaus of the department were overloaded with the burden of daily activities, negligible attention was devoted to the long-range implications of developing problems. An appreciation of the need for policy planning was shared by Presidents and Secretaries of State from the earliest postwar years. State Department personnel as well as most "outside" students of State's behavior supported the idea of establishing a group that would chart the policy direction toward which State's resources could then be applied. However, almost immediately following the creating of the PPS, difficulties were encountered that obstructed the realization of the full planning potential of this staff. The demands of the "thundering present" consumed the energies of State's personnel, including the planning staff. Twelve years after its creation it was observed that the planning staff was able to devote only a limited portion of its time to long-range, broadly focused foreign policy problems. The principal reason for this was that the planners were frequently drafted to assist with "crash" projects or even day-to-day operational duties.[58] President Kennedy attempted to overcome obstacles to planning efforts through establishing a Comprehensive Country Planning System. This system, using interagency consultants, prepared policy papers analyzing the social, political, and economic characteristics of specific nations, with the intention that this would provide the basis for defining America's policy toward these nations. The Comprehensive Country Planning System was a commendable effort to strengthen the planning function, but the conscientious participation of interagency personnel was difficult to sustain.

The traditionally modest role of policy planning in State seriously weakened the effectiveness of the entire department. Long-range policy input to the President was produced only infrequently and useful policy directives accompanied by background rationale were seldom issued to ambassadors. State's personnel were generally uncertain of the relationship between the performance of their daily tasks and long-range policy objectives simply because these objectives were seldom specified in terms other than overused generalizations.

Why has planning been a consistently neglected area of State's activity? One reason is that the numerous tasks of State in relation to the depart-

---

[57] Acheson, *Present at the Creation*, p. 214.
[58] H. Field Haviland, Jr., *The Formulation and Administration of U.S. Foreign Policy* (Washington, D.C.: Brookings Institution, 1960), p. 98.

ment's limited resources (personnel and funds) made planning appear an unjustifiable luxury. Another consideration is that planning was difficult to conduct at a level of specificity that offered useful guidance while at the same time was not so constraining as to cause diplomatic inflexibility. Thus there was a disposition on the part of planners to escape from this difficult task by *allowing* themselves to be drawn into the demands of the moment. Another factor bearing upon this situation is that planning generally occurs when a nation is aware of the need to plan. In other words, foreign policy planning is an activity pursued by nations that intend to assume the offensive in international relations, that intend to act on their own initiative rather than function in a responsive capacity. America was disposed to react rather than initiate, For a nation that had chosen such a role, planning had a less significant contribution to make.[59]

4. Low Domestic Status

The American public tended to view the State Department as an elitist enclave, supporting well-mannered, well-connected, "different" (since their profession was *foreign* affairs) kinds of individuals whose contribution to the security of the nation was marginal at best. "Cookie-pushers in striped pants" was an image that had persisted in the public mind for decades. To the extent that Presidents themselves shared this impression with the public, the usefulness of the Department was seriously undermined. Congress, to the extent that it adopted this point of view, was less willing to make funds available to support the fulfillment of State's authorized functions. Since this view was shared by other executive agencies, especially the Department of Defense and the Central Intelligence Agency, there was an inclination to minimize interaction with the State Department and to work directly with the White House in the formulation and implementation of foreign policy.

State had few supporters and no organized pressure group working to support the department's interests. At the beginning of the 1970s, its

---

[59] The planning function in State was further weakened in mid-1969 when Secretary Rogers disbanded the Policy Planning Staff as a result of the impression that the planners had become increasingly isolated from foreign policy decision-making. A policy and coordination staff was created, headed by a Foreign Service Officer and composed of State Department personnel plus representatives from other government and nongovernment agencies. Some planning activity was to continue, but the policy and coordination staff was also encouraged to maintain regular interaction with the regional and functional bureaus.

A new planning effort was initiated in 1971 with the establishment of the Policy Analysis and Resource Allocation (PARA) system, under the under secretary and the Planning and Coordination Staff. PARA conducts annual policy reviews for major areas of the world, attempting to specify general lines of policy for the future. For example, during 1971, policy reviews were completed that considered America's relations with Canada, North Africa, East Asia, and Western Europe.

budget was less than 1 percent of the budget of the Defense Department and approximately half that of the CIA. From every federal dollar, only 3 percent was spent internationally for nondefense purposes, and of this the State Department's share was one eighth.[60] Because of State's negative image and lack of a significant constituency, "reasonable requests for more funds somehow come out sounding like a cookie pusher's plea for a bigger booze allowance." [61]

5. President-Secretary Relationship

Although the subject of the recent expansion of the President's advisory staff within the Executive Office of the President will be discussed in some detail in the next chapter, it should be mentioned here that the influence of the President's "noncabinet" White House advisers has affected the relationship between the President and his Secretary of State and, as a consequence, has had impact on the foreign policy role of the State Department. The effectiveness of State was inextricably tied to the character of the relationship of the secretary with the President. If the President chose to act largely as his own Secretary of State, as was the case with Presidents Roosevelt and Kennedy, the department was called on less frequently for significant contributions to foreign affairs and, as a direct consequence, the usefulness and potential effectiveness of State's personnel was reduced.[62] However, it should not be concluded that the presence of a strong secretary resolved this problem. Under President Eisenhower, Secretary Dulles' practice of assuming personal responsibility for the formulation and high-level implementation of foreign policy left the personnel of State largely uninvolved in the directing of foreign affairs.

Three generalizations may be made based on postwar relations between Presidents and their Secretaries of State: (1) Active Presidential participation in foreign affairs has resulted in circumventing State, thus contributing to a lowering of morale. (2) Limited Presidential participation or inexperience in foreign affairs has been accompanied by an assertive Secretary of State (Secretaries Dulles and, in some respects, Acheson), undis-

---

[60] *New York Times,* November 12, 1967, p. 78.

[61] William Atwood, "The Labyrinth in Foggy Bottom," *Atlantic Monthly,* February 1967, p. 45.

[62] James F. Byrnes, Secretary of State under Presidents Roosevelt and Truman, indicated that State was seldom used by FDR. For example, en route to Yalta, President Roosevelt did not use State's files and recommendations that had been prepared specifically for the Yalta Conference. James F. Byrnes, *Speaking Frankly* (New York: Harper, 1947), p. 23.

There are numerous reports indicating that President Kennedy bypassed State, and instead, turned to the White House staff that were a part of "Bundy's little State Department." Professor Schlesinger recounts that President Kennedy, upset with State's lack of ideas or new suggestions, referred to the department as a "bowl of jelly." Schlesinger, *Thousand Days,* p. 406.

posed to use or seek advice from departmental subordinates, but, instead, prone to work out problems directly with foreign statesmen. Again, low State morale and deteriorating talents have been the result. (3) The increased influence of non-State Department Presidential advisers in foreign affairs has, understandably, weakened the morale, and thus the potential effectiveness of State's personnel. More and more it has come to be the practice that in the face of developing international crises, the President has turned first to his White House staff for support. To the extent that crises in Asia and the Middle East have been "managed" by the President's White House staff, the skills of State have been eroded through disuse.

Why State's Problems Persist

The question naturally comes to mind as to why these basic problems have plagued the State Department for so long? Why hasn't a progressive personnel program been activated at State? Why have restrictive operating procedures been in effect for decades? Why hasn't the requirement for policy planning been fully appreciated and supported? What has prevented Presidents from fully supporting their Secretaries of State and, as a consequence, tapping the rich professional resources of the department and strengthening its domestic status?

One reason has to do with the position and responsibilities of the Secretary of State. First, it was difficult to attract a person to the position of secretary who could also instigate reform. A weak secretary would be incapable of implementing change and, in addition, would lack the motivation to do so in the first place. Strong secretaries expended their energies in affecting and implementing foreign policy, not in fostering internal administrative reorganization.[63] Beyond these considerations, the dual demands of the secretary's job (advising the President and administering the department) left him little time or energy to implement a major program of aggressive reform. While cognizant of the need for change, most secretaries seem to have been forced by the day-to-day demands of their position to adjust to, rather than reform, existing departmental deficiencies.

A second basic difficulty may be inferred from the persistence of problems that have weakened the department. It centers on the fact that if there were a strong conviction within the executive branch that the values, perceptions, and diplomatic practices traditionally associated with the

---

[63] Secretary Rusk is difficult to classify as either a strong or weak secretary. Whatever skills he possessed as adviser or negotiator were not employed as a vehicle for reform within the department. "The inscrutability which made a good aide and a gifted negotiator made him also a baffling leader. . . . Since his subordinates did not know what he thought, they could not do what he wanted. In consequence, he failed to imbue the Department with positive direction and purpose. He had authority but not command." Schlesinger, *Thousand Days*, p. 435.

State Department offered an important resource vital to the cause of national security, then internal departmental reform would occur without delay. Considering this point somewhat differently, the fact that reform has been needed for so long suggests that succeeding postwar administrations have had reservations concerning the utility of the State Department.

Contrasting State and Defense Approaches to Problem Resolution

The sense of threat described in Chapter 1, and the development of impressive military strength to contend with that threat, as described in Chapter 2, has relegated State and all nonmilitary resources available to the government to a secondary foreign policy role. The responsibility of containment and the complementary strategy of deterrence provoked the development of a military capability that quickly came to be regarded as the principal component of America's national security program. As threats emerged that seemed to call for a rapid response, military advice concerning the appropriate application of military capabilities assumed the major influence in foreign policy decision-making circles. The State Department's nonmilitary advice seemed less and less relevant to the way in which America's international role was perceived. Also, as a result of the United States assigning significant numbers of armed forces to areas of the world that appeared threatened by communism, the impact of policy input from the Defense Department tended to outweigh those coming from State. In Asia, for example, in 1972, the United States maintained approximately 500,000 military personnel in South Korea, South Vietnam, Thailand, Japan, Okinawa, Taiwan, and the Philippines. Because of the presence of United States forces in these areas, developments of almost any kind automatically became military problems, and thus the primary responsibility of the Defense Department. Also, in confronting international conflicts that had not yet developed into military engagements, the State Department would appear cautious in expressing its position, refraining from assertively setting forth its advisory opinion. For example, as the Bay of Pigs plan of action began to unfold in 1961, it has been reported that,

> . . . The Secretary of State failed in refusing to take a strong stand and in not insisting that experts who had a contribution to make should be allowed to make it. Above all, both the Secretary and the Department failed to make the case for political considerations that should have been made. They failed to take up the role of leadership that the President expected of them.[64]

To the extent that America's world outlook was beset by a sense of imminent threat that called for rapid maximization of military strength,

---

[64] Roger Hilsman, *To Move A Nation* (Garden City, New York: Doubleday, 1967). p. 34.

the capabilities of the State Department seemed out of context. State's skills involved time-consuming investigations of the complex social, political, economic (as well as military) aspects of any developing "threat." Not only were State's protracted endeavors and diplomatic engagements time-consuming, the results were viewed as being of questionable utility since they were encumbered with qualifications and exceptions. They lacked the measured neatness and serviceability of the categorical pronouncements provided by the military analyst.[65]

The difference between the military and nonmilitary approach to the resolution of a foreign affairs problem is, in itself, important since it helps explain the weakness and diminished influence of State in policy circles. To further illustrate this difference, a hypothetical problem can be briefly sketched and, with this situation in mind, it is possible to suggest the general outline of what might characterize the approach of the State Department, in contrast to the approach of the Defense Department, in recommending a course of action in a briefing session before the National Security Council.

Assume that Communist-sponsored insurrectionist activity in Northeast Thailand suddenly increased in intensity. The infiltration of Communists into the area also increased significantly—an activity that had been in progress since 1962 with the objective of promoting separatism among the eight million Thai of Lao ethnic origin. Communist terrorist assassinations of local Thai officials, the ambushing of police, and the propagandizing of villages, all clearly backed by Hanoi and Peking, took such an upswing in intensity and frequency that it was clear that the entire Northeastern Plateau of Thailand was about to fall under Communist control.

In response to this threat to the stability of the Thai government, and because of reports that Communist forces were beginning to move southward in the direction of Bangkok, the President of the United States called a meeting of the NSC to seek advice on what might be the most appropriate course of action for the United States to pursue. At the NSC meeting, the State Department spokesman was the first to present his department's position and suggested that three general courses of action be initiated:

1. Forceful statements be issued immediately to Hanoi and Peking demanding that their support of Communist activities in Thailand be halted without delay.

2. Ad hoc study groups be formed to identify sources of popular dis-

---

[65] President Kennedy was sensitive to this point and, according to Sorenson, "at times . . . wished that his Secretary [of State] . . . would assert himself more boldly, recommend solutions more explicitly, offer imaginative alternatives to Pentagon plans more frequently. . . . Rusk at times seemed almost too eager to disprove charges of State Department softness by accepting Defense Department toughness." Sorenson, *Kennedy,* p. 271.

content in all regions of Thailand to specify remedial, and thus anti-Communist, actions that the United States might initiate through AID, Military Assistance Advisory Groups, USIA, and members of the embassy staff stationed in Bangkok.

3. Meetings with the President of Thailand be initiated to determine actions that the Thai government might undertake to contain communism to which the United States might lend diplomatic support, at least during the period of initial response by the Thai government.

The State Department spokesman indicated that counterinsurgency action was a protracted, complicated, subtle undertaking and that the task of reinforcing the link between the Thai people and their government simply could not be accomplished overnight. The State Department expressed reservations and qualifications concerning the probable outcome of any of their recommended actions. No definite promises could be made. The State Department's emphasis was focused on the point that any effort by the United States to unify the Thai people in their opposition to indigenous Communist forces would require at least two or three years of sustained cooperation and aid.

The spokesman for the Department of Defense made the following specific assertions:

1. Bomber attacks should be initiated immediately to interdict the infiltration by Hanoi and Peking of men and supplies into Northeastern Thailand.

2. Increased bombing (protective reaction) raids should be immediately directed against North Vietnamese targets to eliminate supply bases used to support the "offensive" against Thailand and, in addition, to provide a graphic warning that would deter Hanoi's support of the Thai "offensive."

3. Attacks should be initiated immediately against all centers of Communist activity in Northeastern Thailand. Thai military forces, reinforced by the United States military equipment, operating under American air cover, should initiate ground action against the Communist and Communist-support units in the northern areas of the Northeast Plateau, centering on the Udon region of Thailand.

4. Additional elements of the United States Seventh Fleet should be deployed at once to positions off the Thai coast in the Gulf of Siam, Andaman Sea, and the Bay of Bengal, as a deterrent to further Communist aggression.

5. All United States troop withdrawals from Southeast Asia should be halted until the Thai "crisis" was brought to a "manageable" status.

The Defense Department spokesman assured the President and the NSC that if all of the recommended actions were taken, the threat to orderly government in Thailand could be brought under control within six weeks at the longest. Not only would political stability be restored to Thailand, but this rapid, decisive response with force would stand as a warning against further Communist aggression in Asia and elsewhere in the world.

The most apparent generalized differences in the responses advocated by the Department of Defense and those of the Department of State, as reflected by this hypothetical briefing, are summarized below in Figure 9, *Differences in Military and Nonmilitary Approaches to Problem Resolution.*

FIGURE 9
Differences in Military and Nonmilitary Approaches to Conflict Resolution

Defense Department Briefing . . . in contrast to . . .	State Department Briefing
1. Delivery concise and specific— few qualifications or uncertainties.	1. Qualified statements and tentative conclusions.
2. Problem described with appealing simplicity.	2. Emphasis given to social, political, and economic variables and complexities.
3. Events described as case of outright aggression.	3. Events described as local discontent aggravated by external pressures.
4. Aim seen as stability through the use of force.	4. Aim seen as stability through long-term social, political, and economic development.
5. Success promised.	5. No certain, predictable outcome assured.
6. Short-term American involvement predicted.	6. Extended time required to achieve satisfactory outcome.

For a quarter of a century American Presidents and their advisers have had their foreign policy perceptions shaped by the perceived threat of communism and the determination to contain the expansionist tendencies of communism. Feelings of threat and responsibility, combined with an isolationist history, disposed foreign policy decision-makers to find reassurance in the promised advantages of an expanded military capability. Foreign policy decisions made in response to a sense of threat were more deeply affected by the qualities of the Defense Department briefing suggested in Figure 9, than they were by the more qualified advice offered by the State Department. This situation helps explain the tendency of Presidents to emphasize a military response to perceived threats. The related build-up of the Defense Department helps explain the relatively less significant role of the State Department in shaping and implementing America's foreign policy. The less influential position of State also suggests that the President's requirement for a foreign policy advisory and implementation capability that matched his own growing responsibilities in foreign affairs would have to be satisfied by a set of capabilities supplementary to the resources of the State Department. This leads to consideration of the President's White House advisory system.

chapter 4

The Presidential Advisory System

The sense of threat that affected the extent of foreign policy influence exercised by the Defense Department and State Department also affected the Presidency. The threatening international environment of the Cold War meant that the President had to be able to make informed decisions rapidly—and to do this he needed to have immediate access to informed sources of advice and opinion. As mentioned in preceding chapters, the Departments of Defense and State acted in this advisory capacity. However, during the years following World War II, the President came to feel that the advice and information available to him from his cabinet and Congress were not adequate. Presidents from Truman to Nixon turned with increasing frequency to their White House-based advisers for support to develop an improved decision-making capability appropriate for the nuclear age.

The focus of the discussion of the Presidency in this chapter is the advisory system designed to keep the President informed concerning foreign affairs. The chapter describes the relationship between the President and the advisory groups closest to him that attempt to satisfy his information requirements. In a sense the discussion that follows describes the information system that serves the President—the elements that comprise the system, how they operate, how postwar Presidents have used the system, and some of the foreign policy implications of the system itself.

Scope of the President's Power

The Presidency, from the standpoint of the responsibilities of the office and the characteristics of the individual, remains the source of authority and direction for the nation's foreign policy. As Chief of State the President stands responsible for what the nation does or does not do in its relations with other nations.

The dominant position of the President with regard to foreign policy is based on a constitutional delegation of authority. In Article II, Sections 2 and 3 of the Constitution, it is specified that the President (1) "shall have power, by and with the advice and consent of the Senate, to make treaties, provided two-thirds of the Senators present concur," (2) "shall be Commander in Chief of the Army and Navy," and (3) "shall appoint ambassadors," and "shall receive ambassadors and other public ministers."

No absolute powers are granted to the President by the Constitution. The legislative branch is constitutionally authorized to act in a manner that can impose constraints upon any action the President may take in foreign affairs. In regard to treaties, the President is required to seek the advice of the Senate, a constitutional stipulation which, in practice, has involved the Senate's extending or denying its consent to ratification. If two thirds of the Senate do not approve the treaty, and if the President cannot through persuasion win the support of at least 67 Senators, he can then attempt to achieve a similar objective through the device of the executive agreement. The executive agreement, consisting of an agreement between the President and other heads of state without requiring the approval of the Senate, has been used with considerable frequency since the Presidency of Franklin Roosevelt and is a reflection of presidential initiatives in foreign affairs.[1]

With regard to the President's authority as Commander-in-Chief of the armed forces, Congress must first authorize funds to create and maintain the military. It is over this military capability that the President is literally Commander-in-Chief, and it is these forces that he can deploy in a manner considered appropriate from the standpoint of national security.

Finally, the President is constitutionally prohibited from appointing an American ambassador to a foreign post without first obtaining the concurrence of a majority of the Senate. In practice, however, Presidents have usually managed to secure ambassadorial appointments for the men of their choice since the Senate, recognizing the President's responsibility

---

[1] Agreements such as those resulting from the Teheran, Yalta, and Potsdam conferences during World War II are executive agreements and were not considered or approved by the Senate. Although, in theory, Presidents are not bound by the terms of executive agreements negotiated by preceding administrations, in practice Presidents have felt obligated to honor commitments made by their predecessors. Since the end of World War II, over three fourths of the international agreements involving the United States have been executive agreements rather than treaties.

for the conduct of foreign relations, has usually been reluctant to challenge him on this issue. One consideration that exerts an inhibiting influence on the President's freedom of action with regard to the negotiation of international agreements, responsibilties as Commander-in-Chief, and ambassadorial appointments is the realization that the financial backing of Congress is a prerequisite for the success of any Presidential venture in foreign affairs. Presidents will frequently make a considerable effort to explain foreign policy programs to key Congressmen, include Congressmen in foreign delegations, and encourage Congressmen to participate as observers in international conferences, hoping that through increased Congressional understanding it will be possible to build a stronger backing for Presidential programs.[2]

While the influence of Congress on the executive's foreign programs may temper any Presidential tendency to act unilaterally, the carefully designed balance of authority in foreign affairs intended by the framers of the Constitution has not existed during the years since World War II. The President is the initiator, the innovator, clearly the director in foreign policy. Congress may act to restrain the President—a possibility which prompts the President to anticipate the probable responses of Congress before he acts—but the general character of the Presidential-Congressional relationship in foreign policy is that of initiator to respondent. The role of Congress is largely reactionary (in a literal rather than political sense), with the House and Senate modifying, extending, or blocking Presidential proposals, but leaving to the President the responsibility to establish policy and to determine the means by which that policy will be implemented.[3]

---

[2] Some of the potential diplomatic complications of sponsoring visits by Congressmen to foreign posts are suggested by George Kennan's account of a Congressional entourage visiting Moscow. These Congressmen, on their way to visit Premier Stalin after having attended a vodka "tea" in the bowels of the Moscow subway system, began anticipating their interview with questions to Kennan such as, "Who the hell is this guy Stalin anyway?" and "What if I biff the old codger one in the nose?" Kennan's response was, "My heart froze." He then spoke firmly to the Congressmen, calmed them down and got through the meeting between the Congressmen and Stalin with the Americans doing "nothing more disturbing than to leer and wink once or twice at the bewildered dictator." George F. Kennan, *Memoirs, 1925–50* (Boston: Little, Brown and Co., 1967), pp. 275–77.

[3] Professor James Robinson suggests that one of the factors that has tended to diminish the ability of Congress to initiate legislation is the effect of the "information explosion" that has revolutionized policy making, ". . . it is the executive branch, not Congress, that has taken first advantage of the new information techniques; and, in so doing, it has gained advantage over Congress throughout the entire policy-making process. . . ." Professor Robinson points out that "The tendency of Congress to look to the executive for leadership is now endemic throughout all fields of government policy-making (particularly in foreign affairs, in which the constitutional advantage that the executive has always had is now enhanced by the information revolution). Thus, the role of Congress steadily becomes less one of initiating policy alternatives, and more one of modifying, negating, or legitimating proposals that originate with the executive." James A. Robinson, *Congress and Foreign Policy Making* (rev. ed.; Homewood, Illinois: Dorsey Press, 1967), pp. 179–80.

Growth of Presidential Power

One of the most striking developments of postwar American foreign policy is the expanded power and authority of the President. In addition to the traditional sources of Presidential authority in foreign affairs, such as the President's position as head of state which required him to represent the United States in relations with other nations, and the constitutional powers mentioned above, there was from Roosevelt to Nixon a continuing expansion of the active involvement of the President in foreign affairs. Professor William Carleton has suggested that the "sudden stupendous global influence of America constituted a veritable revolution, one of the most dramatic in history." [4] President Nixon, for example, indicated the global scope of America's foreign policy with the statement:

Our responsibilities are not limited to this great continent but include Europe, the Middle East, Southeast Asia, East Asia, many areas whose fates affect the peace of the world. . . .

There will be 400 million people in non-communist Asia relying ever more upon us. . . .

In past times the No. 1 nation was always in that position because of military conquests. But the mantle of leadership fell on American shoulders not by our desire and not for the purposes of conquest. But we have that position today, and how we handle ourselves will determine the chances of world peace.[5]

The clearest recent manifestation of the nation's sense of worldwide responsibility has been the American government's involvement in the Vietnam war. As suggested by President Nixon's statement, America's sense of responsibility is not confined to this single event but is also indicated, for example, by involvement in the 1971 Indian-Pakistani dispute and the Arab-Israeli conflict, President Nixon's visit to Communist China, the NATO alliance, and warnings to the Organization of American States (OAS) members to refrain from making agreements with Castro's Cuba.

There was a causal relationship between America's sense of global responsibility and the greatly increased power of the Chief Executive. Other developments that have contributed to the expansion of Presidential power during the last quarter century include the following.

1. Revolutionary Changes in the External Threats to America's National Security

Nuclear warheads, capable of destroying a major American city in a single strike and capable of reaching American targets in less than 30

---

[4] William G. Carleton, *The Revolution in American Foreign Policy* (2d ed.; New York: Random House, 1967), p. 17.

[5] C. L. Sulzberger interview with President Nixon, *New York Times*, March 10, 1971, p. 14. No transcripts were permitted to be made during this interview and the President's statement quoted above was reconstructed from notes made by Mr. Sulzberger.

minutes, made the nation highly vulnerable to enemy attack.[6] There was no effective physical defense against such an attack. America's only defense, basically a psychological defense, was nuclear deterrence, discussed in Chapter 2. Real and perceived threats to America's security prompted each postwar President to expand and modernize the military capabilities of the nation. The management of the nation's defense capabilities and the responsibility for the nation's security under conditions that required an instant response placed the President at the center of all activities that involved the conduct of relations with allied, neutral, or potentially enemy nations.

2. Expanded Scope of Information Requirements

The United States, being one of the two most powerful nations in the world, came to regard any significant political, military, and economic development in literally any other nation as having actual or potential relevance to America's security. For an information analyst assembling data in an office in the State or Defense Department, almost every event occurring anywhere in the world warranted examination as part of the task of supporting the President in the fulfillment of his foreign affairs responsibilities. The increase in the national security relevance of more and more events meant that the White House became the center to which data collectors and analysts passed increasing volumes of information. Clearly, the President had access to more information than any other single individual or agency in Washington. Access to and control of the broad sweep of information collected by all executive agencies strengthened the President's hand in foreign policy formulation simply because he could claim, or it might be assumed, that he knew more than anyone else.

3. The Exercise of Foreign Policy Initiative

Responsibility for the security of the nation provided the justification, and control of information provided the capability, for the President's exercise of foreign policy initiative. The President, by acting to fulfill his sense of responsibility for the security of the nation, left Congress little choice but to support him—at least initially. Frequently, when Presidential initiative was exercised in foreign affairs, Congress lacked sufficient relevant information to challenge the action of the President. The Truman Doctrine, Marshall Plan, and NATO were all manifestations of executive initiative, as was America's military involvement in the Korean and Vietnam wars.

---

[6] Defense strategists have pointed out that the 30-minute warning period could be reduced to less than five minutes if a missile were fired at an American target from a nuclear armed orbiting satellite.

The President's exercise of foreign policy initiative was also buttressed by his increasing use of emergency powers.[7] Through this power President Roosevelt, during World War II, created a number of federal agencies and initiated domestic actions for which he later sought support from Congress. Six months after the deployment of American troops to Korea President Truman declared the existence of a state of national emergency. With the President's exercise of his emergency powers there developed a broader acceptance of his use of Presidential initiative to preclude the emergence of a national crisis, a type of preventive authority.[8]

4. Availability of Mass Media

Mass media provided the President with direct access to the electorate and during the postwar decades Presidents used mass media with increasing frequency to build public support for their foreign policy programs. The President, when he wished to communicate his position to the public, enjoyed immediate access to all Americans. Any policy statement issued by the President "has behind it all the power of the nation speaking through the voice of one individual." [9] If the President decided that in support of the nation's security it was necessary for him to impose a quarantine against the shipment of Soviet missiles to Cuba, deploy American troops to Southeast Asia, or visit Communist China, he could use nationwide television to announce this fact to the American people, and thereby hope to generate a large body of popular support for his decision.

Power and Personality

The four sources of increased Presidential power just discussed and the flexibility of the constitutional and practical constraints on the President's authority in foreign affairs, suggest that the extent to which the President

---

[7] The President's emergency powers, intended to secure the nation against the consequences of national crisis, are based on two constitutional provisions, the President's role as Commander-in-Chief, and his responsibility to "take care that the laws be faithfully executed." (Article II, Section 3)

[8] It is frequently pointed out that the President's power of initiative is subject to certain checks, primarily those imposed by Congress. However, as President Johnson's press secretary George Reedy has observed, in foreign affairs these checks almost always assume the nature of a review. "Theoretically, Congress can always hamper activities by refusing to grant the necessary appropriations to pay for the acts taken by the executive. It is inconceivable though that Congress would refuse appropriations to support men who are fighting in the name of their country's freedom. It is also inconceivable that Congress would withhold appropriations that are essential to sustain the nation's prestige. And it is even more inconceivable that Congress would fail to approve a president's action against an avowed enemy." George Reedy, *The Twilight of the Presidency* (Cleveland, Ohio: World Publishing Co., 1970), pp. 39–40.

[9] Ibid., p. 41.

can define and act on foreign policy options varies with the energy, objectives, and unique capabilities characteristic of each individual President. Clearly formulated foreign policy objectives, in the hands of a strong, articulate President, have seldom been seriously hampered by constitutional constraints. Forceful, popular Presidents, such as Presidents Roosevelt, Truman, and Kennedy, were usually able to persuade the public, Congress, and the executive bureaucracy to support their foreign policy objectives, especially when these objectives could be described as means to strengthen the nation's security in the face of external threats. What the President can and does do in foreign affairs is closely tied to his personal inclinations. Restraints that inhibit a President's performance are largely those that he *allows* to reduce his sphere of effectiveness. This flexible situation suggests several considerations. First, if a future President should fail to provide forceful foreign policy leadership, possibly because he assigned highest priority to problems in the area of domestic policy, there is no mechanism, set of laws, or executive agency that could assure the effective implementation of America's foreign policy interests, whatever these might be. Second, with an aggressive, expansionist future President, a man "excited" by the prospect of utilizing the nation's strategic military resources to achieve foreign policy objectives, there are no definitely effective constraints that could quickly be brought to bear on the Chief Executive. Third, a responsible, forward looking, basically intelligent President could, nevertheless, be insensitive to the diverse personal and institutional interests that comprise the American political system and, as a result of alienating or aggravating Congress, the State Department, and the public, might seriously limit the utility of his supporting resources and thereby place the implementation of his foreign policy in jeopardy.

The point has been stressed that the scope of responsibility assumed by the President in foreign affairs is largely determined by the inclinations of each individual President. However, despite their diversity in foreign policy style, one consistent characteristic of each of the five Presidents since the pronouncement of the Truman Doctrine in 1947 has been the tendency to make statements and initiate actions that have given to America's foreign policy a continuously expanding range of commitments. The consistency and breadth of this commitment is conveyed by Figure 1 in Chapter 1.

The Burden of Information

As the scope of America's foreign responsibilities has expanded over the past 25 years, American officials have come to believe, with some justification, that events occurring anywhere in the world have some bearing on United States national security. An expanded sense of world responsibility *causes* more events to assume relevance. With more events assuming relevance, there has developed, as suggested above, a requirement for a vastly increased volume of information.

Another factor that has increased the volume of information collected by the government is the radically improved technological means for collecting, analyzing, and storing it. Electronic sensors and photographic satellites have revolutionized collection capabilities. Computer technology has provided analysis and data storing resources of an unprecedented nature. It is interesting to speculate that one reason for the increased requirement for more information about diverse subjects in remote geographic areas is that the United States possesses the technological ability to collect and store such data. In other words, technology, rather than human rationality, determines information requirements.[10]

The President is dependent on information to fulfill his foreign policy responsibilities as well as to lead his political party, to initiate legislation affecting all areas of American life, to administer a bureaucracy of almost three million federal employees, and to represent the interests of all the American people. However, the President, as with all humans, finds that his ability to absorb and efficiently utilize information is restricted to a finite number of hours each day simply because of the limitations of physical stamina. Thus, a problem arises consisting of three elements:

1. The President has only a finite amount of time to devote to his various decision-making responsibilities.

2. Each day thousands of pieces of information from hundreds of agencies and thousands of individuals compete to command the attention of the President.

3. As the responsibilities of the government continue to expand, the President has less time to devote to each of the increasing number of issues about which there is more information. Since the President cannot neglect any area of domestic or foreign responsibility, he has tended to seek help to cope with the pressures that drive him to "spread himself thinner."

Presidents generally, but particularly postwar Presidents, being dependent on information and advice to perform adequately, yet seeking to avoid being inundated by a growing deluge of paper, have worked to develop a system that could offer maximum assurance of making available appropriate information at the appropriate time. Much of this information has concerned national security affairs and it is this aspect of the President's information system to which the discussion that follows will be confined.

---

[10] Harvey Wheeler, in his essay, "The Strategic Calculators," in Nigel Calder, *Unless Peace Comes* (New York: Viking Press, 1968), pp. 103–14, suggests that America has become an interventionist power simply because it possesses military resources that will support such action at any point on the globe.

Basic to the structure of the President's information system is the matter of priorities. From the standpoint of national security, some information is obviously more relevant than other items of information. Information concerning actions by terrorists against the government of South Africa commands a lower priority in eliciting Presidential attention than does news of insurrectionist activity directed against American military bases in Thailand, Okinawa, or South Korea. As might be assumed, the highest priority is assigned to information concerning a direct, and possibly imminent, attack against the United States. These data would be received through a system of warning sensors that would allow the President approximately 15 to 30 minutes to decide what the appropriate American response would be. The enemy's action and the President's reaction must both occur within a time period of less than half an hour.

Second priority is assigned to information concerning a potential direct (but not imminent) attack against the United States. Information from various sources concerning the military capabilities, actions, and intentions of the USSR and Communist China comprise the bulk of such inputs.[11]

Third priority status is given to information indicating that action has taken place or may take place against American personnel or property (extensions of the nation's sovereign territory) in any part of the world. Reports of attacks against American military forces in Asia or Sixth Fleet naval vessels stationed in the Mediterranean represent information of this nature. These first three categories of highest priority information consist primarily of military intelligence.

Fourth priority information is usually of a political or economic nature relating to the stability of America's allied governments. Instability of an ally, for any cause, suggests an indirect threat to the security of the United States. The political instability or defection of a NATO or SEATO ally is an example of the kind of development about which the President must be informed.

A fifth category of information priority concerns the extension (actual or potential) of Communist influence anywhere in the world. Such expansion is viewed as a clear threat to American security.

Finally, the President must be immediately aware of information that suggests the need for Presidential initiative to be taken to achieve a diplomatic advantage. Indications of the political advisability of meeting with another head of state, the advantage of a summit conference, or the appropriateness of issuing a firm, strongly phrased warning to another head

---

[11] Second priority intelligence would, for example, include intelligence gathered through photographic satellites that indicated the USSR was apparently engaged in constructing enlarged concrete missile silos, possibly intended to house new multiple warhead intercontinental missiles. The first-strike implications of this intelligence "find" would be made immediately available to the President.

of state must be available to the White House so that the details justifying the need for action can be assimilated by the President.

The Advisory System

How does the President acquire and disseminate the information that will support him in the fulfillment of his foreign policy responsibilities? Information reaches the President from a large number of diverse sources. It is possible to illustrate the sources of information used by the President by arranging them in the form of concentric circles. (See Figure 10,

FIGURE 10
Presidential "Advisory" Circles

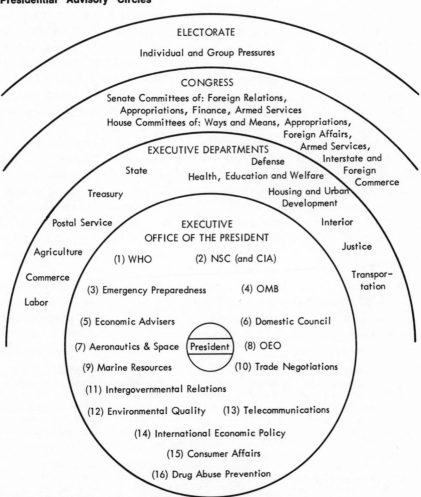

Presidential "Advisory" Circles.) Assuming the President to be located at the center of these circles, the sources of information input farthest removed from the President are the public and Congress. The public, through mass media, pressure groups, and their own individual efforts, convey to the President facts and opinions that affect Presidential decision-making. The impact of public opinion on Presidential decision-making is dependent on the effectiveness of the group through which the opinion is expressed. This effectiveness is, in turn, based on a number of variables such as group size, leadership, cohesiveness, social status, scope of influence, financial resources, political disposition, commitment to group objectives, and ingenuity in designing means to achieve group objectives.

Congress, through both formal (such as committee hearings and voting behavior) and informal (such as breakfast or luncheon meetings with the President) forms of contact, is able to convey essential information to the Chief Executive. Congressmen may also use a more public setting (speeches, articles, television appearances, and press interviews) to convey a point of view to the electorate and the President. The President is most interested in obtaining information from Congress that will enable him to anticipate actions by Congressmen that will affect programs the President is interested in initiating or supporting.[12]

Moving closer to the Presidential center, the twelve executive departments, the heads of which comprise the President's cabinet, and the numerous independent agencies and commissions of the executive branch all interact with the President to keep him informed concerning their specialized areas of responsibility.[13] The two departments most obviously related to matters of national defense are State and Defense.

The groups and individuals closest to the President, those having the most regular and direct contact with the Chief Executive, are the officials of the Executive Office of the President. The 1939 act which established the Executive Office of the President was a response to a study committee's 1937 report that observed, "The President needs help." [14] This conclusion, possibly the shortest scholarly sentence on record, provided the rationale on which was built a Presidential advisory system which by

---

[12] Congressional staff personnel indicate that most requests for information from the executive branch concern procedural or scheduling issues affecting legislation in which the President is interested. (Robinson, *Congress and Foreign Policy*, p. 143.)

[13] There are over 30 independent agencies within the executive branch, including, for example, agencies such as the Federal Trade Commission (1,000 employees), Atomic Energy Commission (7,000 employees), Federal Aviation Administration (45,000 employees), and the National Aeronautics and Space Administration (32,000 employees).

[14] Report of the President's Committee on Administrative Management submitted to President Roosevelt in 1937.

1972 included approximately 4,000 personnel (professional staff and clerks) and operated on an annual budget of $100 million.[15]

The Executive Office of the President consists of 16 advisory offices, each representing an area of executive responsibility and each headed by a Presidential adviser chosen by the President.[16] With regard to American foreign policy, all of these offices (some to only a limited extent) play a role in determining what the policy will be and how it will be implemented. The work of Presidential advisers involving contacts with Congress, press releases, speech writing, and budget recommendations all affect the scope, characteristics and effectiveness of the nation's foreign relations. However, among the 16 groups comprising the Executive Office of the President, the two that serve the President most consistently in the area of foreign affairs are the White House Office and the National Security Council. These offices are the focus of the discussion which follows.

The White House Office

The President's White House Office (WHO) was established by executive order in 1939, with no prescribed set of functions. However, from the outset the basic function of WHO was to insure that the President be adequately and currently informed. The advisers making up WHO do not make decisions for the President but, instead, they assemble, present, and discuss with the President information that will assist him in arriving at the most appropriate decision.[17] In addition to bringing information to the attention of the President, the White House Office disseminates information concerning Presidential decisions to every executive department and agency having related areas of responsibility.

Advisers in WHO are chosen by the President, they are not confirmed

---

[15] See discussion by Louis W. Koenig, "The Invisible Presidency," in Sidney Wise and Richard F. Schier (eds.), *The Presidential office* (New York: Thomas Y. Crowell Co., 1968), and Clinton Rossiter, *The American Presidency* (New York: Harcourt, Brace and World, 1956).

[16] The 16 advisory offices that comprise the Executive Office of the President (as of 1972) consist of the following: (1) White House Office, (2) National Security Council, (3) Office of Emergency Preparedness, (4) Office of Management and Budget, (5) Council of Economic Advisers, (6) Domestic Council, (7) National Aeronautics and Space Council, (8) Office of Economic Opportunity, (9) Office of Science and Technology, (10) Office of Special Representative for Trade Negotiations, (11) Office of Intergovernmental Relations, (12) Council on Environmental Quality, (13) Office of Telecommunications Policy, (14) Council on International Economic Policy, (15) Office of Consumer Affairs, and (16) Special Action Office for Drug Abuse Prevention.

[17] Some of the White House advisers who have "enjoyed" national recognition since the beginning of the Kennedy administration include Theodore Sorenson, Arthur Schlesinger, W.W. Rostow, Pierre Salinger, General Maxwell Taylor, McGeorge Bundy, Lawrence O'Brien, Bill Moyers, Richard Goodwin, Douglass Cater, Henry Kissinger, George Shultz, John Ehrlichman, and Daniel Moynihan.

by the Senate, their appointment is never challenged, and they are protected by "executive privilege" from being required to testify before Congress.[18] They are the President's personal staff, always accessible to him, serving him directly, analyzing and "making manageable" the problems he confronts. Since the problems and tasks of the White House staff correspond precisely with those of the President, they extend to such broad areas of responsibility as national security, domestic affairs, the executive budget, Congressional relations, urban affairs, welfare, speech writing, and the mass media. The White House staff is, in essence, an extension of the President's personality and those who act as his advisers embody a particular personality and philosophy that the President finds congenial and stimulating. Staff members hold their jobs at the President's pleasure, or for as long as the President finds them useful.

The members of the President's staff, according to Theodore Sorenson, Special Counsel to Presidents Kennedy and Johnson, do not replace the role of a cabinet official or block his access to the President. Instead, the usefulness of the President's staff is described as follows:

. . . by working closely with the departmental personnel, by spotting, refining, and redefining issues for the President, they can increase governmental unity rather than splinter responsibility. A good White House staff can give a President that crucial margin of time, analysis, and judgment that makes an unmanageable problem more manageable.[19]

The last sentence of this quotation refers to "a good White House staff" and to a "crucial margin of time." A brief comment is appropriate concerning both of these phrases.

First, a judgment as to whether the members of the White House Office constitute a "good White House staff" can be rendered only by the President. Each President selects his staff on the basis of standards he alone prescribes. These standards are derived from the President's general political outlook, his concept of administrative procedures, the method and style by which he chooses to be advised, and the conditions that he finds most congenial for receiving and transmitting information. The members of the staff are chosen for their ability to help satisfy the President's information requirements, in essence, to talk the President's language.

---

[18] Some members of Congress, in response to the President's decision to use military power in Vietnam, Laos, and Cambodia, were outspoken in their effort to impose restrictions on the President's war-making powers. Hearings were held by a Senate Judiciary subcommittee on legislation to keep the executive branch from withholding information from Congress. Sen. Fulbright, one of the subcommittee's witnesses, charged that the Nixon administration was conducting foreign policy through a White House "superbureau" that was "shielded from Congress and the American people behind a barricade of executive privilege." (*New York Times* July 28, 1971, p. 8.)

[19] Theodore C. Sorenson, *Decision-Making in the White House* (New York: Columbia University Press, 1963), p. 71.

Second, with regard to the "crucial margin of time," the White House Office operates on the assumption that most Presidential decisions are too far-reaching and irrevocable to be made in haste. However, urgent time pressures are frequently present. It is the function of the White House Office first to determine what the margin of time is for any pending decision and then to assist the President to use that time to its maximum advantage. With regard to the 1962 Cuban missile crisis, Sorenson quoted President Kennedy as stating, "If we had to act in the first twenty-four hours, I don't think . . . we would have chosen as prudently as we finally did." [20] But if 24 hours had been the "crucial margin of time," the White House Office, plus other Presidential advisers, would have worked to make the best possible use of those hours from the standpoint of making information available to the President.

As the President's responsibilities expanded and the requirement for advice concerning the numerous areas of federal responsibility increased, so the size of the White House Office grew in the years since 1939. This increase (from three secretaries, a military and naval aid, and 20 clerks under President Hoover, to a total of 1,200 employees under President Nixon) was a reflection of the increased responsibilities of the President and, in addition, a reflection of the changed relationship between the President and his cabinet. The cabinet, only 30 years ago, was thought of as a body of the President's most important and intimate working associates, men who shared the President's broad interests and whose sense of national (apart from departmental or regional) responsibility matched that of the President. This, however, as oberved by Professor Clinton Rossiter, was a relic of a simpler past.[21] Cabinet officers of the 1960s and '70s were heads of vast, complex executive departments, each having special departmental interests to serve. Some, like the Secretary of Defense, had a large constituency of their own, inside and outside of the government. Usually, a cabinet member, as he began his tenure as secretary, regarded his ties to the President as primary, and his ties to his department as secondary. With time in office this concept changed and the secretary soon became a pleader for a specific departmental cause.[22] The special interests of different executive departments conflicted with one another and with the President's concept of national policy. Thus, while department heads formed the upper tier of Presidential advisers, each was bound by the more parochial bureaucratic interests and staff policies of his department. Theodore Sorenson, in describing the inherent limitations of cabinet officials as sources of advice and information, wrote,

---

[20] Ibid., p. 30.

[21] Clinton Rossiter, *The American Presidency*, p. 148.

[22] J.R. Steelman and H. Dewayne Kreager, "The Executive Office as Administrative Coordinator," *Law and Contemporary Problems*, Autumn 1956.

. . . Each department has its own clientele and point of view, its own experts, and bureaucratic interests, its own relations with Congress, and certain subcommittees, its own statutory authority, objectives, and standards of success. . . . The President may ask for a Secretary's best judgment apart from the department's views, but in the mind of the average Secretary . . . the two may be hardly distinguishable.[23]

Thus, on the one hand, the President must have access to information covering all aspects of national and international affairs to make appropriate decisions. On the other hand, cabinet members and agency heads, by virtue of their more specific and limited responsibilities, have found it difficult to think always in terms of the "big picture." This has caused the President to expect varied and often conflicting recommendations from his cabinet members, recommendations that require careful sorting, analysis, and matching against the President's own conception of the nation's foreign and domestic objectives before a final executive decision can be made. In this setting, the President has required someone to do the sorting, analysis, and matching for him. The White House Office, with no departmental allegiances, came to assume the primary responsibility for directly assisting the President in the fulfillment of his domestic and foreign functions.

Presidential Use of the White House Office

Presidents have differed widely in utilization of the White House Office. Some, like President Truman, have maintained an informal relationship with the White House staff. Each staff member (there were approximately ten during the last year of the Truman administration) enjoyed equal and direct access to the President. At times President Truman was urged to establish an advisory system that specified a clearer hierarchical relationship among staff personnel. However, it seems that whatever system he did establish he was likely to ignore. He remained "incurably informal and accessible." [24] The President's advisers did provide significant support and useful information, however, as suggested by the estimate that President Truman spent "as much as one-half to two-thirds of

---

[23] Sorenson, *Decision-Making*, pp. 68–69. Cabinet officers have testified how their huge executive departments continue to conduct programs designed to serve objectives defined by past Presidents. For example, some of Franklin Roosevelt's appointees to federal positions, promoted with time to senior civil service jobs, contributed in the 1970s to the perpetuation of practices and views to which President Nixon's own 2,500 appointees were forced to adjust.

[24] Richard E. Neustadt, *Presidential Power* (New York: John Wiley and Sons, Inc., 1960), p. 172.

One formal practice President Truman did adhere to was, once having reached a decision, he insisted that a written record be made of this decision. President Truman believed that the oral rendering of decisions tended to increase the probability that the decision would be interpreted according to the particular predilections of his listener.

his time" studying and discussing advisory reports from his staff before making a decision.[25]

Under President Eisenhower, the informal character of the Presidential staff relationship changed radically. The close interaction of President Truman and his staff that made the President equally accessible to each member of his staff was abandoned. In its place was organized a White House Office with the character of a formal, hierarchical agency with the Assistant to the President cast in a role resembling a chief-of-staff.[26] This change from the informal to the formal gave unprecedented order to the White House Office, making it resemble the chain of command structure with which President Eisenhower was familiar and, because of his military background, presumably most comfortable. The individual around whom the chief-of-staff function developed was Sherman Adams, former Governor of New Hampshire. Mr. Adams, as The Assistant to the President, made the White House Office a clearing house for policy matters.[27] The role of primary importance performed by Adams was to select, arrange, and transmit information to the President that he (Adams) considered important. Through Adams was filtered virtually every problem, question, or request. The staff commanded by Adams was divided into functional units that handled Presidential appointment schedules, the press, liaison with Congress, liaison with executive departments, legal questions, the writing of speeches and papers, and day-to-day economic problems.

In his role as chief-of-staff of White House operations, Sherman Adams took orders only from the President. The heads of executive departments and agencies approached the President only through the chief-of-staff.[28] Policy proposals for the President's decision were all submitted to the President through Sherman Adams. Each policy proposal was prepared in writing and was the result of extensive staff study. When a proposal was ready to be submitted to the President for action, the papers on

---

[25] Anthony Leviero, "How the President Makes Decisions," *New York Times Magazine,* October 8, 1950, pp. 14–15, 62, 64–66.

[26] See discussion in Wilfred E. Binkley, *The Man in the White House* (Baltimore, Maryland: Johns Hopkins Press, 1958), especially p. 216.

[27] Sherman Adams, viewing himself as first among "equals," prefixed the word "The" to his title, a change that accurately reflected his position as the most influential of the White House staff.

[28] There were two exceptions to this situation. The first was Secretary of State John Foster Dulles who might "telephone the President twenty-five or thirty times a week, drop in at the White House three or four times in addition, and, on weekends, if Eisenhower was in town, stop in on Sunday afternoons." Lewis E. Koenig, *The Invisible Presidency* (New York: Rinehart and Co., 1960), p. 376. The second exception was the Secretary of Treasury George Humphrey whose advice, it is reported, was sought on foreign as well as domestic problems. (*New York Times,* February 3, 1957, p. 8). President Eisenhower once said, "In Cabinet meetings I always wait for George Humphrey to speak. I sit back and listen to others talk while he doesn't say anything. But I know when he speaks he will say just what I am thinking." Richard Rovere, "Eisenhower: A Trial Balance," *Reporter,* April 12, 1955, pp. 14–20.

which it was based were accompanied by a one-page, double-spaced synopsis prepared by Adams. "If a proposition can't be stated in one page," President Eisenhower declared, "it isn't worth saying." [29]

One of the key functions served by The Assistant to the President was that of a buffer between the President and the vast volume of information that pressed in upon the White House. From the mass of documents and papers that entered the White House each day, Mr. Adams would select those which he decided the President should see. Adams also acted as an information buffer by his constant efforts to keep people and their problems from the President, leaving him free for other things. Adams is reported to have said, "I count the day lost when I have not found some way of lightening the President's load." [30] By determining whom the President saw and what he read, Adams was able to control the elaborate staff system through which information was channeled up from the executive departments to the President's desk.

The system by which the White House Office was to transmit information to and from the President was designed to spare the President the routine paper work and conferences that preceded the formulation of policy recommendation. Beyond this, President Eisenhower insisted that the conflicts concerning policy be resolved before they reached his desk. He wanted to hear only consensus, not the opinions or unresolved differences of his staff members.

In addition to transmitting information to the President, Adams acted to implement Presidential decisions. He did this through the members of the President's cabinet, during and after cabinet meetings. [31] One of the strongest inducements used by Adams to stimulate policy implementation by executive department heads was the "Action Status Report," a statement prepared by the departments at least every three months. This re-

[29] Charles Murphy, "Eisenhower's White House," *Fortune,* July 1953, p. 77. The President would not be bothered with paper work. What he preferred, and what assured Presidential consideration, was, at the end of a paper, to have Sherman Adams initial the phrase, "O.K., S.A." The President then could, with assurance, initial this paper, "D.D.E."

[30] Neustadt, *Presidential Power,* p. 159.

[31] Traditionally, the essence of cabinet meetings was their informality. Discussion, the exchange of conflicting points of view, and the relaxed atmosphere of cabinet gatherings provided the information, opinion, and stimulation that Presidents Roosevelt and Truman valued so highly. Under Eisenhower, cabinet meetings became systematically planned and rigidly controlled. Agenda for meetings were prepared under White House Office supervision. For each item to be discussed, elaborate cabinet papers, running 50 pages or longer, were assembled and circulated in advance. The cabinet member making a "presentation" was rehearsed by the cabinet secretary. Visual aids in the form of charts, slides, and even films were made ready. A system of flashing lights was installed in the cabinet room to enable the cabinet secretary to maintain a tight time schedule for the various presentations. Following the cabinet meeting the cabinet secretary would brief the departmental assistants and attempt to determine the extent to which cabinet decisions had been carried out. Richard Fenno, *The President's Cabinet* (Cambridge, Massachusetts: Harvard University Press, 1959), p. 111, and R. E. Neustadt, Review, *Reporter,* June 11, 1959, pp. 38–40.

port indicated how far the departments had progressed toward implementing Presidential decisions. Action Status Reports were reviewed at all cabinet meetings. The prospect of being exposed before the President as delinquent motivated executive departments to fulfill their commitment to the President.

An evaluation of the system designed to transmit information to President Eisenhower suggests that the President may have been spared too much. Within the mechanical apparatus presided over by Sherman Adams the President was insulated from the information and pressures that stimulate insight and develop sensitivity. It was the opinion of one student of the White House system under President Eisenhower that, "By blocking citizens and communications from reaching the President, by limiting debate and discussion, and by arrogating decisions into his own hands, Adams kept the President from securing a knowledge of harsh realities which it was the duty of the Chief Executive to have." [32]

Under President Kennedy no attempt was made to replace Sherman Adams. President Kennedy's approach to information gathering precluded the excessive reliance on any single person for advice, or the filtering of policy proposals through a chief-of-staff. President Kennedy preferred to work directly and informally through ad hoc task forces that he created to deal with national and international problems. Such a task force would usually include members of the White House Office, plus the Attorney General (Robert Kennedy), the Secretaries of Defense and State, and the Chairman of the Joint Chiefs of Staff.

President Kennedy's White House staff reported directly to him, each member having direct access to the President. Informal, unscheduled exchanges of information and directives between the President and his staff characterized operating relationships under President Kennedy. Although disposed to receive and transmit information on a person-to-person basis, President Kennedy also held numerous organized meetings with his cabinet, National Security Council, and White House assistants. Theodore Sorenson reported that President Kennedy believed that there were a number of advantages associated with organized meetings involving a number of advisers. These advantages may be summarized as follows: (1) Such meetings reflect a degree of order and regularity which inspire increased public confidence; (2) they increase the esprit de corps of the participants; (3) organized meetings serve to keep open the channels of communication; and (4) through meetings and the interaction of many minds it is possible to air diverse points of view, to hear alternatives, to expose errors, and to challenge assumptions. [33]

In holding organized meetings of his staff, President Kennedy learned

---

[32] Koenig, *The Invisible Presidency,* p. 358.

[33] Sorenson, *Decision-Making,* pp. 58–59. Point 1, above, is particularly interesting since it suggests the attention President Kennedy tended to give to the political implications of the way things might appear in the public's eye.

that it was necessary for him to weigh carefully his own words. If he hinted too early in the proceedings at the direction of his own thought, the weight of his authority and the understandable desire of advisers to side with the President could have the effect of cutting off productive debate. For example, it was reported that President Kennedy, upon learning on his return from a midweek trip in October 1962, that the deliberations of the NSC executive committee over the Cuban missile crisis had been more spirited and frank in his absence, asked the committee to hold other preliminary sessions without him.[34]

As a consequence of President Kennedy's actively seeking new and diverse sources of information, the volume of information entering the White House during the Kennedy years probably reached an unprecedented high point.[35] Theodore Sorenson has described how the inevitable tides of official memoranda, reports, cables, intelligence briefings, analyses, and numerous other government documents forced the President to become subject to a "drowning in paper." [36] In speaking of the difficult balance between the President's almost limitless information requirements and the limitations of any human to assimilate information, Sorenson wrote: "While he [the President] cannot permit himself to be submerged in detail, he cannot afford to know so little as to shut out perspective and new inspiration." [37]

The methods by which Presidents Eisenhower and Kennedy used their White House Office as a source of information represent procedural extremes: the structured, relatively inflexible, mechanistic, centralized information system, as opposed to the more open, decentralized, informal system. President Johnson adopted an approach to information gathering and dissemination that tended to conform to the Kennedy end of the spectrum, although President Johnson was less accessible, less an "open door man" than President Kennedy. President Johnson tended to feel most comfortable in a more closed, person-to-person type contact with a restricted number of familiar advisers. President Nixon, on the other hand, adopted practices that were closer to those developed by President Eisenhower. Orderly, prescheduled meetings, reviewing reports that reflect the

---

[34] Ibid., p. 60.

[35] As an active gatherer of information input, President Kennedy tended to resemble President Roosevelt. Roosevelt's approach to requiring information, which might have been regarded as an ideal model by President Kennedy, was described by Arthur M. Schlesinger in *The Coming of the New Deal*. Professor Schlesinger suggests that, "The first task of an executive, as he [Roosevelt] evidently saw it, was to guarantee himself an effective flow of information and ideas. . . . Roosevelt's persistent effort therefore was to check and balance information acquired through official channels by information acquired through a myriad of private, informal and unorthodox channels and espionage networks." Arthur M. Schlesinger, *The Coming of the New Deal*, in *The Age of Roosevelt* (Boston: Houghton-Mifflin, 1957–60), vol. 3.

[36] Sorenson, *Decision-Making*, p. 37.

[37] Ibid., p. 38.

positions of systematically canvassed executive department officials, suggest the emphasis that was placed on a more programmed, centralized approach to information gathering and dissemination.[38]

Before discussing the National Security Council as an information channel to and from the President, two concluding statements concerning the future of the White House Office may be made. First, the importance of the White House Office as a channel of information to and from the President will continue to increase. In the early 1970s, with the changed role of the President's cabinet as an advisory body, the White House staff has been the only body of government officials who have been required by their job to think on a national, rather than a departmental or regional, level. This fact, coupled with the expanded authority and responsibility of the President for national leadership, has placed a greater responsibility upon the White House Office for decision-making support.

Second, the structure of the White House Office will become more fixed. Each President will continue to shape the White House Office according to his own needs. However, with increases in staff size, and as various WHO responsibilities persist from administration to administration, more and more structural characteristics will assume permanence. The main reason for anticipating a more rigorously structured White House Office is the increasing pressure of time constraints under which the President must make decisions. As Presidential authority and responsibility have expanded, the number of decisions that Presidents must make has increased and, as a consequence, time available for each decision has decreased. In order to satisfy the pressing requirements imposed by time, the President must be able to regard the White House staff as a channel that is constantly prepared to transmit information rapidly, the content of which conforms to the broad and complex pattern of Presidential responsibilities. For a larger and busier White House staff to fulfill this role, it will be required to function within a less flexible organizational structure.

The National Security Council

The second group within the Executive Office of the President to be considered is the National Security Council (NSC). As its name suggests, the main function of the NSC is to advise the President in formulating policy affecting national security. More specifically, the 1947 statute creating the NSC stipulated that its function was " . . . to advise the President with respect to the integration of domestic, foreign, and military policies relating to the national security so as to enable the military services and

---

[38] Additional observations concerning President Nixon's methods of conducting relations with his advisers are included in the discussion of the National Security Council that follows.

other departments and agencies of the government to cooperate more effectively in matters involving the national security." [39] President Nixon has indicated that the NSC will be used as the principal forum for consideration of policy issues about which he must make decisions. Examples of subjects on which the NSC might advise the President include the antiballistic missile system and its foreign policy implications, the prospects for extended Soviet influence in the Middle East, future sources of disunity within the NATO alliance, 1973 to 1980, or a proposed United States negotiating position for the Strategic Arms Limitation Talks.

As with these hypothetical topics, few problems or issues to which the NSC has addressed itself have been exclusively military problems and thereby the sole responsibility of the Department of Defense. It has also been true that, from the standpoint of the President, almost all foreign policy problems have been related, in one way or another, to the issue of national security. A decision as to how and under what circumstances the Defense Department proposes to use its nuclear capability would have the deepest foreign policy implications. A military policy toward North and South Vietnam, including the kinds or weapons and numbers of military personnel that might be introduced into these areas, could provoke (as was witnessed during the 1960s and '70s) serious domestic as well as international political effects. One essential function served by the NSC has been that of bringing the government's military and political positions closer together. The Departments of State and Defense have constituted a kind of partnership in the area of national security policy. One of the objectives of the NSC was to provide those conditions that would best assure the establishment of a coordinated position, supported by State and Defense, and approved by the President.

The membership of the National Security Council gives to this body the utmost prestige and authority. The choice of membership is another reflection of the intention to bring together the federal institutions for defense and diplomacy. The statutory NSC membership includes the President (Chairman), Vice President, Secretary of State, Secretary of Defense, and the Director of the Office of Emergency Preparedness.[40] The Chairman of the Joint Chiefs of Staff and the Director of the Central Intelligence Agency act as advisers to the council.[41] Officials from other

[39] National Security Act of 1947, Title I, Section 101 (a).

[40] The Office of Emergency Preparedness, one of the 16 offices within the Executive Office of the President, was concerned with developing and planning the emergency use of material and human resources for civil defense, stabilization of the economy in an emergency, and planning for rehabilitation after an enemy attack.

[41] From the standpoint of military advice within the NSC it is interesting to note, as pointed out by Professor Morton Halperin, that the President could influence the selection of all officials who participate in NSC meetings except that of the Chairman of the JCS, whom it was necessary to choose from a small group of senior career military officers. Compared with the range and freedom of choice the President enjoyed in

executive agencies have been frequently invited by the President to participate in NSC meetings to the extent that their responsibilities have been related to the agenda topics scheduled for a particular meeting. The heads of the Atomic Energy Commission, the FBI, the Attorney General, the Director of the President's Office of Management and Budget, and the Secretary of the Treasury have been frequent participants in NSC discussions.

The council, consisting of the highest ranking civilian officials concerned with diplomatic and military planning, is responsible for making national policy recommendations to the President which, when approved by the President, define national policy in a manner that provides clear, coordinated guidelines for policy implementation. One intention of the 1947 legislation was to make policy sufficiently well-defined so that, for example, guidance would be provided to the State Department for the conduct of international negotiations. State, as a participant in NSC deliberations, would gain a realistic appreciation of the nation's military capabilities and then, it was reasoned, would be in a position to use this knowledge to secure negotiating advantages. Similarly, the Defense Department and the JSC would be able to prepare strategic and logistic plans in support of agreed diplomatic policy.

The frequency of full NSC meetings has varied with each President. President Eisenhower's NSC, being addicted to a more routine, rigidly scheduled existence, met once a week. Policy papers were prepared according to fixed formats, meetings followed a formal procedure, NSC personnel adhered to prespecified roles and there was a tendency to measure accomplishment by the number of policy papers produced over a fixed period of time. Under Presidents Kennedy and Johnson, with a more relaxed, impromptu relationship existing between advisers and President, NSC meetings occurred with less frequency and regularity. President Nixon, during his first year as President, held full NSC meetings almost every week. Meetings were more formal than those conducted by Presidents Kennedy and Johnson, but not as rigidly structured as President Eisenhower's. However, by 1971, as the operations of Dr. Kissinger's NSC system became more routinized and as the advisory relationship between the President and his National Security Affairs adviser became closer, full meetings of the NSC were held less frequently, averaging only one a month during 1971.

At no time under any President have transcripts been made of NSC discussions. This practice was intended to encourage free discussion. The

---

appointing noncareer people to subcabinet and ambassadorial posts, he was extremely limited in his choice of men to appoint to senior military positions or overseas military commands. Of relevance to the discussion in this chapter is the fact that the President had difficulty gaining access to alternative sources of military advice. (See Morton H. Halperin, "The President and the Military," *Foreign Affairs,* January 1972, pp. 310–24.)

council members never voted on an issue since the purpose of the meeting was not to solidify a consensus of support for a particular policy, but instead, to create an atmosphere of discussion from which the President could draw opinion and advice to help him arrive at an informed decision. Generally, although this has varied from President to President, an effort has been made to maintain sufficient informality so that the President is able to witness the expression of diverse views by his top department and agency officials. In such a "give and take" atmosphere the relevant issues and diverse facets of a problem can be more sharply defined for the President than would probably be the case if the same points of view were described in voluminous memoranda or briefing papers. Also, from the standpoint of achieving effective implementation of Presidential decisions, the open discussion among top-level officials and the President provide agency officials with a more precise, common understanding of the content and intention of executive decisions.

The President's Special Assistant for National Security Affairs

The National Security Council is supported by a staff of professional and clerical personnel that has steadily grown in both size and foreign policy influence under each successive postwar President. In early 1973, the NSC staff was the largest in history and included approximately 50 professional foreign affairs specialists, policy and program analysts, and coordinators, supported by a clerical staff of nearly 200 additional personnel. The NSC staff is (as of February 1973) headed by the President's Special Assistant for National Security Affairs who, under President Nixon, is Dr. Henry Kissinger. The steadily expanded functions of the NSC staff and the abilities of the men Presidents have chosen as their Special Assistant for National Security Affairs have enabled this group of White House personnel to become one of the President's major sources of foreign policy advice and support.

Under President Kennedy, and for the first years of the Johnson administration, the position of Special Assistant to the President for National Security Affairs was held by McGeorge Bundy. It was during this period that several factors converged that caused the President's National Security Affairs adviser to exercise a significantly increased foreign policy influence. First and most basic was the active foreign affairs involvement, accelerated by the Vietnam war, of the President and his National Security Affairs adviser. Second was McGeorge Bundy's natural assertiveness in expressing his policy views. Third was the relatively passive role played by Secretary of State Dean Rusk. The advisory influence that was acquired by Mr. Bundy was retained and exercised by his successor, Walt Whitman Rostow. The Vietnam war, which persisted through the Kennedy and Johnson administrations and into the Nixon administration, provided the basis for a close operating relationship between the President and his national security affairs adviser. Under President Nixon, Dr. Henry Kissinger, in the tradition of his predecessors Bundy and Rostow, further strengthened and expanded the importance of this advisory position. Dr. Kissinger, as the President's Special Assistant for National Security Affairs, has become *the* person responsible for keeping the President informed concerning matters of national security.

The Kissinger staff, as had been true of the Bundy and Rostow staffs, collects and analyzes information to support the National Security Affairs adviser by (1) providing information concerning issues that the adviser might wish to bring to the President's attention; (2) providing support to the adviser in his efforts to respond to Presidential requests for information; and (3) helping the adviser decide which issues should be brought to the attention of the National Security Council and, following such a decision, collecting, integrating, and analyzing relevant information.

Dr. Kissinger prepares the agenda for all President Nixon's NSC meetings. Prior to each NSC session he informs the appropriate officials of concerned executive agencies of the subject to be considered at the meeting and then attempts to anticipate the policy position that it is most probable that the invited agency representative would support. Thus, when he meets with President Nixon one or two days prior to any NSC meeting he could brief the President on the subject to be discussed and the probable disposition of council participants toward the issues involved.

In addition to briefing the President on matters relevant to specific NSC meetings, Dr. Kissinger confers with the President on an average of one hour every day. These daily meetings with the President usually commence with an intelligence briefing on the critical international developments of the preceding 24 hours. The President and his adviser then discuss pressing key foreign policy and defense questions such as Vietnam, relations with Communist China, the Arab-Israeli war, or the strategic advantages and political implications of a Defense Department proposal for a new military weapons system. In addition to keeping the President informed, the President's National Security Affairs adviser is equally concerned with motivating executive branch officials to implement Presidential decisions. He spends a large portion of his 15-hour day in contact with other agencies of the federal bureaucracy overseeing on-going efforts in support of the President's foreign policy. Dr. Kissinger said that "I used to think that a President just had to make a decision and issue orders, but it isn't as simple as that. You have to find ways to make the bureaucracy want to do what the President wants to do." [42]

---

[42] Stewart Alsop, "The Powerful Dr. Kissinger," *Newsweek*, June 16, 1969, p. 108.

Operations of the NSC System

The operations of the National Security Council system, which involve the activities carried out by both the staff and the official members of the National Security Council, change with each President. However, under President Nixon and Dr. Kissinger, the operations of the NSC system have been more elaborate and far reaching than has been the case under any preceding President.

The principal components of Dr. Kissinger's NSC system consist of eight groups or committees.[43] All work to support the NSC and all are responsible for functions which, to be effectively carried out, require the coordinated interaction of at least several executive agencies and departments. (See Figure 11, *The National Security Council System.*)

The first group to be considered within the NSC system is the NSC Senior Review Group, of which Dr. Kissinger himself is chairman. The membership of the Senior Review Group includes the Undersecretary of State and the Deputy Secretary of Defense, the Director of the Central Intelligence Agency, and the Chairman of the Joint Chiefs of Staff. Directors of other agencies are included when an issue relevant to their area of responsibility is being considered. The Senior Review Group is literally a reviewing body, determining which issues, studies, or proposals should be forwarded to the NSC for consideration, determining how information to the council should be organized and presented, and making sure that all realistic alternatives are made known to council members.

Most research papers considered by the Senior Review Group are prepared by a second category of interdepartmental committees within the NSC system, the six Interdepartmental Groups (IGs). (See Figure 11.) Each research paper prepared by one of the IGs is either initiated by an Interdepartmental Group and passed on to the Senior Review Group for consideration or prepared by an IG in response to a request from the President or his National Security Affairs adviser.[44] The six Interdepartmental Groups correspond to the five regional (Europe, East Asia, Latin

---

[43] Two intelligence advisory groups also within the NSC system are the NSC Intelligence Committee and the Net Assessment Group. Both are described in Chapter 5.

[44] Studies undertaken by one of the Interdepartmental Groups are usually initiated by a National Security Study Memo (NSSM) signed by the President or Dr. Kissinger. (Approximately 150 completed NSSMs were produced during the first three years of the Nixon administration.) After a completed study is considered by the NSC and a decision reached by the President, a National Security Decision Memo (NSDM) is issued indicating what, how, and by whom the President's decision is to be implemented. There are occasions when an IG study, after being considered by Dr. Kissinger and the Senior Review Group, will be forwarded for consideration to the NSC Undersecretaries Committee, headed by the Undersecretary of State and including the President's National Security Affairs adviser as a member (see Figure 11). Subjects referred to the Undersecretaries Committee usually concerned operational, as distinct from policy, matters pertaining to overseas interdepartmental activities and thus do not usually require consideration by the President or the NSC.

FIGURE 11
The National Security Council System

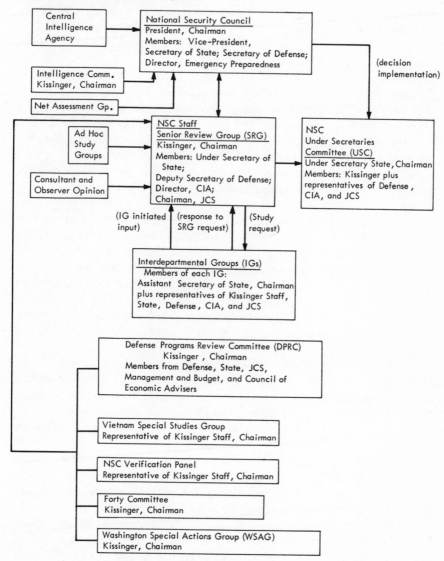

America, Africa, Near East and South Asia) and one functional (Politico-Military) bureaus of the Department of State. The chairman of each Interdepartmental Group is the Assistant Secretary of State from the corresponding bureau of the State Department. The membership of each NSC IG includes a representative of Dr. Kissinger's NSC staff as well as representatives of the Departments of Defense and State, CIA, JCS, and other concerned agencies. To facilitate an efficient working relationship, the membership of each Interdepartmental Group parallels that of the NSC Senior Review Group.

A third group within the NSC system is the NSC Undersecretaries Committee (USC), the principal function of which is to coordinate the implementation of Presidential decisions. There are occasions when Dr. Kissinger's Senior Review Group will consider problems that, because they are primarily operational in nature, would not be sent to the NSC for consideration but, instead, are sent from the SRG directly to the Undersecretaries Committee for implementation. Again, as with the IGs, the agencies represented within the USC match those of the SRG.

In addition to the Senior Review Group, the IGs and the Undersecretaries Committee, Dr. Kissinger's NSC system includes the following five groups:

(1) The Defense Programs Review Committee (DPRC), created in November 1969, headed by Dr. Kissinger, and including as members the Undersecretary of State, Deputy Secretary of Defense, Chairman of the JCS, Director of the Office of Management and Budget, and the Chairman of the Council of Economic Advisers. The mission of DPRC is to attempt to anticipate the diverse political and economic implications, both foreign and domestic, of any alterations in American defense spending, budgeting, and force levels. In other words, DPRC is to keep the annual Defense budget compatible with foreign policy objectives.

(2) The Vietnam Special Studies Group, headed by a deputy to the National Security Affairs adviser. This group is responsible for assembling all significant data related to the American involvement in the Vietnam war and American participation in the Paris peace negotiations.

(3) The Verification Panel, a group with the primary responsibility for monitoring all sessions of the Strategic Arms Limitations Talks. Daily activities of the American and Soviet negotiators are followed by a member of Dr. Kissinger's staff while the broader coordination of support within other concerned federal agencies is carried out by the Deputy Director of the Arms Control and Disarmament Agency.

(4) The Forty Committee, a group, headed by Dr. Kissinger, which supervises the covert intelligence operations sponsored by the United States government.[45] The task of supervising the operations of the Central Intelligence Agency is discussed further in Chapter 5.

(5) The Washington Special Actions Group (WSAG), headed by Dr. Kissinger, and including as members the Director of CIA, the Deputy

---

[45] There were some exceptions to this grant of responsibility. For example, supervision of CIA and Green Beret missions in Cambodia and Laos was the responsibility of the Washington Special Actions Groups (WSAG).

Secretary of Defense, the Chairman of the JCS, and the Undersecretary of State for Political Affairs. WSAG is the operations center closest to the President, responsible for responding to sudden international crises and emergencies directly related to American security. WSAG monitored such critical past events as the movement of Soviet submarines in Cuban waters in 1969, the USSR-China border conflict in the Ussuri River region in 1969, the Jordan crisis in 1970, the Indian-Pakistan war in 1971, and the Cambodian and Laotian invasions.[46] One analyst of NSC staff operations suggested that WSAG and the Verification Panel had become President Nixon's "innermost councils of war," comparable to President Kennedy's "Excom" advisory group that worked closely with the President during the 1962 Cuban missile crisis.[47] The basic components of the NSC system and their operating relationship are depicted in Figure 11.

Finally, an element of the NSC system not indicated in Figure 11 but which should be mentioned pertains to matters of military policy and planning. Under President Kennedy, General Maxwell D. Taylor was the President's military adviser from April 1961 (following the abortive Cuban Bay of Pigs invasion) until he was appointed Chairman of the Joint Chiefs of Staff in late 1962. General Taylor's advice to the President concerning military affairs was intended to place the information regularly received from the JCS and Defense Department in the broader context of the President's national defense policy. However, there was no replacement for General Taylor after he went to the JCS. As additional military advisers to the President, under Presidents Kennedy and Johnson, three General grade officers, one from each of the armed services, were attached to the White House Office. These officers performed liaison work between the armed services and the White House and presented briefings concerning defense matters and strategic intelligence. The armed services attached importance to their White House officers since they provided a means of bringing military information and advice to the President outside the normal channels of the Chiefs of Staff and the Secretary of Defense. President Johnson, in early 1964, reduced the number of White House military aides to one, and this arrangement has continued under President Nixon. However, under President Nixon, the senior White House military adviser is assigned to Dr. Kissinger's National Security Council staff and thus no longer works directly for the President.

Implications of the NSC System

Two observations may be drawn from the discussion of the NSC system developed by Dr. Kissinger. One pertains to the breadth of the informa-

---

[46] For a discussion of the NSC staff operations under Dr. Kissinger, see John P. Leacacos," Kissinger's Apparat," *Foreign Policy*, Winter, 1971–72, pp. 3–27.

[47] Ibid., p. 9.

tion base from which the NSC is able to draw both opinion and fact in order to serve the President's decision-making responsibilities. Sources of information input to the NSC consist of the following: (1) the knowledge of the participating full NSC members, especially the Secretaries of Defense and State; (2) the advisory input of the Chairman of the Joint Chiefs of Staff, the Director of the CIA, and other participating agency heads; (3) draft policy papers produced by the six Interdepartmental Groups (NSSMs), the Vietnam Special Studies Group, the Verification Panel, and WSAG; (4) observer statements (such as those of a senior foreign service officer or military field commander); and (5) consultant opinion.[48]

The second observation concerns the pervasiveness and authority of the President's National Security Affairs adviser. Despite the breadth of the NSC information base, most of the information that the NSC system collects and processes is ultimately screened by Dr. Kissinger before it reaches the President. He also prepares and personally presents information reports to the President, compressing NSC studies into short statements and discussing the implications of these summaries with the President. Dr. Kissinger also exercises direct or indirect (through a deputy NSC staff member) influence over all units that comprise the NSC system. The foreign policy influence implicit in carrying out these responsibilities appears to be unprecedented and suggests a conflict with the assertion made in the preceding chapter that one of the two basic functions of the Secretary of State was that of being the adviser to the President in matters of foreign policy. After considering the functions and activities of the National Security Council system, it appears that the President's Special Assistant for National Security Affairs and his NSC staff have become the principal source of advice used by the President in the formulation of foreign policy.

The question naturally comes to mind as to the relative importance of the foreign policy advisory role played by the President's Special Assistant for National Security Affairs as opposed to the role played by the President's Secretary of State. This question will be discussed further in Chapter 7, but at this point the following observations may be made. First, it is possible that the trend toward more advisory influence being exercised by the President's National Security Affairs adviser could be changed with a new President. The advisory roles of the Secretary of State and National Security Affairs adviser are entirely dependent on Presidential preference. As suggested, the authority and responsibilities of all Presidential advisers are scaled to meet the particular needs and mode of operation of each President.

---

[48] The principal documentary input from the intelligence "community" to the NSC is the National Intelligence Estimate (NIE). This estimate, the final version of which is assembled by CIA, is based on intelligence data from the Defense Intelligence Agency, the Joint Staff, AEC, and FBI.

Second, advisory influence is a relative consideration, and is difficult to measure precisely. It is evident from the discussion above and from Figure 11 that the Scretary of State, Undersecretary of State, the Assistant Secretaries of State, and a number of State's career officers hold important positions within the Kissinger NSC system. Because of this and because of the secretary's continuing relationship with the President, the State Department will continue to provide advisory support to the President.

Third, the trend toward increased foreign policy advisory assistance exercised by the NSC and the President's National Security Affairs adviser —a trend that began with McGeorge Bundy under President Kennedy and which continued into the Nixon administration—suggests that unless some significant changes occur within the Department of State, the relationship of the Secretary of State with the President will be permanently altered by the influence recently acquired and exercised by the President's White House-based foreign policy staff.

The Future of the White House Information System

It was suggested that the future structure of the President's White House Office will become more fixed and tend to vary less with each future President. The same will probably be true of the NSC system. The functional orientation of the groups comprising the NSC system will change as foreign policy issues of critical importance change. It does appear likely, however, that the basic tasks involved in information processing will continue and a White House foreign affairs staff will be required to manage the appropriate dissemination of information to and from the President. One change that may occur is a reinvestment of authority in the Secretary of State, reinvesting in him the status of the President's principal adviser in foreign affairs. Before continuing the discussion of this subject (see Chapter 7) it is important to consider the functions and foreign policy significance of another source of foreign affairs information used by the President, the Central Intelligence Agency.

chapter 5

Intelligence and Foreign Policy

The National Security Act of 1947 which established the National Security Council also created the Central Intelligence Agency (CIA). The 1947 act stipulated that the CIA was to report directly to the NSC and to provide it with information, advice, and recommendations concerning matters of national security. The CIA furnished the basic intelligence input to the NSC, intelligence which was used by the NSC to fulfill partially its advisory responsibility to the President. Thus, because the Central Intelligence Agency constituted an important additional source of advisory input to the President (see Figure 11), consideration of the agency in this chapter represents a continuation of the discussion of the Presidential advisory system.

Not only does CIA's significant role as the intelligence arm of the President justify a consideration of the operations of this agency, but a number of the activities in which the CIA appeared to have been involved since 1947 call for an attempt to assess the impact of these activities on America's foreign policy. In fact, over the past quarter century CIA acquired a domestic and international reputation so sinister that its positive contribution to American foreign policy seems overshadowed by the threatening implications of its foreign operations. Carl T. Rowen, former director of USIA and former Ambassador to Finland, stated that " . . . during a recent tour of East Africa and Southeast Asia, it was made clear to me that suspicion and fear of the CIA has become a sort of Achilles heel of American foreign policy." [1] To many students, academi-

---

[1] *New York Times*, April 25, 1966, p. 20.

cians, Congressmen, and even government officials, the CIA appears as an invisible empire, committed to conspiratorial acts and other forms of "secret" behavior that are incompatible with the traditions of a democracy. President Truman, almost 20 years after he had established the CIA, publicly expressed his concern about the agency's changed role:

> For some time I have been disturbed by the way CIA has been diverted from its original assignment. It has become an operational and at times a policy-making arm of the government. . . . We have grown up as a nation respected for our free institutions and for our ability to maintain a free and open society. There is something about the way the CIA has been functioning that is casting a shadow over our historic position. . . .[2]

To many who have observed the agency's operations over the years, the CIA has come to appear as a policy liability rather than an asset that enhances the nation's security as was initially intended.

In the following discussion, the functions of the Central Intelligence Agency are described, the intelligence functions of other executive agencies are reviewed, and some of the CIA's operations are considered. One aspect of the agency's operations to which some attention is given is the relation between secrecy, or the restriction of information, and the freedom of action exercised by the agency. The implications of the relationship between secrecy and freedom from controls allowed the CIA to enjoy a degree of operational autonomy that had a significant effect on the character and effectiveness of United States foreign policy in the 1970s. Some of the effects of the CIA's operations on America's foreign policy are considered as are some of the means by which the President and Congress attempted to maintain compatibility between agency operations and foreign policy objectives.

Creation of the CIA

While Congress was preparing to pass the National Security Act of 1947 and thereby establish the CIA, Allen W. Dulles (brother of John Foster), Director of CIA from 1953 to 1961, justified the need for such an agency:

> The State Department, irrespective of the form in which the Central Intelligence Agency is cast, will collect and process its own information as a basis for the day-to-day conduct of its work. The armed services intelligence agencies will do likewise. But for the proper judging of the situation in any foreign country it is important that information should be processed by an agency whose duty it is to weigh facts, and to draw conclusions from these facts, without having either the facts or the conclusions warped by the inevitable and

---

[2] *Washington Post*, December 22, 1963, quoted by Roger Hilsman, *To Move A Nation* (Garden City, New York: Doubleday, 1967), p. 63.

even proper prejudices of the men whose duty it is to determine policy and who, having once determined a policy, are too likely to be blind to any facts which might tend to prove the policy to be faulty. The Central Intelligence Agency should have nothing to do with policy.[3]

Mr. Dulles's description of what the ideal CIA should be contrasted sharply with what President Truman said the CIA had actually become. It is also interesting to note the emphasis given by Mr. Dulles to the need to separate the activities of the agency from the activities of those men who determined policy.

Congress, in creating the CIA, authorized it to perform the following functions:

1. To keep the NSC informed concerning the various intelligence activities of the executive departments and agencies that comprised the so-called intelligence community, the members of which are described below.

2. To recommend to the NSC methods of coordinating the intelligence activities of the various government agencies.

3. To correlate, evaluate, and disseminate to appropriate government agencies intelligence relating to national security.

4. To centralize intelligence services that were common to all intelligence operations within the government.

5. And, finally, a "catch-all" function that came to assume some significance, "to perform such other functions and duties related to intelligence affecting the national security as the National Security Council may from time to time direct." [4]

These five functions suggest a role for the CIA that was largely administrative, primarily directed toward facilitating the effectiveness of other operations within the executive branch of the government.[5] It may

---

[3] Allen W. Dulles, "Intelligence Is Our First Line of Defense," in Young Hum Kim, *The Central Intelligence Agency: Problems of Secrecy in a Democracy* (Lexington, Massachusetts: D. C. Heath and Co., 1968), p. 33.

[4] The 1947 National Security Act also stipulated that the CIA "shall have no police, subpoena, law enforcement powers, or internal security functions." However, on the basis of fulfilling its authorized responsibilities, CIA's role was broadened to include certain domestic operations. Each increment of broadened responsibility was authorized by the National Security Council and was based on an interpretation of CIA's right to "perform such other functions and duties related to intelligence affecting the national security. . . ." (See point 5, above.) For example, the CIA was authorized to brief and debrief scholars, students, businessmen, and tourists traveling to and from Communist countries. The CIA was also authorized to sign contracts with colleges and universities to employ faculty for agency-sponsored research. For an interesting account of the CIA–National Student Association and the CIA–labor union relationship, see "A Short Account of International Students and the Cold War with Particular Reference to the NSA, CIA, Etc.," *Ramparts*, March 1967, and "Three Tales of the CIA," *Ramparts*, April 1967.

[5] There was bound to be some duplication of effort in the intelligence operations

be noted that in the above listing of functions, the agency was not specifically authorized to collect intelligence, but instead, it was to be the *central* intelligence agency for coordination, evaluation, and dissemination. However, during the quarter century since the establishment of the CIA, the agency gradually became the government's major collector, as well as analyzer and disseminator of intelligence. It was largely through the broad interpretation of the fifth function of the agency, authorizing the CIA to perform "other functions" affecting national security, that the agency's activities gradually expanded. The NSC frequently decided that through the centralized administration of certain intelligence activities maximum efficiency and security could be achieved. For example, on the basis of the delicate nature of certain intelligence missions, the political implications of some intelligence operations, and the frequent requirement for specially trained personnel, the NSC would decide that a single, centralized program under the CIA's direction could best serve the requirements of all other intelligence agencies as well as the cause of national security.

The most apparent public reflection of the dominance of the Central Intelligence Agency in collecting and analyzing foreign intelligence was the position of the Director of the CIA as Chairman of the United States Intelligence Board (USIB), a group comprised of representatives of all the intelligence agencies in Washington described below. USIB was responsible for overseeing and integrating the substantive as well as the operational tasks of all of the government's foreign intelligence activities. For example, USIB supervised the National Reconnaissance Program which operated earth-orbiting photographic satellites and the National Photo Interpretation Center which analyzed the intelligence acquired through satellite photography. The results of USIB's integrating efforts were intelligence estimates (National Intelligence Estimates) which were made available to the National Security Council.[6] Supervisory responsibility for USIB's output gave the CIA a dominant position with regard to the primary purpose of the government's diverse intelligence operations, i.e., keeping the President informed.

---

conducted by the various agencies comprising the intelligence community. It should be mentioned, however, that some of this duplication was intentional and desirable. What in other lines of work might be regarded as redundancy, in intelligence was regarded as the process of validation. What was efficient for business (singleness of effort and avoidance of duplication) was not necessarily most advantageous for effective and reliable intelligence operations. The sources and content of intelligence reports required extended checking and rechecking to achieve maximum verification, a process that was facilitated by comparing intelligence items collected through several agencies.

[6] The National Intelligence Estimate (NIE) represented a consensus among the agencies comprising the intelligence community. If any participating agency held a dissenting opinion concerning a NIE estimate or conclusion, this dissenting viewpoint was accommodated by a NIE footnote.

The Director of the CIA was appointed by the President and was the senior intelligence adviser to the President and Congress. The director was also the President's representative on the United States Intelligence Board. His third function was to administer the CIA itself. As a significant part of this threefold responsibility, the director established data collection priorities for USIB members and (at least in theory) reviewed all intelligence that was channelled to the President.[7]

The rationale for the creation of the Central Intelligence Agency was the conviction held by some executive branch officials, supported by Congress, that the more the President and his National Security Council advisers knew about the intentions of other nations, the better the cause of national security would be served. National security was obviously strengthened by the ability to anticipate the actions of other nations. However, it was reasoned, accurate predictions of what other nations might do depended not only on the analysis of public statements and observable behavior, but also on a capability to collect information that another government might not choose to make available. Two operational difficulties arose in connection with this line of reasoning. First, to be effective, America's intelligence activities required some degree of secrecy and the ability to be speedily implemented if the need should arise. Second, the practice of secrecy and rapid implementation precluded the opportunity for free and open discussion prior to the decision to act and thus conflicted with the openness that characterized a democratic political system. These considerations created a basis for many of the subsequent difficulties that the CIA encountered in its efforts to gain acceptance and support within certain areas of the legislative and executive branches of the government. Further difficulty was related to the fact that intelligence collection involved intervening in the internal affairs of other nations. Although the United States might be convinced that national security interests required the collection of certain intelligence concerning the internal affairs of other nations, a serious question arose as to how far the President could go in approving the clandestine violation of treaties and national borders, financing political coups, and influencing officials within foreign governments before serious damage was done to the ideas of freedom and self-government for all which the United States had espoused for so many years. Before considering these questions, however, it is appropriate to describe briefly the functions of the intelligence community.

---

[7] Richard Helms, Director of the CIA from 1966 through 1972, joined the agency when it was established in 1947, worked directly under former CIA Directors Allen Dulles, John McCone, and Vice Admiral William Raborn, and in 1966 became the first career intelligence specialist to direct the agency. For an interesting discussion of Richard Helms and his responsibilities, see Benjamin Welles, "H-L-S- of the CIA," *New York Times Magazine,* April 18, 1971, pp. 34–48, 52–54. Helms' successor as CIA Director is James R. Schlesinger, former chairman of the Atomic Energy Commission.

The Intelligence Community

In 1972, Washington's intelligence community consisted of approximately a dozen government agencies, employed 200,000 people, and spent $6 billion a year.[8] The main agency members of the intelligence community, in addition to the Central Intelligence Agency, included the following:

(1) The State Department's Intelligence and Research (INR), (note Figure 5, *Organization of the Department of State*) was a small (300 personnel) intelligence operation that collected and analyzed intelligence largely through the efforts of its career foreign service officers stationed abroad.

(2) The Defense Department's Defense Intelligence Agency (DIA) (note Figure 3, *Organization of the Department of Defense*) was created in 1961, by Secretary of Defense Robert McNamara in an effort to coordinate the military intelligence programs conducted by each of the three military services. However, in 1972, the army, navy, and air force continued to exercise considerable service autonomy. The air force alone maintained an intelligence staff of 60,000 personnel who operated under a budget of $2.8 billion, most of which was used to maintain the service's reconnaissance satellite intelligence collection program. In 1971, a further effort was made to strengthen intelligence coordination among the services and to reduce intelligence collection costs by establishing the position of Assistant Secretary of Defense for Intelligence. The DIA, compared with air force intelligence, operated on a relatively modest annual budget of $100 million and a staff of approximately 5,500 members.

(3) The Defense Department's National Security Agency (NSA) was the nation's cryptological command responsible for intercepting and decoding messages sent within or between other governments and constructing codes used to transmit messages to American intelligence agents operating in foreign areas.[9] NSA's annual budget of $1 billion was used to operate one of the government's largest computer systems which, in NSA's case, was used to break codes and encrypt messages. NSA employed 110,000 persons, 20,000 of whom were linguists, intelligence analysts, and mathematicians.

(4) The Federal Bureau of Investigation (FBI) was responsible for all counterespionage activity within the United States. The FBI's counterespionage program was relevant to the government's foreign intelligence

---

[8] It was estimated that the three military services (army, navy, and air force) spent annually almost $5 billion of this total. "The New Espionage American Style," *Newsweek*, November 22, 1971, p. 32. Many of the estimates of intelligence community funds and personnel mentioned below were derived from this article, pp. 28–40.

[9] An "example" of an encrypted message was on the small highway sign pointing toward CIA's headquarters in Langley, Virginia, a message which read "Fairbank Highway Research Station."

collection effort since by determining the objective of "enemy" intelligence efforts conducted within the United States, it was possible to make certain assumptions concerning the data limitations and intelligence collection priorities of the "enemy" nation.

(5) The Atomic Energy Commission's intelligence effort analyzed data concerning nuclear developments and the status of on-going nuclear research within other nations. Highest priority requirements were assigned to the collection of intelligence concerning characteristics of the nuclear weapons and the weapons research and testing programs of the four actual, and all "threshold," nuclear nations.[10]

To promote further integration among the agencies of the intelligence community President Nixon, in late 1971, delegated to the Director of the CIA a broader overall supervisory role in the direction of "community-wide responsibilities" in America's foreign intelligence gathering operations. The director remained Chairman of USIB and he was also made Chairman of a new committee, the Intelligence Resources Advisory Committee, administratively attached to USIB and composed of representatives from State, Defense, CIA, and the Office of Management and Budget.

The main function of the Intelligence Resources Advisory Committee was to review the overall expenses of intelligence operations and to then specify actions whereby costs could be reduced to a point well below the 1972 figure of $6 billion. The ultimate objective of the committee was to prepare a consolidated and reduced budget applicable to all federal operations in foreign intelligence.[11]

Other groups established in the early 1970s in an effort to integrate and supervise the government's intelligence operations were the NSC Intelligence Committee, the Net Assessment Group, and the Forty Committee, each a part of the national security system described above in Chapter 4. The NSC Intelligence Committee reported directly to the NSC. It was headed by Dr. Kissinger and its membership included the Director of the CIA, the Attorney General, the Undersecretary of State, the Deputy Secretary of Defense, and the Chairman of the JCS. The committee was to provide direction and guidance in determining national intelligence requirements and evaluate intelligence products on the basis of stipulated intelligence requirements. The Net Assessment Group was headed by a member of Dr. Kissinger's staff and was responsible for the evaluation of all intelligence products as well as producing "net assessments," or com-

---

[10] The Treasury Department, also a member of USIB, had intelligence responsibilities that concerned international traffic in drugs and economic intelligence.

[11] President Nixon instructed CIA's Director to trim the nation's intelligence expenses by $1 billion. The focus of potential "cuts" appeared to be the large total defense intelligence budget. (*New York Times*, November 7, 1971, p. 55.)

parisons of American capabilities with those of potential enemies. The Forty Committee was headed by Dr. Kissinger and was to function as a link between the President and the covert operations of the CIA. It is now appropriate to describe some of the characteristics and operations of the CIA itself, the principal channel through which foreign intelligence was transmitted to the President.

Activities of the CIA

The Central Intelligence Agency's human and technological sensor system for collecting, interpreting, and disseminating intelligence was supported by an annual budget of close to $1 billion and an estimated 15,000 employees (plus an estimated 30,000 foreign personnel stationed abroad) who were assigned to the four basic directorates of the agency.[12]

(1) *The Directorate of Science and Technology* collected and analyzed foreign intelligence concerning developments in science, technology, and weaponry, especially intelligence pertaining to Communist nations or nations accepting scientific and military aid from Communist nations. Intelligence collection requirements of the highest priority pertained to the offensive and defensive capabilities of the Soviet Union and Communist China and it was the task of the Directorate of Science and Technology to attempt to satisfy these requirements. Within this highest priority category, there were rigorous collection requirements for information pertaining to the latest innovations in nuclear weapons technology, especially the status of programs for such advanced weaponry as orbiting satellites armed with nuclear weapons and intercontinental missiles equipped with multiple nuclear warheads.

(2) *The Directorate of Support* was the agency's service division. It handled administrative and personnel matters, procured equipment, developed and maintained CIA communications systems, provided for the security measures (including CIA codes) that were a part of every intelligence collection effort, and maintained logistic support for all foreign operations. For example, it was the Directorate of Support that developed

---

[12] The description of the CIA's organization and activities is largely conjectural, having been abstracted and assembled from scholarly and journalistic statements rather than being based on official documents or sources. For a useful analysis of the CIA's activities and resources, see *New York Times,* April 25–29, 1966. The actual budget of the CIA was difficult to ascertain since it did not appear as a formal line item in the federal budget. Instead, the CIA funds were covered by appropriations listed for other federal agencies. The fact that government officials outside of the CIA were not privileged to know the precise amount of money available to the agency for the support of specific intelligence operations severely hampered the effective monitoring of agency activities.

a highly sensitive device that was capable of picking up, at considerable distances, indoor conversation by recording the window vibrations caused by the voices of individual speakers within a room.[13]

(3) *The Directorate of Plans* carried out covert operations and, as a consequence, came to be known as the division of "dirty tricks." The main activities of the Plans Directorate were espionage and subversion, responsibilities that reflected the fact that the scope of the agency's mission had been expanded beyond intelligence collection and involved subversive actions intended to affect the internal affairs of other nations. For example, it became generally accepted that the directorate was involved with the overthrow of the left-wing Mossadegh government in Iran in 1953, the downfall of the left-oriented government in Guatemala in 1954, the effort to obtain Khrushchev's secret anti-Stalin speech delivered at a closed session of the 20th Communist Party Congress in Moscow in 1956, the planning of the ill-fated Bay of Pigs invasion in 1961, and, in the 1970s, the planning and organizing of anti-Communist activity in Laos, Cambodia, Thailand, and South Vietnam.[14]

(4) *The Directorate of Intelligence* assembled intelligence collected through the analysis of "open" sources (such as radio broadcasts, interviews with selected Americans returning from abroad, the foreign press and professional journals, and official pronouncements by key government figures) and also analyzed and evaluated intelligence acquired through covert methods. By drawing from the professional resources of the agency's linguists, scientists, geographers, engineers, psychiatrists, and social scientists, the directorate produced daily and periodic intelligence reports for the NSC as well as detailed studies concerning regional, social, economic, military, and political problems. The types of subjects for which the directorate assumed responsibility ranged from life-expectancy studies of foreign leaders and anthropological studies of Vietnamese and Laotian hill tribes, to studies examining the present and future political stability of the Politburo of the Communist party of the USSR. In a basic sense, in addition to providing the central analytical capability of the agency, the directorate provided the channel for transmitting the results of the agency's analytical efforts to the National Security Council, and possibly, depending on the level of "criticality" assigned to the intelligence item, to the President.

---

[13] It was reported that this capability was "improved" to the extent that the same window "bugging" technique could interpret the sound emitted by typewriter keys. (*New York Times*, April 27, 1966, p. 1.)

[14] The Plans Directorate has also engaged in domestic operations, under authorization granted by classified NSC directives. For example, the CIA, on behalf of national security, was authorized to question persons within the United States, provided the CIA first checked with the FBI (a provision frequently ignored).

Methods of Intelligence Collection

Although there were a large and varied number of specific techniques and practices by which each of the directorates of the CIA collected foreign intelligence, four general methods of collection were regularly employed. The first collection method was the use of the intelligence agent. It should be made immediately clear that, despite a widespread popular impression, only an estimated 20 percent of the CIA's intelligence was obtained through agency spies or special agents. The so-called deep cover agent did exist, but his or her utility to the agency was far more limited, and the potential for detrimental political repercussions if "un-covered" was far greater than is generally assumed.[15] Agents employed the techniques of blackmail, spying, financing coups, assassination, and "buying" officials within other governments. The use of any of these covert techniques to achieve American objectives affected the way other governments regarded the United States.[16] Not only was antagonism toward the United States generated within other countries by these forms of intervention, but the techniques themselves conflicted with the ideals of freedom and self-determination that the United States espoused for itself and all other nations. The adverse repercussions from the use of agents restricted their use, as did the fact that the utility of the agent was significantly diminished by the development of other modern techniques of intelligence gathering and analysis.

A second method for acquiring intelligence, and one that has under-gone significant refinement and improvement since 1947, was referred to in the discussion of the Directorate of Intelligence, i.e., the use of profes-sionally trained intelligence analysts to scrutinize information made acces-sible by other nations through mass media and official sources. Perhaps as much as 50 percent of the CIA's intelligence was derived through analysis of such sources.[17]

---

[15] The deep cover agent was usually required to assume a completely different per-sonal identity, profession, and social life in order to fulfill his intelligence mission. His true identity was known to only a limited number of agency personnel. The psychologi-cal strains of such a career were understandably great and thus the rate of pay and personnel turnover were relatively high. In contrast to the deep cover agent was the CIA "spook" attached to the United States embassy whose function was known to most members of the country team as well as to many officials of the host country.

[16] Roger Hilsman, Assistant Secretary of State for the Far East under President Kennedy, indicated that the word "covert" did not refer to an action that was com-pletely secret, but one that was "plausibly deniable." It was the general practice for the guilty nation to deny any involvement when its covert agent was caught in the process of collecting intelligence. Thus, when President Eisenhower in 1960 accepted responsi-bility for America's violating Soviet air space when one of the CIA's U-2 spy planes was sent over the USSR, he deviated from accepted international convention.

[17] Kremlinology has come to be publicized as one analytical method for producing political intelligence. Through an analysis of numerous fragments of information de-

The third collection method, the acquisition of intelligence through technological means, provided a great volume of highly reliable data to the agency. Technology enabled CIA to intercept and analyze messages, and through "spy" satellites, referred to above, to gather photographic intelligence for any point on the surface of the earth. Most of the intelligence requirements of the Directorate of Science and Technology were satisfied by technological collection techniques. The photographic satellite largely replaced the U-2 spy plane, a high-speed aircraft with cameras carried in its under-carriage to take photographs of the earth from 14 miles altitude, but which also proved to be vulnerable to surface-to-air missiles fired by the nation (USSR, Cuba, Communist China) over which the spy plane flew. The fact that the U-2 aircraft was both vulnerable and provocative as an intelligence collection device made it a candidate for early retirement. Photographic intelligence was collected through the use of orbiting satellites which housed high-powered black and white, color, and TV cameras that made film records of troop movements, missile installations, weapons production and storage centers, and other items of strategic significance. Periodically each satellite would release reels of photographs that provided accurate images of "target" areas on the surface of the earth. Photography released from orbiting satellites was collected in mid-air by air force crews and brought to the National Photo Interpretation Center in Washington for analysis and interpretation.

Other technological devices for intelligence collection, most developed under the Directorate of Support, included infra-red cameras for night photography, radiation counters to detect and analyze nuclear weapons tests, heat sensors to record rocket launches, and an infra-red sensor and microwave radar to detect submerged nuclear submarines, the location of which was "given away" by the slightly warmer water they left in the wake of their nuclear reactors. The agency also made extensive use of radio and radar equipment to intercept electronic communication.

A fourth method of acquiring intelligence was through interviewing individuals (refugees, tourists, scholars, political officials) who had first-hand experiences in foreign areas. The reliability and accuracy of intelligence gathered from such sources varied considerably, and it was the task

---

rived from overt and covert sources, insights are provided concerning the relative positions of power and influence held by key officials within the Soviet bureaucracy. Useful "indicators" for the Kremlinologist include such factors as the order in which officials are listed in official publications, their hierarchical status as revealed by official photographs (who stood next to whom at official ceremonies), who attended which formal and informal gatherings, the applause and approval received by specific individuals at Communist party functions, etc. One clear indication of General Secretary Brezhnev's primacy within the Soviet political system was derived from an analysis of the attention, time, and policy statements allotted to him during the 24th Communist Party Congress in the spring of 1971.

of CIA analysts attached primarily to the Directorate of Intelligence to assess the validity of this intelligence input.

Intelligence Operations and Foreign Policy

Concern over the relationship between the CIA's foreign operations and America's foreign policy objectives has existed within both the legislative and executive branches of the government since the early 1950s. The 1953 incident in Iran, referred to above, in which CIA participated in the overthrow of the Mossadegh government, reflected a tendency on the part of an agency with responsibilities limited to the collection, analysis, and dissemination of intelligence, to extend its functions to include active participation in an effort to shape the course of events within another nation. Since 1953 there have been reports of CIA personnel being involved in efforts to bring about desirable, from an American point of view, resolutions of political problems in Central America, Latin America, the Middle East, Southeast and Eastern Asia, Africa, and the Communist nations of Eastern Europe and the USSR.

For example, in the description of the functions of the Directorate of Plans, it was mentioned that the directorate had been involved in efforts to organize anti-Communist activity in Laos, as well as other Southeast Asian countries. The CIA, by late 1971, following efforts initiated in 1962, maintained a 30,000 man "irregular" anti-Communist army in Laos, trained, equipped, supported, and advised by the agency. This force was supplemented by Thai "volunteers" recruited and paid by the CIA. In fiscal year 1970, the CIA spent $70 million in support of this "irregular" Laotian army.[18] CIA training took place in Thailand and the irregulars were transported to and from Laos in planes of Air America, an air operation in Laos supported by American intelligence agencies.[19]

The CIA's insistence on secrecy and rapid response placed the agency in the position of determining for itself what actions were consistent with the nation's foreign policy objectives, and then reporting its actions (or having its actions reported by others) after the fact. In other words, by insisting that secrecy was mandatory if its mission was to be fulfilled, the CIA was able to determine what techniques it would employ to implement the President's foreign policy. Another example of a CIA operation helps to illustrate this point. In August 1962, the Central Intelligence Agency

---

[18] In addition to this amount, in the same year the United States government had spent $162 million in military aid to Laos plus $52 million for economic aid. The total amount of aid to Laos in 1971 was 25 times as large as when United States assistance began in 1962.

[19] Description of the CIA's Laotian operations was provided in a report prepared by the agency. See *New York Times*, August 3, 1971, pp. 1, 8.

carried out a scheme that involved the contamination of some 14,000 sacks of Cuban sugar that had been off-loaded from a British freighter while the freighter was being repaired in the harbor of San Juan, Puerto Rico. This shipment of Cuban sugar was bound for the Soviet Union. The CIA contamination plot had not been cleared by President Kennedy, and when a White House aide saw an intelligence report indicating what the CIA had done, he quickly informed the President who immediately ordered the contaminated sugar to be impounded in Puerto Rico. It was reported that President Kennedy was "furious" because the operation had taken place on American territory, because it could provide the USSR with some effective anti-American propaganda, and because it could set a precedent for chemical sabotage.[20] When, after the fact, the CIA was pressed for an explanation, the agency indicated that its rationale for this operation was based on the assumption that, in line with American policy toward Cuba, it was desirable to sabotage the Cuban economy where and when feasible. However, at the same time, the President had as one of his broad foreign policy objectives the intention to support and initiate actions that would improve American-Soviet relations.

There were other CIA-sponsored operations that conflicted with broader Presidential objectives. In 1960, CIA chose to continue U-2 intelligence missions over the USSR, despite the fact that President Eisenhower was in the process of attempting to create an atmosphere of Soviet-American cooperation as a prelude to a planned summit conference with Premier Khrushchev in Paris. The shooting down of the U-2 aircraft by the USSR and the capturing of the American pilot provided the Soviet Union with an incident that they used to justify their withdrawal from the planned conference and to vilify the United States. The collapse of the Bay of Pigs invasion of April 1961, an operation planned, organized, and supported by the CIA, was not only embarrassing to President Kennedy but was detrimental to the ability of a new President to make credible the noninterventionist character of his foreign policy objectives. The interventionist activities of the CIA seem to have recurred from time to time during the 1960s and into the 1970s. It might be assumed, for example, that the presence of CIA "spooks" as a part of the American country team in foreign nations could jeopardize the President's efforts to encourage foreign governments to develop closer relations with the United States.

Whether the CIA's operations did or did not clash with the President's foreign policy objectives, *all* CIA operations had the potential for creating such a conflict. It was therefore necessary that some form of control be provided so that the President could be assured that all CIA operations

---

[20] *New York Times*, April 28, 1966, p. 1.

were compatible with his view as to how the nation's foreign policy could be most effectively supported.

Executive and Legislative "Controls"

The sensitive relationship between the CIA's foreign operations and the nation's foreign policy, plus the expanded role of intelligence operations in the 1970s, provoked a number of suggestions from within and outside the government for a more effective system of constraints that could be imposed on the CIA's operations. From Congress alone, during the quarter century of the CIA's existence, there were over 200 resolutions introduced for tighter Congressional controls, and all were defeated or put aside by committees. Similarly, a series of suggested "reforms" have come from ad hoc Presidentially appointed study groups. By 1972, as a result of a series of efforts by the legislative and executive branches, the following groups existed:

1. *The Forty Committee,* described in the preceding chapter as a part of the NSC system, was established by President Nixon to review and approve all CIA covert intelligence operations before they had "gone operational." The Committee was also to keep the President informed of all important CIA operations. Its four members were the President's Special Assistant for National Security Affairs, chairman, the Director of the CIA, the Deputy Undersecretary of State for Political Affairs, and the Deputy Secretary of Defense.

The purpose of creating the Forty Committee was to keep CIA operations compatible with the President's foreign policy objectives. Prior to the Forty Committee, the 54-12 Special Group (a name reflecting the fact that the Group was created in December 1954) attempted to perform the same functions of keeping Presidents Eisenhower, Kennedy, and Johnson aware of the programs their intelligence agency intended to carry out. Because of the close working relationship among President Eisenhower, Secretary of State Dulles, and CIA Director Allen Dulles, the Special Group was largely inactive during the Eisenhower administration. The Special Group met more frequently following the abortive 1961 Bay of Pigs invasion, but it never became an effective control mechanism. It generally met only once a week, its members were preoccupied by the demands of their primary departmental responsibilities, and the CIA did not insist that the President take time from his numerous other tasks to review the agency's operational plans.

The Forty Committee under President Nixon met approximately once a week. As a part of the National Security Council system it worked in conjunction with the Washington Special Actions Group in an effort to supervise all covert intelligence operations.

2. *The Office of Management and Budget (OMB)*, in the Executive Office of the President, was a second group that "watched" the CIA, mainly through attempts to supervise the funding of agency operations. The OMB, however, usually having access to only a general statement of a CIA project proposal, was frequently not in a position to anticipate accurately the possible foreign policy repercussions of the agency's proposals. Thus, funds continued to be approved with limited comprehension of their ultimate use. Funds appropriated by Congress to specific executive agencies, such as the Defense Department, could subsequently be rerouted to the CIA. This rerouting would occur to enable the CIA to undertake activities which the 1947 National Security Act suggested, i.e., ". . . other functions and duties related to intelligence affecting the national security as the National Security Council may from time to time direct." [21]

3. *The Foreign Intelligence Advisory Board,* made up of nationally recognized citizens (scientists, administrators, academicians, military officers) appointed by the President, was to review agency budget requests and operations and make recommendations for administrative and operational reform to the President. However, as with the Forty Committee, all of the members had other demanding, full-time positions, they met even less frequently than the Forty Committee, and thus were not in a position to exercise effective supervision over agency operations.

Congressional controls over the CIA were, in practice, no more effective than were executive controls. The Appropriations Committees and the Armed Services Committees of both Houses of Congress established intelligence subcommittees. Together, these four intelligence subcommittees comprised a "watchdog" body to supervise agency activities. However, neither Congress nor the CIA have been disposed to hold subcommittee meetings on a regular basis. The infrequent meetings that were held took place in secret session and no records of subcommittee actions were made available to the public. One member of the House Armed Services Committee did make his opinion public by stating, "As you may know, we have a subcommittee on the CIA. I was a member of that Committee for four years. . . . We met annually—once a year, for a period of two hours in which we accomplished nothing." [22] The general laxness of Con-

---

[21] In early 1972 it was reported that several senators responsible for monitoring CIA operations had urged that effective control be imposed on the CIA's access to funds initially allocated to other agencies to help prevent United States involvement in Cambodia from developing surreptitiously as it had in Laos, and to halt the CIA's funding of Thai troops in Laos. It was stressed that any such funding, if it were to be undertaken at all, should be handled in a manner that would enable officials in other agencies concerned with foreign affairs to be cognizant of the purposes for which federal funds were being spent abroad. (*New York Times,* February 13, 1972, p. 3.)

[22] Congressman Walter Norblad, cited by Representative John V. Lindsay, in "An Inquiry into the Darkness of the Cloak, the Sharpness of the Dagger," *Esquire,* March

gressional controls was due to several factors: (1) The individual chairmen of the House and Senate committees were Congressmen who tended to regard the CIA as an effective means of strengthening America's national security, and were thus favorably disposed toward the agency. As a consequence, the Congressmen appointed to the intelligence subcommittees have reflected a similar attitude. (2) In practice, the four intelligence subcommittees spent much of their time protecting the agency from its critics rather than controlling its operations. (3) The subcommittees tended to believe that their oversight responsibilities were fulfilled if the CIA periodically reported to them. This arrangement allowed the initiative to rest with the CIA and thus it was mainly the agency that decided what Congress needed to know. (4) Congressmen have not wished to be encumbered with information concerning the CIA's covert actions and plans. Such knowledge could inhibit a Congressman's freedom to speak openly. Many Congressmen reasoned that if they were not aware of a classified item they would not be able to lapse into a security violation. Also, it could prove to be politically embarrassing if it became known that a Congressmen had been aware of a covert CIA scheme that subsequently proved detrimental to American foreign policy.[23]

One recurring suggestion by a limited number of senators and representatives for strengthening the ability of Congress to oversee the activities of the CIA has been to create a joint standing committee on foreign intelligence. The model for such a committee was the Joint Committee on Atomic Energy which monitored the Atomic Energy Commission. The proposed joint committee could continue to include members of the House and Senate Committees on Appropriations and Armed Services, and add members from the House and Senate Government Operations Committees, the Senate Foreign Relations Committee, and the House Foreign Affairs Committee. Supporters of this proposed change believed that such a well-staffed joint committee, including representatives from more of the relevant Congressional committees and being in regular session, could exercise more effective surveillance over the CIA and could help rebuild the prestige of the nation's intelligence operations within

---

1964, p. 109. See discussion of Congress' monitoring of the CIA's activities in Paul W. Blackstock, *The Strategy of Subversion* (Chicago: Quadrangle Books, 1964), chap. 12.

[23] Concerned over the deficiencies of Congress' ability to oversee the CIA's operations, Sen. Fulbright, in 1966, attempted to have Congress approve a new, nine-man Senate Committee on Intelligence Operations. Membership would have included three senators each from the Appropriations, Armed Services, and Foreign Relations Committees. Sen. Russell, then Chairman of the Armed Services Committee, oppposed the Fulbright proposal because this alteration would have made intelligence leaks more possible and intelligence sources around the world, fearing exposure, would have denied their information to the United States. Subsequently, in response to this proposal, it was agreed to permit three members of the Senate Foreign Relations Committee to participate as guests on the Oversight Committee.

both Congress and the executive bureaucracy.[24] To date, there has been no effective support within Congress for the establishment of such a joint committee.

Basis for Agency Influence

What are some of the sources of the CIA's strength? What has allowed the agency to enjoy the autonomy it has exercised and what was the basis for its expanded scope of operations and its influence within foreign policy circles?

First, the Cold War in general made a central intelligence gathering agency seem vital to the security of the nation. Specifically, because of the threat posed by world communism, the ability to determine "enemy" capabilities and intentions became a prime requirement for national security. Allen Dulles, Director of the CIA for eight years, expressed this point with clarity in 1963. Mr. Dulles wrote that the United States had three "assets" to employ against the Soviet threat.[25] The first asset was America's foreign policy itself, which was the responsibility of the State Department. Second was the American "defense posture" with which the United States could "convince the Free World that we and our Allies are both strong enough and ready enough to meet the Soviet military challenge, and that we can protect, and are willing to protect, the free countries of the world, by force if need be. . . ."[26] Then Mr. Dulles indicated that the third component of America's ability to challenge Communist expansion was the mission of his intelligence agency:

> The third element is what the intelligence service must help to provide: (1) It must give our own government timely information as to the Communist targets, that is to say, the countries which the Communists have put high on their schedule for subversive attack. (2) It must penetrate the vital elements of their subversive apparatus as it begins to attack target countries and must provide our government with an analysis of the techniques in use and with information on the persons being subverted or infiltrated into local government. (3) It must, wherever possible, help to build up the local defenses against penetration by keeping target countries aware of the nature and extent of their peril and by assisting their internal security service wherever this can best be done, or possibly only be done, on a covert basis.
>
> Many of the countries most seriously threatened do not have internal police or security services adequate to the task of obtaining timely warning of the peril of Communist subversion. For this they often need help and they can only

---

[24] For a review of the arguments for and against the creation of such a joint committee, see discussion in Harry Howe Ransom, *Can American Democracy Survive Cold War?* (Garden City, New York: Doubleday Anchor Book, 1964), chaps. 7 and 8.

[25] Allen Dulles, *The Craft of Intelligence* (New York: Harper and Row, 1963), pp. 231–34.

[26] Ibid., p. 231.

get it from a country like the United States, which has the resources and techniques to aid them. . . .

Wherever we can, we must help to shore up both the will to resist and confidence in the ability to resist. By now we have had a good many years of experience in combating Communism. We know its techniques, we know a good many of the actual "operators" who run these attempts at takeover. Whenever we are given the opportunity to help, we should assist in building up the ability of threatened countries and do it long before the Communist penetration drives a country to the point of no return.[27]

The fact that the agency was viewed as an essential component of the nation's defenses strengthened its position within the executive branch.

Second, the CIA was not required to make most of its plans and operations known to nonagency officials within the government. The agency's rationale for not being more accountable to other executive agencies and Congress was that increased openness could compromise clandestine sources and thus jeopardize covert operations overseas.[28] Through secrecy the agency enjoyed autonomy, and autonomy was a source of potential influence. The fact that information about the CIA was restricted made it different from the Department of Defense, for example, which seemed comparatively "public" with its service rivalries, budget conflicts with Congress, and its political visibility. It was also different from the Department of State with its "open" diplomatic involvement and its frequent need to respond to public criticism of its international operations. The CIA's secrecy gave it a relative advantage of pursuing its own projects and supporting its own point of view.

Third, the CIA's power was strengthened by its command of the facts. The agency, through its own agents, clandestine sources, and covert operations, had access to a great volume of diversified information, some of which it occasionally chose to deny to other agencies for "security" reasons. The following justifications were used for the imposition of restraints on the dissemination of information:

1. The maintenance of national security. A Top Secret classification indicated that the disclosure of information contained in the document

---

[27] Ibid., pp. 231–32. This statement by Allen Dulles not only tied the mission of the CIA to the requirement to contain communism, but it also embodied many of the key elements of America's Cold War approach to international relations. For example, it reflected America's view of aggressive communism, the requirement to stand up against communism, the willingness of America to protect the free nations of the world (by force if necessary) and, when asked, the disposition of the United States to help other nations build up their ability to resist communist subversion.

[28] The security classification of information (Top Secret, Secret, Confidential, etc.) was justified not only on the basis of preventing other governments from knowing the content of the information the United States had collected and the conclusions that were drawn from this information, but also because of the need to protect the human sources and mechanical techniques through which the United States had acquired the information.

so designated could result in "exceptionally grave" damage to the security of the United States. Secret and Confidential classifications suggested lower levels of security importance but they also had the effect of limiting the distribution of information.

2. The concept of "need to know." Access to information was restricted by the agency's determination of who *needed* to have access to specific items of information.[29] The implementation of the "need to know" was administered through the use of document headings such as LIMDIS (Limited Distribution), EXDIS (Exclusive Distribution), and NODIS (No Distribution).

3. The urgency of information. The need to expedite the handling of a specific "critical" item of information had the effect of restricting the accessibility of information. Terms varying from Critic (indicating imminent enemy action), to indicators of less urgent information such as Flash, Immediate Priority, and Routine designated the relative urgency of messages.

Through having, or appearing to have, access to more facts than any other agency, the CIA was frequently in a position to present an impressive case in support of a particular foreign policy recommendation. As suggested by Professor Ransom,

Knowledge . . . conveys power. Secret knowledge can become secret power. A secret intelligence apparatus, claiming superior knowledge from undisclosed sources, and operating—because of legitimate secrecy claims—outside the normal checkreins of the American governmental system can wield invisible power either in the policy-making process or in clandestine operations in other countries.[30]

A fourth source of agency strength was the fact that individual CIA personnel were stationed in foreign areas for longer periods of time than were most other government employees. This enabled them to develop an impressive set of contacts (both in terms of numbers and political status), and as a result, CIA influence abroad was frequently stronger than that exercised by overseas personnel attached to other federal agencies. In the words of Roger Hilsman,

---

[29] The concept of "need to know" meant, in practice, that intelligence bearing a security classification could be made known to an employee of any agency only if he needed to know the contents of an intelligence item to fulfill the requirements of the specific task assigned him. Other colleagues within the same agency, although "cleared" for classified data, did not have access to such intelligence unless they too had a "need to know." Sometimes for special projects, such as the Paris peace talks concerning the Vietnam war, a code name was also added to a report and this determined a set distribution list for messages relating to this special project. For example, in 1968 when W. Averell Harriman and Cyrus Vance were United States negotiators in the Paris peace talks, the acronym HA VAN was used to control the distribution of messages concerning the event.

[30] Ransom, *Can American Democracy Survive Cold War?*, p. 168.

Indeed, because the CIA could keep its men in a particular country longer than most ambassadors stay, CIA station chiefs frequently had been able to make closer friendships with prime ministers and kings and presidents than ambassadors did, and thus be more influential. In many countries, especially the more backward countries on the firing line of Communist expansionism, where money is used freely in ways that the State Department budget does not provide for and where intrigue is a way of life, most nationals of the country sincerely believed that it was the CIA station chief who really represented the United States.[31]

Finally, CIA personnel included a large staff of well-educated, professionally trained, dedicated, diligent intelligence analysts representing almost 300 fields of specialization. Over half of these analysts held advanced academic degrees. Not only did the CIA possess quality personnel, but there were usually more of them to be assigned to a given problem or geographic area than were available to other agencies with comparable responsibilities. While, at times, State, Defense, AID, or ACDA might not have sufficient qualified personnel to attend an interdepartmental meeting, the CIA usually had enough trained personnel to prepare relevant studies and present a well-formulated program at such a meeting.

Secrecy and Foreign Policy

From the foregoing discussion it is possible to identify several generally accepted assumptions regarding American intelligence operations. First, there was a legitimate requirement for foreign intelligence. Because of the breadth of America's international commitments, the President required rapid access to accurate information concerning all areas of the world, especially hostile areas. Second, the role of intelligence operations had expanded. As the nation's international presence increased, there was a corresponding increase in the on-going programs supported by America's intelligence community. Third, effective intelligence operations required secrecy for two reasons: to protect the techniques of intelligence collection and to guard the content of intelligence. Fourth, the agency that was the source of secret information was in a position to exercise considerable influence in the formulation of foreign policy. Finally, because of the intelligence agency's potential and actual influence on policy, there was the need to impose some executive control on intelligence operations.

These five assumptions provided a basis for the following dilemma: there was a need for an effective intelligence gathering capability that required secrecy to be effective; secrecy permitted institutional autonomy; it was necessary to reduce autonomy through effective executive controls; executive controls violated secrecy and thereby reduced effectiveness.

---

[31] Hilsman, *To Move A Nation*, pp. 64–65.

From the CIA side of this dilemma, intelligence officials have urged that the members of the executive and legislative branches of the government accept intelligence plans and operations on faith. Former CIA Director Helms expressed the intelligence agency position as follows:

If we disclosed how much we know, the opposition is handed on a platter highly damaging indications of how and where we obtained the information, in what way his security is vulnerable, and who may have helped us. He can seal off the breach in his defenses, roll up the agents, and shut off the flow of information.

I cannot give you an easy answer to the objections raised by those who consider intelligence work incompatible with democratic principles. The nation must to a degree take it on faith that we too are honorable men devoted to her service. I can assure you that we are, but I am precluded from demonstrating it to the public.[32]

On the President's side of this dilemma there were some different considerations. First, for the American political system's traditional checks, balances, and restraints to be operative, officials within each of the three branches of government had to be cognizant of the activities of *all* government officials. It was not consistent with the traditional functioning of democratic government to have a component of the nation's foreign affairs capability accepted, as Mr. Helms suggested, purely "on faith."

Second, with regard to the conduct of foreign affairs, since the President was the responsible official, he required some control over intelligence operations. It was necessary for the President to determine the extent to which the need for foreign intelligence required him to approve the covert violation of treaty agreements, support political coups, buy political influence, and generally intervene in the domestic affairs of other nations.

Third, from the standpoint of Presidential decision-making, secrecy required the President to arrive at decisions by a process that limited the number of contacts and sources of advice he might find useful. Security precautions precluded his tapping, examining, and cross-checking as many sources as possible for the expression of sound judgement before he reached a decision. Obviously, in some instances secrecy was mandatory. Whenever secrecy was mandatory, however, the chance was increased that some potentially useful source of information would be denied to the President.

Finally, secrecy tended to undermine confidence among government officials of different executive agencies and between the government and the public and the government and the press. This point is developed further in Chapter 7.

---

[32] *New York Times,* April 15, 1971, p. 30. This speech by Mr. Helms to the American Society of Newspaper Editors was his first public address since he was appointed director of the CIA in 1966.

Ultimate Presidential Responsibility

The foreign policy implications of America's intelligence operations acquired an increasingly clearer focus during the years since 1947. Along with this growing awareness, the need to insure the tight coordination of the CIA's activities with the President's foreign policy objectives also became more apparent. Since the administrative mechanisms for legislative and excutive control existed, while real control was minimal at best, it appeared that the actual achievement of foreign policy coordination was dependent on the *will* to enforce control. In the final analysis, this responsibility centered on the President, supported by his White House staff. It seemed, based on developments within the NSC system discussed above, that further efforts in this direction had been initiated. Stronger and more rigorously enforced Congressional control was probably not the answer. In fact, an arrangement of controls that required Congress to be informed in advance of CIA's operations could be interpreted as a violation of the Constitutional freedom of the executive branch under the separation of powers and of the President's right to conduct the nation's foreign affairs. While the responsibility for controlling the CIA rested with the President, the exercise of effective executive control required the cooperation of the Director of the Central Intelligence Agency. A cooperative—and forceful —director working closely with the support of a determined President, could create a situation which conformed to the initial intention of the 1947 National Security Act, to provide the President with the intelligence data he required to reach informed policy decisions.

chapter **6**

Arms, the Bureaucracy, and
Foreign Policy:
The Strategic Arms Limitation Talks

A New Seriousness

America's unmatched military strength had a profound impact on the nation's international behavior. Nuclear superiority, complemented by an unparalleled logistic and technical ability to equip, deploy, and support American military forces in any part of the world, led American officials to believe they could assume and fulfill a responsibility of unprecedented scope, i.e., resisting communism (or political movements described as being Communist) anywhere in the world. America's worldwide efforts acquired the character of an anti-Communist crusade and culminated in a program of global interventionism to contain communism. Military capabilities provided the basis for establishing military alliances and attempting to make deterrence "work." They also led the United States to believe it could fight in Korea and in Vietnam, and win. However, the impact of these "no-win" war experiences aggravated basic doubts concerning the utility of physical power in the nuclear era.[1]

During the late 1960s and early 1970s, American officials began to consider a shift away from the policies of the past quarter century, policies

---

[1] For a lucid, compelling elaboration of these observations, see Ronald Steel, *Pax Americana* (New York: Viking Press, 1970), especially chap. 1 and 2.

that had been intricately tied to the development and maintenance of military superiority. Four basic factors contributed to the disposition toward policy change: (1) the financial cost of the arms race, a cost that consumed close to 50 percent of the federal budget; (2) the questionable utility of military power, power sufficient "to destroy most human life on the planet within a matter of minutes, yet [insufficient to enable America to] win a guerrilla war against peasants in black pajamas"; [2] (3) the atmosphere of tension, suspicion, and hostility which, itself, was conducive to the outbreak of nuclear war and the destruction of America; and (4) the growing skepticism concerning transcendent military status combined with interventionist tendencies as the most effective means for achieving extended world influence. America's "heavy-handed" protective practices suggested to some "lesser" nations the possibility of being suffocated by America's bounty, especially with Vietnam as a graphic example of how America "helps" a besieged nation, an observation discussed further in Chapter 7.

All of these factors suggested the need for policy change. Although the subject of policy change is developed more fully in the following chapter, it is appropriate to mention at this point that the first step toward developing alternatives to the dependence on arms for national security was the reducing of arms and defense appropriations and the strengthening of other resources within the country which might, in the long run, better serve America's national interests. Moving toward arms limitations was viewed as involving considerable risks, but one insight gained from the long years of the Cold War was the fact that there were also risks associated with the arms race in the form of war through accident, miscalculation, or misperception. Neither a policy of increasing or decreasing arms offered the assurance of absolute security. However, by the late 1960s, it appeared possible to some officials that more advantages and more security could be achieved through moving beyond the Cold War along the uncharted path toward disarmament than through a perpetuation of the practices of the past 25 years.

SALT and Foreign Policy

The focus of the discussion in this chapter is the Strategic Arms Limitation Talks (SALT), negotiations between the United States and the Soviet Union that began in Helsinki in late 1969 and which, after 2½ years of bilateral discussions, resulted in the first international agreement to limit nuclear arms. SALT was chosen as the focus for discussion for three reasons. First, SALT represents the strongest effort to date by the executive branch to achieve an international agreement limiting nuclear arms. SALT suggested a new level of seriousness in arms negotiations and a new

---

[2] Ibid., p. 13.

level of determination by the President to loosen America's foreign policy from the bind of the Cold War.

Second, the subject of SALT negotiations—that of nuclear arms—resides at the heart of America's foreign policy. America's principle postwar means of promoting national security and resolving international conflict has been its military capabilities. If, as was the case with SALT, American policy makers began to support self-imposed programs to limit or restrict what had previously been regarded as the central source of foreign policy strength, such a development warrants serious consideration.

The third reason for looking at SALT is that the process of negotiation highlights some important characteristics of the formulation and implementation of American foreign policy. In the preceding four chapters the principal agencies and officials involved in foreign policy were discussed. By viewing SALT as a case study, the same agencies can be seen as they interact in the process of shaping policy. Thus, the primary objective of discussing SALT is not to convey a detailed comprehension of the talks themselves, but to use SALT to illustrate some of the basic and recurring factors that shaped United States foreign policy during the Cold War years and that will continue to do so for some time to come.

In the discussion that follows, some background experiences related to America's postwar involvement in disarmament attempts are described. These experiences were selected to illustrate varying attitudes toward disarmament within the executive branch. This discussion is followed by a description of some of the developments within which SALT took place. The objectives sought and issues confronted by American and Soviet negotiators at SALT are then set forth. With these selected issues in mind, it is possible to isolate and set forth some recurring and persistent considerations pertaining to foreign policy in general.

Opinion Differences Within the Executive Branch

The first step taken by the United States in the direction of placing controls on atomic weapons occurred on June 14, 1946, when a two-phase proposal was presented to the newly created Atomic Energy Commission of the United Nations.[3] At that time the United States held an atomic

---

[3] This United States proposal was commonly referred to as the Baruch plan, named for Bernard Baruch, an adviser to President Truman, who presented it to the UN Atomic Energy Commission. The first phase of the plan called for the establishment of an International Atomic Development Authority which would own, control, and operate all nuclear energy facilities from mine to finished product. This international authority would also inspect all nuclear activities. After an inspection system was established, the second phase of the plan was to be implemented which called for the cessation of all production of nuclear weapons and the destruction of all nuclear stockpiles. Soviet Foreign Minister Molotov denounced the Baruch plan, insisting that nuclear weapons first be destroyed and then, following this action, a nationally operated inspection system could be established. This American-Soviet difference over the

weapons monopoly and, through its UN proposal, was indirectly suggesting that the USSR accept as a permanent condition the second rank status of a nonnuclear power. The Soviet Union refused.

Following the erosion of America's monopoly on nuclear weapons from 1949 to 1953, and with the USSR beginning to participate vigorously in the competitive quest for superiority in weaponry, American Presidents began to refer publicly to disarmament as a primary objective of American foreign policy.[4] For example, in 1957, at a Presidential news conference, President Eisenhower said,

> I just want to take this occasion to say one more word about disarmament. It seems to me that the more any intelligent man thinks about the possibilities of war today, the more he should understand you have got to work on this business of disarmament. We must, at the same time, though, keep our minds open and keep exploring every field, every facet of the whole great field, to see if something can't be done. It just has to be done in the interest of the United States.[5]

Further, at the same conference, with reference to the subject of international tension, the President continued,

> That has got to be diminished or there is going to be no progress. At the same time there has got to be progress in some kind of disarmament or there is going to be no reduction in world tensions.[6]

Presidents Kennedy, Johnson, and Nixon extended this support for disarmament and arms control, describing them as prime objectives of America's foreign policy. President Nixon, in a 1970 report to Congress, stated that, "There is no area in which we and the Soviet Union—as well as others—have a greater common interest than in reaching agreement with regard to arms control."[7]

---

sequence of events leading to disarmament remained a problem in all the years following 1946; the United States urging the creation of an inspection system and only then beginning to limit arms, the USSR wanting an initial destruction of arms, to be followed by the creation of an inspection system.

[4] The term disarmament, as used in the discussion that follows, refers to any plan or system for the reduction or elimination of armaments and armed forces. The term arms control, on the other hand, does not involve the reduction or elimination of arms but, instead, refers to arrangements for the control over the use of weapons or the limitation of their number. This would include agreements designed to prevent wars through accident or miscalculation (such as the Hot Line Agreement of 1963), agreements designed to restrict the effects of weapons testing that are harmful to human life (such as the Limited Test Ban Treaty of 1963), and agreements designed to restrict the development and dissemination of nuclear weapons (such as the Outer Space Treaty of 1967 and the Non-Proliferation Treaty of 1968). To date, on the basis of these definitions, the United States has not participated in any disarmament treaties or agreements affecting its nuclear weapons stockpiles. All agreements, including the discussions covered by the Strategic Arms Limitation Talks, are related to arms control issues.

[5] *New York Times*, May 23, 1957, p. 14.

[6] Ibid., p. 14.

[7] *Documents on Disarmament* (Washington, D.C.: United States Arms Control and Disarmament Agency, December 1971), p. 67.

Although the four most recent Presidents publicly declared their support of disarmament as a prime objective of American foreign policy, a perceptible reflection of this professed concern was very slow to develop within the government at levels below that of the Chief Executive. The disparity between the relative importance the President attached to the quest for disarmament, and the reservations or outright opposition of selected executive branch officials was first evident during the Eisenhower years. Resistance to disarmament, most apparent during the Eisenhower administration, persisted through the 1960s and the administrations of Presidents Kennedy, Johnson, and Nixon.

In mid-March 1955, President Eisenhower announced that he had created the White House staff position of Special Assistant to the President for Disarmament to facilitate progress toward disarmament. Harold Stassen, appointed by the President to fill this position, assembled a staff of over 50 professional and clerical personnel to supersede (and transfer to the White House) the modest four-man disarmament research effort that had been operating quietly within the Department of State.[8]

While President Eisenhower spoke of the need to achieve progress toward disarmament, executives within his administration with responsibilities directly related to disarmament matters worked to resist any arrangements that would limit the nation's military strength and thereby render America vulnerable to Soviet aggression. First, in 1957, Secretary of State Dulles brought Mr. Stassen's disarmament organization (reduced in size by over 50 percent) under the administrative direction of the Department of State, an action that led to Mr. Stassen's resignation in early 1958. In taking this action, Secretary Dulles appeared to have been motivated primarily by two considerations. One was his distaste for the leading role Mr. Stassen had assumed in disarmament affairs, an area of responsibility over which the State Department had previously exercised full authority.[9] The second reason for initiating this action was Secretary

---

[8] One of President Eisenhower's intentions in establishing the Stassen disarmament group was to bring together for the first time a permanent, experienced body of disarmament experts to replace the ad hoc negotiators the United States had been dispatching to disarmament conferences. This Presidential intention, however, was not fulfilled at any time prior to the creation of the Arms Control and Disarmament Agency in 1961. For example, in early 1960, with a ten-nation arms control conference only one month away, Italian, French and British allies came to Washington to agree on a unified position. The United States had formulated no disarmament plan, which three weeks later prompted then-senator John F. Kennedy to point out, "We are meeting next week in Geneva with nine other nations in an East-West Disarmament Conference, but (except to the extent we will accept the broad British proposals) we have prepared no plan for our conferees." Seymour Melman (ed.), *Disarmament, Its Politics and Economics* (Boston: American Academy of Arts and Sciences, 1962), p. 180.

[9] Secretary Dulles held sufficient influence to implement this action. As suggested, his control over foreign affairs, including disarmament, was firm and all-pervasive. In the words of Saville Davis, managing editor of the *Christian Science Monitor*, "It is clear that the key to the decision-making process on arms control in Washington during

Dulles's inability to relate disarmament or arms control to the concept of national security, an inability compatible with a mentality that had espoused the concept of massive retaliation.

Although the tone of the resistance to disarmament became less shrill following the death of Secretary Dulles in 1959, the absence of effective support continued. Secretary of State Dean Rusk expressed the point of view under both Presidents Johnson and Kennedy that it was unrealistic to anticipate responsible diplomatic exchange with the Soviet Union when the "Soviets have not yet abandoned their aim of world revolution." [10] Thus, according to Secretary Rusk, it was important to maintain military strength, ". . . for no nation now free could long remain free if military power was not available to deter agression." [11] Following the first year of the Johnson administration, the secretary's deep preoccupation with America's involvement in the Vietnam war made the issue of disarmament an almost irrelevant consideration among the President's top officials. As had been true of President Eisenhower, Presidents Kennedy and Johnson expressed on a number of occasions the need to achieve progress toward disarmament, but once again, administrative officials immediately below the chief executive level either lacked a personal commitment to this objective or found that their energies were expended in implementing other aspects of foreign policy.

Opposition to disarmament also came from the Defense Department, opposition which, in 1957, perhaps assumed its most outspoken quality in statements issued by Admiral Arthur W. Radford, Chairman of the Joint Chiefs of Staff. In reacting to the possibility of an arms control agreement with the Soviet Union, Admiral Radford announced that, "We can't trust the Russians on this or anything. The Communists have broken their word with every country with which they have ever had an agreement." [12] Six days later, in apparent reaction to this statement, President Eisenhower almost seemed to plead, "there has got to be prog-

---

this period is to be found in the thought processes, the methods of working, the policy concepts of Foster Dulles." (Saville Davis, "Recent Policy Making in the United States Government," *Daedalus*, Fall, 1960, p. 954.) Although Secretary Dulles did not comment publicly on the President's appointment of Mr. Stassen as his disarmament adviser, it was assumed by one Washington writer that Mr. Dulles was "not overjoyed by this development." (Richard H. Rovere, *The Eisenhower Years* (New York: Farrar Straus and Co., 1956), p. 265.)

[10] Dean Rusk, "Foreign Policy and the American Citizen," *Department of State Bulletin*, December 30, 1963, p. 994.

[11] ———, *The Winds of Freedom* (Boston: Beacon Press, 1963), p. 46.

[12] *New York Times*, May 20, 1957, p. 1. The fervor with which Admiral Radford and Defense Department officials opposed a disarmament agreement was noted by a number of Washington observers. James Reston commented that, "Some members of the Joint Chiefs of Staff, particularly the Chairman, Admiral Arthur W. Radford," regarded agreements with the Soviet Union as "worthless" while other members of the Joint Chiefs were concerned that prolonged disarmament talks might be to the disadvantage of the military budget. (*New York Times*, May 28, 1957, p. 13.)

ress in some kind of disarmament."[13] Another vigorous opponent of disarmament within the Defense Department at the time was Assistant Secretary of Defense Donald Quarles. Because the Quarles point of view persisted in government circles for at least a decade following the assistant secretary's departure, it is useful to savor the quality of his unequivocal dismissal of disarmament. In 1955 Quarles made the point that, in the future, the United States was going to base its security

. . . not on the abolition of power, but on the retention of an overwhelming air-atomic power; not on "disarmament" in the old-fashioned sense, but on the capability to retaliate; not on "banning" or "destroying" atomic bombs, but on retaining them in such quantities that no nation could hope to start a major war without being destroyed by atomic and hydrogen retaliation; not on international monopolies of atomic power or "fool proof" inspection systems, but on mutual surveillance designed to prevent surprise attack by either side.[14]

Similar views, although expressed with greater restraint, were held by Defense Secretaries Neil McElroy and Thomas Gates, both of whom found opportunities to voice their opposition to the nuclear weapons test ban.

The Defense Department's consistent opposition to reduction in armaments centered around the conviction that such action would (1) seriously weaken the strategy of deterrence, a consequence which was viewed as completely unacceptable; (2) retard or halt the development of more advanced weaponry, i.e., a diverse range of more powerful, accurate, and reliable weapons; and (3) leave the United States unable to detect enemy violations of any arms agreement, violations that were believed to be inevitable due to the Soviet addiction to cheating.

On the surface of government affairs it appeared that, with the change of Presidential administrations in 1960, attitudes toward disarmament within the Defense Department corresponded more closely to the President's stated position than had been the case under President Eisenhower. However, upon closer analysis, while outspoken opposition to disarmament became less sharp, the rationale for Defense Department resistance remained unchanged. Twelve years later, in 1972, the Defense Department's position reflected the same outlook that had persisted during the two preceding decades. The department's categorical imperative, expressed by JCS Chairman Admiral Thomas Moorer, on the eve of President Nixon's departure for his visit to Communist China, was that the United States must always maintain enough nuclear power "to cope with both China and the USSR simultaneously."[15]

---

[13] *New York Times*, May 26, 1957, p. 1.

[14] Secretary Quarles quoted by James Reston, *New York Times*, September 6, 1955, p. 8. Secretary Quarles completed his statement by indicating that the United States was assuming the essential wickedness and acquisitiveness of man in general and the Communists in particular.

[15] *New York Times*, February 18, 1972, p. 35.

Another executive agency that played a major role in the shaping of disarmament decisions was the Atomic Energy Commission (AEC), the mission of which was to design, develop, and test nuclear weapons. The participation of the AEC in policy decisions during the Eisenhower administration was largely due to the articulate and assertive character of the chairman of the commission, Admiral Lewis Strauss.[16] Admiral Strauss consistently opposed American participation in arms control or disarmament agreements, a position he adhered to rigorously during the 1958–61 United States-USSR nuclear test ban negotiations.[17] When asked by Sen. Hubert Humphrey why he opposed the test ban, Admiral Strauss answered, "We now have a variety of kinds, sizes, weights of weapons designed to accomplish various specific tasks. Further tests will result in the perfection of still more precise weapons and many of those which we will need will be destined to prevent incoming attack." [18]

Although President Eisenhower expressed support for a suspension of nuclear weapons tests under certain conditions (conditions which he left unspecified), Admiral Strauss, reinforced by nationally recognized scientists such as Dr. Edward Teller, frequently referred to as "the father of the H-Bomb," and Dr. Ernest O. Lawrence, former director of the University of California Radiation Laboratory, plus other members of the AEC, resisted efforts to achieve such an agreement.[19] Secretary Dulles added his support to the AEC position of resisting the suspension of nuclear weapons tests, stating that the Unitied States needed further testing in order to develop smaller, cleaner tactical weapons "in fairness to our responsibilities and our duties to the American people" and "perhaps to humanity." [20]

Admiral Strauss's successor as Chairman of the AEC was John McCone, a declared opponent of any agreement on nuclear tests that involved a long and uncontrolled moratorium on small underground explosions. Thus, a change in the leadership of the AEC did not alter the commission's disposition to oppose the realization of a disarmament or arms control agree-

---

[16] A "feeling" for Admiral Strauss's opposition to disarmament is provided by his statement that the personnel of the AEC who were engaged in developing nuclear weapons were "sustained by the earnest belief that the achievements in the area of atomic armament have been a deterrent to aggression." U.S. Senate Committee on Foreign Relations, Subcommittee on Disarmament, *Hearings on Control and Reduction of Armament* (part 3, March 7, 1956), p. 117.

[17] Nuclear test ban negotiations, terminated on September 1, 1961 when the Soviet Union resumed nuclear testing, were a prelude to the negotiations that culminated in the Limited Nuclear Test Ban Treaty of 1963.

[18] *Subcommittee Hearings*, part 3, March 7, 1956, p. 124.

[19] Two nuclear physicists, both members of the President's Scientific Advisory Committee, stated that Dr. Teller and Admiral Strauss "had deliberately undertaken to sabotage in advance any attempt to negotiate a [test] suspension." Charles J. Murphy, "Nuclear Inspection: A Near Miss," *Fortune*, March 1959, p. 156.

[20] *New York Times*, April 2, 1958, p. 6. The term "cleaner" with reference to nuclear weapons describes a bomb that produces less, or no, radioactive fallout following detonation.

ment. With regard to the AEC's practice of attempting to exert influence on disarmament planning and negotiations, Sen. Humphrey pointed out that:

> The A.E.C. seems to have difficulty in remembering that it was not created to be a policy-making body in the area of foreign relations. . . . The A.E.C. is allowed to continue to oppose the official position of the United States and to inject its own views on foreign policy due to a lack of leadership at the top.[21]

Under the administrations of Presidents Kennedy and Johnson, the chairman and other officials of the Atomic Energy Commission refrained from public expression of opposition to disarmament.

Several summary observations are appropriate at this point. First, the Departments of State and Defense, and the AEC, during the 1950s and 1960s, were directed by officials who failed to contribute effective support to, and at times opposed, the President's efforts to achieve some form of arms control or disarmament. Second, the basic reason for this resistance was the fact that nuclear deterrence, as pointed out in Chapter 2, stood as the sanctioned strategy designed to assure national security. The credibility, and thus the effectiveness, of deterrence was related to the maintenance and continued development of an impressive weapons capability, a condition which in the minds of many government officials stood in conflict with the Presidentially espoused objective of disarmament. Third, under Presidents Eisenhower, Kennedy, Johnson, and Nixon the Defense Department's resistance remained tied to the three part conviction described above, i.e., arms limitation or reduction would weaken deterrence, restrict weapons development, and allow the USSR to gain a weapons advantage through cheating. The conceptual linkage between Admiral Radford in the mid-50s and Secretary Laird almost 20 years later remained undistorted by the passage of time and shifting international relationships. Finally, just as was the case during the 1950s and 1960s, the proceedings at the Strategic Arms Limitation Talks (as will be evident in the discussion that follows) revealed a continuing dependence on arms for security and a continued resistance to arms control by the Department of Defense and the Joint Chiefs.

It is interesting to note that, prior to President Kennedy's creation of the Arms Control and Disarmament Agency in 1961, the only potentially effective organization for disarmament was that which operated for three years under Mr. Stassen as part of the President's White House Office. This disarmament group had sufficient relevant professional skills, direct access to the President and Secretary of State, funds with which to initiate disarmament research, and organizational stability, so that it constituted a potentially adequate resource to support the President's interest in dis-

---

[21] *U.S. Congressional Record,* 86th Congress, 1st session, August 18, 1959, p. 16136.

armament. The positive attributes of the Stassen office provided organizational guidance for the subsequent design of ACDA. One other characteristic of the Stassen organization was that it was located in the White House, close to the President. As indicated in Chapter 4, a similar organizational arrangement was revived by President Nixon with the creation of the Verification Panel which was made part of the National Security System. In the area of arms control, ACDA looked to the White House for policy directives just as, in the area of foreign policy in general, the State Department took its lead from Dr. Kissinger's White House operations.

SALT: Part of a Continuum

The Strategic Arms Limitation Talks between the United States and the Soviet Union began November 17, 1969, in Helsinki, Finland. After two and one half years of negotiations, the two nuclear superpowers reached an agreement on May 26, 1972, which for the first time limited the number of defensive and offensive nuclear missiles that either power could acquire. This unprecedented bilateral agreement represented the most advanced step taken by either power in the long effort to place controls on nuclear arsenals. It was also the latest step in the long process that began 26 years before with the Baruch proposal. Along the way there had been many frustrations, obstacles, and unfulfilled efforts toward achieving an agreement that would actually limit or reduce arms stockpiles. On the other hand, there had also been a number of positive accomplishments.

It was this protracted and diversified set of experiences that provided the basis from which professional confidence and official persistence developed and thereby contributed to the realization of the SALT achievements of 1972. Long experience in joint efforts to devise acceptable methods for controlling arms had made the concept of arms control appear less of a departure from the familiar, and, as a result, less threatening to national security. Earlier arms control agreements had softened official resistance and wariness and created a negotiating atmosphere without which it probably would not have been possible to take the step at SALT finally agreed to by President Nixon and General Secretary Brezhnev. The most significant earlier achievements, all of which controlled the use and dissemination of arms but did not limit their number, included the following:

1. *The Antarctic Treaty,* December 1959, prohibited the establishment of military bases and the testing of any weapons in Antarctica. The treaty included provisions for inspection, permitting on-site inspections of Soviet installations in the Antarctic. Sixteen nations, including the United States and the USSR, have acceded to this treaty.

2. *The Hot Line,* or Direct Communications Agreement, June 1963, a bilateral agreement between the United States and the Soviet Union,

provided two direct communication circuits for immediate contact between Washington and Moscow to lessen the dangers of war resulting from error or misunderstanding. During the fifth round of SALT (July–September 1971) at Helsinki, the United States and the Soviet Union agreed to modernize and make more secure this communications link by using space satellite communication systems rather than the more vulnerable ground-based communication network.

3. *The Limited Test-Ban Treaty*, August 1963, prohibited nuclear weapons testing in the atmosphere, underwater, and in space. One hundred five nations have acceded to this treaty, the only nuclear powers not participating being France and Communist China.[22]

4. *The Outer Space Treaty*, January 1967, prohibited the installation of weapons on celestial bodies (such as the moon) and the placing into orbit of any objects carrying nuclear weapons. Sixty nations, including the United States and the Soviet Union, have acceded to this treaty.

5. *The Treaty for the Prohibition of Nuclear Weapons in Latin America*, February 1967, provided for the maintenance of Latin America as a nuclear-free zone. Only Latin American countries could become parties to the treaty and 19 have acceded. The United States and Great Britain indicated that they respected the denuclearized status of Latin America and agreed not to use or threaten to use nuclear weapons against any party to the treaty.

6. *The Non-Proliferation Treaty*, July 1968, provided that nations possessing nuclear weapons would not transfer these weapons to any nonnuclear power. Each nonnuclear nation agreed not to acquire nuclear weapons and the nuclear powers agreed to continue efforts to curb their nuclear arms.[23] In addition, nonnuclear nations agreed to arrange with the International Atomic Energy Agency (IAEA) a means to prevent the diversion of nuclear material from peaceful to military purposes. Seventy-one nations, including the nuclear powers of the United States, Soviet Union, and Great Britain, have acceded to the treaty. The "threshold" or near-nuclear nations that have not ratified this treaty include West Germany, Japan, India, Israel, Pakistan, and South Africa.

---

[22] Underground testing was permitted as such explosions did not cause "radioactive debris to be present outside the territorial limits of the state under whose jurisdiction or control such explosion is conducted." To date, a comprehensive test ban, prohibiting all nuclear weapons tests, has not been achieved because of the problem of verification. The USSR has rejected on-site inspections which the United States has insisted are necessary in order to insure that the terms of a comprehensive test ban are being adhered to. The United States and the USSR believed that a ban on testing in the atmosphere, underwater, and in space could be adequately verified without onsite inspections.

[23] Following the signing of the SALT accords, Soviet and American spokesmen indicated that SALT testified to the fact that the two nuclear superpowers were living up to their pledge expressed in the Non-Proliferation Treaty to restrict their nuclear stockpiles in exchange for the renunciation of nuclear arms by nonnuclear nations.

7. *The Seabed Arms Control Treaty*, February 1971, prohibited the placing of nuclear weapons or other weapons of mass destruction on the seabed beyond a 12-mile coastal "seabed zone." Nineteen nations have acceded to the treaty, including the United States, the USSR, and Great Britain.[24]

In January 1967, at the same time as the treaty prohibiting the placement of weapons in space, President Johnson attempted to achieve progress on a more ambitious level—that of placing limits on the number of nuclear arms possessed by the United States and the Soviet Union. The President, in a secret letter to Premier Kosygin, suggested that the USSR join the United States in exploring this sensitive subject. This letter was the first step in the protracted effort which, five years later, resulted in an agreement to limit arms. A month following the dispatch of President Johnson's letter, Soviet Premier Kosygin expressed interest, but nothing further developed. Then, a year later, another favorable response came from Soviet Foreign Minister Gromyko. A year and a half after President Johnson's 1967 letter, on August 19, 1968, the USSR invited President Johnson to come to Moscow in early October to begin arms discussions. The possibility of further exchanges at this time was disrupted by the move of Soviet and Warsaw Pact troops into Czechoslovakia in August 1968. Following the invasion of Czechoslovakia, in the fall of 1968, President Johnson, still hoping to be the first American President to visit Moscow, tried to reactivate Soviet interest in arms discussions but the USSR procrastinated, knowing a new American President would be elected in November. Immediately following the inauguration of President Nixon, the Soviet Union again indicated interest in arms negotiations with the statement:

The Soviet government has proposed that all the nuclear powers begin negotiating at once on halting the production of nuclear weapons, reducing nuclear stockpiles and subsequently banning and eliminating nuclear weapons completely. The Soviet government has also proposed that agreement be reached on mutual limitation and subsequent curtailment of strategic systems for the delivery of nuclear weapons.[25]

---

[24] The Seabed Treaty was to come into effect when 22 nations had ratified, including the three nuclear nations which had already done so.

In addition to the seven agreements cited it should be noted that since 1962, and separate from SALT, the Geneva disarmament conference (the Conference of the Committee on Disarmament or CCD) was the world's principal forum for negotiating multilateral arms control agreements. The United States and the Soviet Union were permanent co-chairmen of the CCD. Twenty-six nations were members (but France, a member, never participated). In August 1971, the United States and the Soviet Union submitted identical draft texts to the CCD which prohibited the development, production, and stockpiling of biological weapons and toxins, and both nations pledged to conduct negotiations on measures for prohibiting the development, production, and stockpiling of chemical weapons.

[25] *Current Digest of the Soviet Press*, February 5, 1969, pp. 6–7.

Following further discussion between American and Soviet officials, it was agreed that both nations would hold a preliminary one-month arms session in mid-November 1969, to be followed by a second round of more substantive discussions, beginning on April 16, 1970. The United States delegation was headed by Gerard C. Smith, Director of ACDA, the Soviet delegation by Deputy Foreign Minister Vladimir S. Semyonov.

In May 1972, at the Nixon-Brezhnev Moscow Summit Conference, the conference at which the SALT agreements were signed, a series of other agreements for cooperation were also concluded. These included an agreement for cooperative American-Soviet research on environmental problems; an agreement for coordinated research in cancer, heart disease, and environmental health; an agreement for joint space exploration; an agreement for scientific and technical cooperation; the creation of a joint American-Soviet trade commission; and an agreement to prevent incidents at sea involving American and Soviet naval vessels.[26]

These agreements, all requiring extensive time and labor to draw up and negotiate, contributed to an atmosphere of cooperation and were a reflection of the direction in which American-Soviet relations had already begun to move. Thus, SALT took place in a negotiating setting that gave it maximum opportunity for success.

SALT: Objectives

The United States agreed to participate in SALT to achieve the following three basic objectives. First, to contribute to the stability of the United States-USSR strategic relationship through agreed limitations on strategic nuclear weapons. The fulfillment of this objective would strengthen international stability as well as promote American national security. The second basic objective was to halt the upward spiral of nuclear arms stockpiles and, as a consequence, lessen the tensions, uncertainties, and costs of an unrestrained continuation of the strategic arms race. The third objective was to increase the security of the United States through reducing the risks of a nuclear war.[27] Two additional subobjectives were, first, to enhance the stature of the United States in the eyes of the other nations

---

[26] It is interesting to note that a number of these areas of cooperation were specified by Secretary Brezhnev at the 24th Congress of the Communist Party of the Soviet Union, March 31, 1971. At that time, Secretary Brezhnev indicated the willingness of the USSR to engage in research with other nations in areas such as conservation of the environment, prevention of disease, development of transportation and communications, development of natural resources, and the exploration of space and the oceans. The agreements of May 1972, over a year later, represent, in a sense, the outcome of a responsiveness to earlier Soviet overtures.

[27] This summary assessment of SALT objectives is drawn from the discussion in *Documents on Disarmament—1969* (Washington, D.C.: Arms Control and Disarmament Agency, 1970), p. 534.

of the world by acting to support agreements that would reduce the threat of war; second, to help set a precedent for strategic arms limitations that would begin to have the effect of encouraging the participation of Chinese Communist officials in arms discussions, or at least to create sufficient diplomatic pressure to make the Chinese sensitive to some international constraints on arms.

With regard to America's pursuit of its SALT objectives, President Nixon advised Ambassador Smith: "For our part we will be guided by the concept of maintaining 'sufficiency' in the forces required to protect ourselves and our allies."[28] President Nixon thought of "sufficiency" in weaponry as a less provocative (from the standpoint of the arms race) and a less open-ended term than "superiority." Sufficiency in nuclear power also suggested a level of weaponry that was quantitatively less than that required by superiority yet sufficient to protect the United States without necessarily representing a numerical edge over the USSR. President Nixon pointed out that the United States would maintain a sufficiency in arms "to deny other countries the ability to impose their will on the United States and its allies under the weight of strategic military superiority." President Nixon went on to state that the Unitied States had reached the stage where it was conceivable that security could be achieved through strategic arms limitations.[29] Secretary Brezhnev had stressed the need for "equal security" in the nuclear era, a condition under which neither side had a unilateral advantage. The concepts of "sufficiency" and "equal security" suggested a shared American-Soviet outlook that made it appear conceivable that the time was at hand when arms negotiators might arrive at some mutually acceptable ceiling for weapons stockpiles.

SALT: Terms and Numbers

What weapons were actually possessed by the United States and the USSR that gave rise to the objectives just discussed? To provide some familiarity with the military "hardware" to which the objectives of SALT were related, the following three tables are included. Figure 12, *Glossary of Strategic Terms*, provides some assistance in translating terms used at SALT and in the field of national security affairs. Figure 13, *Strategic Nuclear Weapons Balance*, indicates some of the characteristics of the nuclear weapons which, for the United States, represented "sufficiency" and for the USSR, "equal security." Figure 14, *The Arms Race*, depicts the relative American and Soviet rate of arms acquisition between 1964 and 1972.

---

[28] Ibid., p. 737.
[29] U.S. Arms Control and Disarmament Agency, *Tenth Annual Report to Congress* (Washington, D.C.; January 1, 1970–December 31, 1970), p. 5.

FIGURE 12
Glossary of Strategic Terms

ABM (Antiballistic Missile Defense)—System of radars, missile intercepters, and control network to track and destroy incoming ballistic missile warheads. The United States system, called Safeguard, was being developed to protect land based missile sites in North Dakota and Montana. A Soviet system utilizing 64 missile intercepters has been deployed around Moscow.

ASW (Antisubmarine Warfare)—Location and destruction of enemy submarines by aircraft, surface vessels, and submarines. Generally thought to be less than adequate at its present stage of development, ASW will become increasingly important in the coming decades as the nuclear powers rely more heavily on their undersea strategic forces.

B-1 AMSA (Advanced Manned Strategic Aircraft)—Long range U.S. supersonic bomber intended to replace the B-52s. Cost of each B-1 is $30 million (each B-52 cost $8 million).

FOBS (Fractional Orbital Bombardment System)—System tested by Soviet Union for delivering a nuclear warhead by launching it into a low earth orbit instead of sending it into a higher ballistic trajectory thus avoiding detection by radar until the very last portion of the flight path. Fractional orbit avoids violation of the 1967 outerspace treaty.

Hardening—The protection of land based missiles and facilities against nuclear attack by enclosing them in underground silos of concrete and steel.

ICBM (Intercontinental Ballistic Missile)—Large land-based missile capable of launching nuclear warheads into trajectories of between 5,500 and 8,000 nautical miles. These solid and liquid fueled missiles are a major component of the U.S. and USSR arsenals. (See Figures 13 and 14.)

IRBM and MRBM (Intermediate Range and Medium Range Ballistic Missiles)—Land based ballistic missiles with ranges of 2,000 to 4,000 nautical miles (IRBM) and 1,500 nautical miles (MRBM).

KT and MT (Kilotons and Megatons)—A measure of the destructive power of an atomic or nuclear weapon by comparing it to the equivalent energy released by 1,000 tons of TNT (for one kiloton) or 1,000,000 tons of TNT (for one megaton).

Land Mobile Missiles—Missiles placed on trucks or trains. This technique, designed to reduce the vulnerability of land-based missiles through making them mobile, has been used by the USSR and may be developed further as stationary land-based offensive missiles become more vulnerable to attack because of advances in missile accuracy and warhead technology (See MIRV.)

MIRV (Multiple Independently Targetable Reentry Vehicle)—A system capable of directing a number of warheads (also decoys and penetration aids) into separate preprogrammed trajectories after being launched by only one booster. The U.S. has deployed MIRVs on its Minuteman III land-based missiles (three 200-KT warheads) and on its Poseidon sea-based missiles (ten 50-KT warheads). (See Figure 13.)

MRV (Multiple Reentry Vehicle)—Several warheads launched by a single missile that cannot be directed to separate targets. The U.S. sea-based Polaris is equipped with three 200-KT warheads, and it is believed the giant Soviet land-based SS-9 is being equipped with a MVR containing three 5-MT warheads. (See Figure 13.)

SLBM (Sea Launched Ballistic Missiles)—Missile in Polaris and Poseidon nuclear submarines (U.S.) and on surface vessels and in both diesel and nuclear powered submarines (USSR). (See Figures 13 and 14.)

SAM (Surface to Air Missile Defense System)—Short-range missiles deployed extensively in the USSR and designed for use against strategic bombers.

SRAM (Short Range Attack Missile)—Air-borne short range (60–75 miles)

FIGURE 12—(Continued)

Glossary of Strategic Terms—(Continued)

missile with nuclear warhead for attack against land target. Sometimes called a "standoff missile" this weapon allows bombers such as the U.S. B-52 to deliver nuclear warheads at a greater distance from the target area.

Strategic Bombers—Medium range and long range jet aircraft capable of carrying up to 25 MT of thermonuclear weapons.

Trident-ULMS (Undersea Long Range Missile System)—A new submarine being developed by the U.S. Navy which will carry much longer range missiles allowing the submarine more freedom of movement since it can patrol at greater distances from the enemy. (Cost of each submarine is $1 billion. Cost of conventional World War II submarine was $4.7 million.)

Verification—Technique for assessing the strategic capabilities of the other side, including the use of external sources of information, such as reconnaissance satellites and electronic sensors, as well as other methods of intelligence collection.

SALT: Negotiations [30]

During the two and one half years of SALT negotiations there were seven rounds of meetings, each round lasting from one to four months. The seven rounds involved a total of almost 100 sessions between American and Soviet delegates. Each of the seven rounds alternated between Helsinki, the site of the first round, and Vienna.[31] Within each city the location of each session alternated between the American and Soviet embassies.

There were approximately 60 members of the American delegation to SALT, plus scores of security personnel, secretaries, advisers, families, and hundreds of journalists. Working-level delegations usually met twice a week for a one-hour session that involved the active participation of approximately a dozen delegates from each nation. A more casual gathering over soft drinks took place following each one-hour meeting, with delegates of military, scientific, or diplomatic background seeking out their counterparts from the other nation's delegation. At formal, ambassadorial-level sessions, it was arranged so that Ambassadors Smith and Semyonov were the only participants who made statements. Each spoke once, reading a prepared statement with a copy in the original language being handed to the other delegation on the other side of a long table. There was no discussion at these formal meetings, no improvisation, and no public record was made available. All questions were withheld and were

---

[30] See Appendix C, *Selected Chronology, Strategic Arms Limitation Talks,* for a more detailed chronology of the SALT proceedings.

[31] This alternating arrangement represented one of the first compromises reached between the American and Soviet delegations. The USSR preferred that negotiations be held in Helsinki, wishing to favor their neighbor Finland and sensitive to Austria's criticism of the USSR's 1968 invasion of Czechoslovakia; the Americans preferred the comfort and space of the Vienna embassy.

FIGURE 13
Strategic Nuclear Weapons Balance

UNITED STATES

Weapon Name	Number Available *	Range (Statute Miles)	Warhead Yield
ICBM:			
Titan 2	54	7,250	5-10 MT
Minuteman 1	⎰ 900	⎱ 8,000	1 MT
Minuteman 2			1-2 MT
Minuteman 3 †	100		Three 200-KT
SLBM:			
Polaris A2	160	1,750	800 KT
Polaris A3	432	2,880	1 MT or three 200-KT
Poseidon †	64	2,880	Ten 50-KT

SOVIET UNION

Weapon Name	Number Available *	Range (Statute Miles)	Warhead Yield
ICBM:			
SS-7	220	6,900	5 MT
SS-8	210	6,900	5 MT
SS-9	280	7,500	Three 5-MT or one 20-25 MT
SS-11	900	6,500	1-2 MT
SS-13	8	5,000	1 MT
SS-N-4 (diesel)		350	⎫
SS-N-5 (diesel and nuclear)	⎰ 230	750	⎬ MT range
SS-N-6 (nuclear)	420	1,750	⎭

† Minuteman 3 and Poseidon in process of being adapted for MIRV missiles, each missile carrying from three to ten nuclear warheads. Each Poseidon and Polaris submarine carried 16 missiles.
* All numbers of available weapons are estimates based on Institute for Strategic Studies, *The Military Balance,* 1970–71 and 1971–72, and *SALT and the Strategic Arms Race,* Washington, D.C.: Center Survey for the Study of Power and Peace, January 15, 1972.

FIGURE 14
The Arms Race *

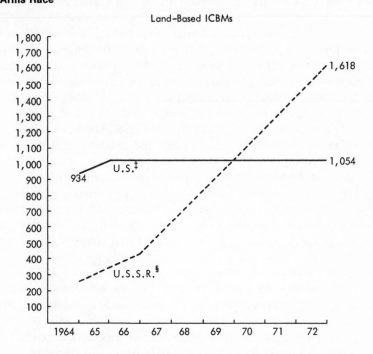

Land–Based ICBMs

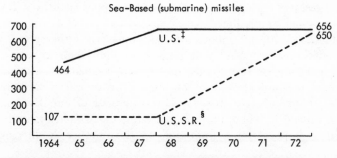

Sea–Based (submarine) missiles

* Offensive nuclear weapons estimates from *New York Times,* May 27, 1972, p. 1.
† Estimates for sea-based missiles do not reflect additional numbers nearing operational status. This would boost the total to 710 for the United States, and 950 for the USSR.
‡ For the United States, post-1967 period represents qualitative, not quantitative improvement.
§ Sharp acceleration of rate of Soviet weapons production following 1967.

presented at a subsequent meeting, with answers to each question provided at a later meeting, thus allowing time for negotiators to consult officials in their respective capitals. Separate technical sessions occurred almost daily and these meetings also alternated between American and Soviet embassies.

Early in SALT the negotiating focus was placed on both offensive and defensive strategic nuclear weapons.[32] In fact, in early 1969, well before the talks began, Secretary of State William Rogers mentioned the willingness of the United States to abandon its proposed ABM system if, during the arms limitation talks, the USSR indicated a willingness to do the same.[33] During the first round of SALT (mid-November to late December 1969) there were no formal proposals set forth. Soviet negotiators did indicate their wish to discuss limitations on America's heavy bombers and tactical fighter bombers based in Europe and aboard aircraft carriers because they were capable of attacking the USSR. The United States was unwilling to comply with this Soviet wish and indicated that these topics could only be included as part of an East-West European settlement that would also include Soviet IRBM's targeted on Western Europe.

During the second and longest round of talks, running from April 16 to August 14, 1970, debate centered on whether the arms talks should first concentrate on achieving an agreement on defensive weapons alone and, once having accomplished this, move on to a consideration of offensive weapons; or whether discussions should simply persist until an agreement was reached covering both offensive and defensive weapons. The USSR preferred that efforts be devoted first to achieving a defensive limitation since that appeared to be the most realistic negotiating objective at the outset of the talks. Early in the second round President Nixon indicated that the American delegation would support the position that both nations be permitted a restricted ABM system and, at the same time, numerical ceilings be imposed on offensive weapons such as ICBMs and submarine launched missiles.[34]

On May 20, 1970, one month after the opening of the second round, the United States proposed that both sides limit their missile defense systems to a ring of sites (consisting of approximately 100 launching missiles each) to protect Washington and Moscow and, in addition, that both sides freeze at early 1970 levels the number of offensive land and sea based missiles.[35] Then, two months later, the United States formally presented a proposal for a limitation on the number of offensive and

---

[32] During the first sessions of SALT much of the discussion centered on efforts to define strategic weapons. The USSR defined a strategic offensive weapon as any weapon that could reach the other's territory. This definition included American fighter-bombers stationed in Western Europe and aboard Sixth Fleet aircraft carriers in the Mediterranean. The United States did not accept the Soviet definition and defined strategic as only applicable to missiles based on the national territory of each of the SALT participants, on submarines at sea, or carried by strategic bombers. The more restricted American definition prevailed and provided the working basis for subsequent discussion. As indicated below, it was later agreed that strategic bombers would not be included in SALT discussions.

[33] *New York Times,* March 28, 1969, p. 1.

[34] *New York Times,* April 17, 1970, p. 1.

[35] *New York Times,* May 20, 1970, p. 13.

defensive missile systems which would not deny either nation the opportunity to improve the capabilities (range, accuracy, destructive potential, etc.) of the restricted number of strategic weapons permitted to
each nation.[36] This meant, for example, that the USSR would be free to
refine and improve the accuracy of its SS-9 missile, but the number of
SS-9s was not to exceed a yet-to-be-specified ceiling. No effort was made
to freeze or prohibit the testing or deployment of MIRV.[37] This American
proposal incorporated the need to impose limitations on both offensive and
defensive capabilities, a negotiating requirement that was underscored the
following year (February 1971) when President Nixon said that "to limit
only one side of the offense-defense equation could rechannel to arms
competition rather than effectively curtail it." [38] One negotiating tactic
adhered to by the United States during SALT was to convey to Soviet
officials the clear impression that unless an American-Soviet agreement
stipulated otherwise, the United States was determined to proceed with
the expansion of its ABM system. Six months earlier, the Senate had lent
credibility to this assertion by supporting the expansion of the ABM system from two Safeguard sites (Montana and North Dakota) to four sites
(adding sites in Missouri and Wyoming). Both President Nixon and Dr.
Kissinger believed that continued funding of the expansion of America's
ABM system was vital to provide the United States with a negotiating
"bargaining chip" that could be used to elicit concessions from the USSR
which might, for example, involve Soviet acceptance of a SS-9 ceiling.[39]

On May 20, 1971 (at the end of the fourth round of discussion), the
Soviet and United States governments simultaneously announced that a
negotiating framework had been agreed upon: both nations would concentrate on reaching an agreement to limit the deployment of antiballistic
missile systems, and in line with the American interest, this effort would
also include "certain measures" intended to limit offensive strategic
weapons. This Soviet concession (the USSR had supported a proposal for
a one-site ABM defense only agreement) followed a series of secret Nixon-
Brezhnev letters, a correspondence so secret that Ambassador Smith first

---

[36] *New York Times,* July 25, 1970, p. 1.

[37] The reasons for the early Soviet rejection of the Baruch proposal would have
probably been applied to a MIRV ban: first, the United States would have required
on-site inspection and the USSR would have rejected this condition; second, the
USSR had not tested a MIRV and thus a MIRV ban in 1970 would have made
permanent the American advantage.

[38] *New York Times,* February 26, 1971, p. 1.

[39] It is possible to view the USSR as having its own bargaining chip in the form
of an expanding SS-9 capability, over which the United States expressed concern
during 1971. In late 1970, through satellite reconnaissance, the United States became aware of the Soviet construction of five clusters, four holes each, of new ICBM
sites, each hole large enough to house the Soviet SS-9. These sites were along the
arc of the Soviet offensive missile system from the Polish border to the Chinese
frontier.

learned of it in early May when Deputy Minister Semyonov proposed the ICBM freeze as well as an ABM treaty. This interim accord regarding negotiating priorities permitted personnel attached to both delegations (scientists, economists, political scientists, technicians, and diplomats) to develop specific, detailed positions in preparation for the final phase of moving toward a formal arms agreement.[40] The American-Soviet agreement of May 20, 1971, set the direction for the final agreement of SALT, signed in Moscow one year later by President Nixon and Secretary Brezhnev.

SALT: Agreements

The important provisions of the two SALT agreements signed on May 26, 1972, consisted of the following:

First Agreement: The Anti-Ballistic Missile Treaty. This treaty was of unlimited duration. The treaty required ratification by the United States Senate but the United States and the USSR pledged immediate adherence to the terms of the treaty. The treaty stipulated that the United States and the Soviet Union were both limited to two ABM complexes, one for the national capitals of Washington and Moscow, and the second to protect one field of intercontinental ballistic missiles. Each site would consist of 100 ABMs, or a total of 200 ABMs for each country. The United States ICBM protection site would be at Grand Forks, North Dakota. The location of the comparable Soviet site was unidentified, but would be at least 800 miles from Moscow.[41]

Second Agreement: The Offensive Strategic Weapons Agreement. This was an executive agreement of five years' duration and thus did not require two thirds Senate approval.[42] The agreement limited all ICBMs to those under construction or deployed at the time of signing the agreement. In accordance with the agreement, the USSR was permitted to

---

[40] During the fifth round of talks (July–September 1971) in Helsinki, two agreements were reached. The first (as mentioned above) was to modernize the Hot Line to increase both the capability and reliability of the communications link. The second agreement was related to the avoidance of an accidental outbreak of nuclear war. The United States and the USSR pledged (1) to take all precautions necessary to guard against accidental or unauthorized use of nuclear weapons; (2) to provide arrangements for rapid communication should the danger of nuclear war arise from nuclear incidents or from detection of unidentified objects on early warning systems; and (3) to provide advance notification of certain planned missile launches.

[41] The USSR agreed to place its second 100-launcher defensive missile site in the area east of the Ural Mountains. This geographic separation of the two defensive sites would match the pattern of the American sites and it would preclude the two Soviet sites being used together to protect the two thirds of the Soviet population and industry that was concentrated in European Russia.

[42] Although an executive agreement does not normally require Congressional approval, this executive agreement required majority support from Congress before it could be effective. This was a condition attached to all arms control and disarmament agreements when Congress approved the establishment of ACDA in 1961.

maintain 1,618 operational ICBMs. This total included a subtotal of 313 large SS-9 missiles. The United States was permitted to maintain 1,054 operational ICBMs. This total included 1,000 Minutemen and 54 Titan missiles. The agreement froze construction of submarine launched ballistic missiles on all nuclear submarines at 1972 levels. This permitted the United States a ceiling of 710 ballistic missile launchers on 44 nuclear-powered submarines. The Soviet Union was allowed 950 ballistic missile launchers on 62 nuclear-powered submarines.[43]

Neither arms agreement placed limitations on *qualitative* improvements in either offensive or defensive systems. Thus, in a special qualitative sense, the arms race could continue with both nations making efforts to place a maximum number of warheads on each missile permitted under SALT, to improve missile guidance systems, propellants, and penetration capabilities. Since the agreement to limit offensive weapons also placed restrictions on the enlargement of missile silos, each nation, if it chose to increase its offensive strength, was forced to do this by developing techniques to store the most powerful weapons possible in each existing silo.[44]

Each nation had the right to withdraw from either agreement by giving six months' notice if it concluded that its "supreme interests" were in jeopardy. Neither agreement provided for on-site inspection to check against violations, and the task of monitoring adherence to the agreements was left to reconnaissance satellites and electronic intelligence devices. Both nations agreed "not to interfere with the national technical means of vertification of the other party." They also agreed not to provide anti-missile defenses to allies. In addition, the offensive missile agreement stated that neither nation would resort to "deliberate concealment measures which impede vertification."

Opposition in Congress to the two SALT accords, although limited, centered mainly upon the following points: (1) the quantitative arms advantage that appeared to be granted to the USSR; (2) the lack of good faith on the part of Soviet negotiators; (3) the efforts on the part of some members of the executive branch to couple SALT agreements with requests for increased funds for strategic arms. Members of the executive branch, in support of the bargaining chip thesis, insisted that the United

---

[43] It was reported that the Joint Chiefs of Staff informed President Nixon that they could not support an offensive arms agreement unless the USSR included submarine-launched missiles. President Nixon discussed this issue with Secretary Brezhnev and a Soviet agreement was reached when Dr. Kissinger was in Moscow in late April 1972, preceding the May summit meeting.

[44] Intelligence reports in mid-1972 indicated that the USSR was developing a missile more powerful than the SS-9. The new missile would be capable of carrying 20 nuclear warheads of up to one megaton each. These missiles could be launched from existing SS-9 silos, or silos enlarged by not more than 15 percent of their original size, thus not violating the SALT agreement. Such a capability would increase the number of warheads the USSR could launch from 1,618 in 1972 to 7,318, but would not violate the terms of the SALT agreement.

States must improve its arms capabilities to the extent permitted by SALT so that the USSR would have some motive to negotiate further arms reductions. Some Congressmen, on the other hand, believed that increased defense spending on strategic weapons would diminish the value of SALT, escalate the arms race, and waste taxpayers money [45] Sen. James L. Buckley, Conservative-Republican of New York, said he had "grave misgivings" over the agreement's provisions on defensive missiles. Sen. Henry M. Jackson, Democrat of Washington, the leading opponent of SALT, stated that, "The present agreements are likely to lead to an accelerated technological arms race with great uncertainties, profound instabilities and considerable costs." He stressed that the numerical advantage given to the USSR in nuclear missiles meant that "we don't even have parity" and this fact "must be a principal focus of an intensive Congressional inquiry." [46]

In response to actual and anticipated Congressional criticism, Dr. Kissinger, in support of the administration, pointed out that the United States had an advantage of 460 strategic bombers while the USSR had only 140. Also, by the end of 1972, the United States would possess 5,700 nuclear warheads, compared to the 2,500 held by the USSR. In addition to the 5,700 warheads stored on American soil, there were an estimated additional 7,000 warheads stored at American air bases in Europe. Further, America's MIRV capability meant that despite a quantitative inferiority in missile launchers, the United States could, during the next five years, enjoy a superiority in actual warheads that could be individually directed against enemy targets. Basically, Dr. Kissinger argued that parity in weaponry did exist between the United States and the Soviet Union. While the USSR had a slight quantitative advantage over the United States, the United States enjoyed a qualitative lead in a number of areas of weapons technology: accuracy, reliability, retargetability, multiple warheads, solid fuel rockets, plus a wide variety of penetration aids for strategic missiles and bombers. For the USSR to match or exceed American qualitative superiority in these areas, it would require an extremely costly crash program of research and development, exactly the type of expense and effort the USSR sought to avoid through a commitment to the SALT agreements.

Despite criticism from some sections of Congress, SALT enjoyed support from the leaders of most groups that held responsibility for initial consideration of the agreements. Support of the agreements came from Senate Majority Leader Mike Mansfield, House Speaker Carl Albert, Representative F. Edward Hébert (Chairman, House Armed Services

---

[45] Senators Fulbright (Democrat, Arkansas), Symington (Democrat, Missouri), Pell (Democrat, Rhode Island), and Proxmire (Democrat, Wisconsin) expressed such views. Sen. Fulbright said that "More force, greater spending and additional weapons will not make either side more secure." (*New York Times*, June 15, 1972, p. 9.)

[46] *New York Times*, May 27, 1972, p. 10; and June 1, 1972, p. 16.

Committee), Sen. John C. Stennis (Chairman, Senate Armed Services Committee), and Sen. J. William Fulbright (Chairman, Senate Foreign Relations Committee), all of whom worked for Congressional approval.[47]

The SALT agreements of May 1972 were not, as stated by Ambassador Smith, " . . . the end of the road by any means, but they are a very solid step forward." [48] President Nixon spoke forcefully in support of "Phase 2" for SALT, hoping that his strong advocacy would encourage backing by Congress and thus make it possible for SALT II to take place. In the President's words:

Now what we have to do is to really go forward with the second step. And that is why the Phase 2 of the arms control limitation which we hope will begin in October [1972], provided the Congress approves the ones that we have before them at the present time, Phase 2, which will be a permanent arms control agreement on all offensive nuclear weapons. . . . Phase 1 is the break-through and Phase 2 is the culmination.[49]

SALT: Considerations Relevant to American Foreign Policy

The SALT agreements were significant developments in themselves and, for this reason, warrant serious study. Beyond this, the process of arriving at the agreements provides a useful source from which to extract a number of recurring characteristics and pertinent considerations related to American foreign policy in the nuclear age. Some of the identifiable characteristics of American foreign policy were shaped during the long Cold War years and persist, intact, at the present time. Others suggest a cautious tendency to deviate from Cold War practices. These were evident at SALT and, as suggested in the following chapter, will probably have a greater impact on policy during the next decade.

The observations discussed below, all of which were evident at SALT, are categorized in terms of, first, those that apply to international negotiations in general; second, characteristics of American foreign policy at the present time; and third, those that impede policy change.

Characteristics of Negotiations in General

1. *Three prerequisites for successful negotiations are time, compromise, and mutual advantage.*

---

[47] On August 3, 1972, the Senate approved the Anti-Ballistic Missile Treaty by a vote of 88–2, and, by the same vote, approved the Offensive Strategic Weapons Agreement in mid-September. The House approved this agreement on September 26, 1972, by a vote of 306–4.

[48] *New York Times,* May 27, 1972, p. 1. SALT II sessions began in Geneva, November 21, 1972.

[49] Presidential News Conference, *New York Times,* July 1, 1972, p. 8. At this news conference, President Nixon stated that if SALT were not approved by the Congress it would be necessary for him to have to ask Congress for an increase in the defense budget of $15 billion for fiscal year 1973.

A. Successful international negotiations, necessarily involving issues of national interest, require time and patience. This is especially true when the issue of arms limitations is involved. The conviction that increased security is attainable through increased arms stands as a revered maxim of international affairs and, in the 20th century, has been underscored by the Cold War behavior of the nuclear superpowers. When two nations agree to subject themselves to a limitation of arms, such an event represents a significant departure from the tradition of centuries, and as such, calls for caution and a gradual, i.e., "responsible," step-by-step approach to negotiation.[50] It took (and probably required) 13 years to progress from the 1959 Antarctic Treaty to the SALT agreements of 1972. It is unrealistic to imagine that a move away from the atmosphere of the Cold War could ever be negotiated in haste.

B. The negotiating process necessarily involves compromise and the granting of concessions. This fact of negotiating life was clearly visible at SALT. For example, on the American side, in order to reach an arms agreement, United States negotiators (1) accepted a Soviet numerical superiority in land-based ICBM launchers, (2) agreed to postpone a discussion of MIRV limitations (since the USSR believed that such an agreement at such a time would place them at a strategic disadvantage), (3) agreed not to include the USSR's IRBMs in SALT discussions. In turn, on the Soviet side, the USSR made negotiating concessions when it (1) agreed not to discuss at SALT any American tactical offensive units located near the USSR (some 500 American fighter-bombers stationed in West Germany and nuclear-armed aircraft carriers attached to the Sixth Fleet in the Mediterranean), (2) agreed to impose a numerical ceiling on their own SS-9 missiles, (3) agreed to shift from concentrating exclusively on defensive weapons to a discussion of defensive *and* offensive weapons, (4) agreed to accept, under certain conditions, a ceiling on submarine-based missile launchers, and (5) agreed not to include limitations on strategic bombers (B-52s) in initial discussions.

C. A sense of mutual advantage is the most stable basis for international negotiations and agreements. The most workable, long-term, least violated international treaties have always been those that the participating nations have found most useful, i.e., those most closely related to the national advantages of the treaty participants. Treaties of a functional nature, for example treaties involving commercial shipping agreements, exchange of technical data, health regulations, and postal, air, and communications regulations are treaties to which nations adhere with reasonable regularity.

---

[50] It was reported that, in 1970, the USSR was unresponsive to an American proposal for a major (50 percent) reduction in nuclear arms, phased over a seven-year period. The USSR considered such a proposal as premature and supported a concentration on a defensive arms "freeze" in the initial phase of negotiation. (*New York Times,* June 18, 1972, p. 16.)

These are treaties of mutual advantage and nations adhere to their terms because it is to their advantage to do so. With regard to SALT, the two basic motives behind the Soviet and American agreements were to alleviate the economic burden of the arms race and to reduce the threat of nuclear war. Here resided the basis for mutual advantage.

2. *Secrecy stands as a fixed part of the negotiating process.* The practice of closed sessions for international negotiations remains a prerequisite for the achievement of diplomatic objectives. Without some prearranged opportunity for secret (nonpublic) negotiations, the intrusion of public and press opinion would, under a democratic political system, force negotiators to assume positions calculated to look best from the standpoint of public reaction rather than be best from the standpoint of negotiating possibilities.[51] In the 1970s the suspicions and anxieties provoked by the East-West Cold War confrontation continued to affect American-Soviet negotiations and some privacy for negotiation was mandatory if predetermined negotiating objectives were to have a chance of being realized. President Johnson's 1967 secret letter to Premier Kosygin, the closed SALT sessions, and the guarded diplomatic exchanges at Helsinki and Vienna were examples of the adherence to secrecy in the process of reaching agreement. SALT involved two highly sensitive areas, American-Soviet relations in general, and arms reduction in particular. It would have been literally impossible for any meaningful arms agreements to emerge from SALT if some provisions for secrecy had not been maintained.[52]

3. *Foreign policy officials must perceive the world through the eyes of the other nation.* It has always been to the advantage of the diplomat to be able to see the world as it is seen by other statesmen. The requirements of modern diplomacy impose the same burden on negotiators; i.e., to be able to put oneself in the position of the man on the other side of the negotiating table. It is necessary to comprehend the other nation in sufficient depth to enable one to think in terms of that nation's foreign policy

---

[51] The prevalence of and justification for diplomatic secrecy is a constant aspect of international negotiation. When President Nixon conducted meetings with leaders of China in Peking in early 1972, he apologized to reporters for the secrecy imposed in these discussions and justified this action by saying that secrecy was needed to build mutual trust at the beginning of a new diplomatic relationship. (*New York Times*, February 16, 1972, p. 1.) Also, in early 1972, the State Department stated that American-Chinese meetings in Paris (concerning a settlement of the Vietnam war) required secrecy to insure their ultimate success. (*New York Times*, March 14, 1972, p. 16.)

[52] Sir Harold Nicholson, in his book *Diplomacy*, discussed the subject of secrecy in diplomacy and stressed the difference between foreign policy and negotiation. He believed that foreign policy should never be secret and the public should be fully aware of the policy to which their government was committing them. On the other hand, negotiations "must always be confidential." The approach of the United States to SALT conformed to the Nicholson advice. Sir Harold Nicholson, *Diplomacy* (New York: Oxford University Press, 1963), p. 138.

objectives, to assess the resources available for the fulfillment of these objectives, and to identify the social weaknesses that diminish the ability of that nation to utilize fully its human and physical resources. For example, with regard to the USSR at SALT, it was important to assess the significance of factional differences within the Soviet Politburo and determine how these might affect Secretary's Brezhnev's negotiating position, how a Soviet concession to the United States might affect Soviet-Chinese relations, how a Nixon-Brezhnev agreement might affect Soviet relations with its Communist ally of North Vietnam.[53] A careful analysis of the political dynamics affecting the decision-making of the "other side" can enhance the probability that American actions and responses will be appropriately conceived and geared to the reality of the other nation's perceptions, rather than being encumbered with the more lofty but baseless hopes of what *should* be.

4. *Foreign policy is not indifferent to propaganda advantage.* A nation's statements concerning foreign policy objectives are affected by, sometimes motivated by, the desire to shape world public opinion. Nations seek to have their foreign policy pronouncements elicit as much positive response as possible. During the 1950s, 1960s, and into the 70s and SALT, America's official statements concerning its quest for disarmament served, in part, the national interest of having the United States viewed as a nation committed to the pursuit of peace, a nation seeking to avoid international violence. It was propagandistically advantageous to generate an image of the United States as a nation that not only supported the ideal of disarmament, but also would act to serve this cause if it were not for the aggressive inclinations of international communism that compelled America to build up its arms. Theodore Sorensen reports that President Kennedy's initial interest in disarmament was "largely for propaganda reasons —a desire to influence neutral nations and world opinion." [54] It was Arthur Schlesinger's opinion that President Kennedy saw disarmament "primarily as a measure of political warfare." [55] Presidents Johnson and Nixon were also not immune to the propaganda potential associated with support for disarmament.

Although Presidents have not been repelled by the prospective propaganda advantages of foreign policy statements, it is possible to dis-

---

[53] Two weeks following the SALT agreements, it was revealed in *Pravda*, the Communist party newspaper, that within the party's decision-making apparatus there had been opposition to the decision to proceed with the summit talks with President Nixon due to the United States' mining the ports of North Vietnam shortly before the Nixon-Brezhnev meeting. An awareness of the existence of factions in high places should help shape the content, timing, and presentation of American negotiating proposals at possible future SALT meetings.

[54] Theodore Sorensen, *Kennedy* (New York: Harper and Row, 1965), p. 518.

[55] Arthur M. Schlesinger, *A Thousand Days* (Boston: Houghton Mifflin Co., 1965), p. 479.

tinguish statements based on the motive of propaganda advantage from statements based on the conviction that national security can be achieved through an active pursuit of a stated policy objective. If, beyond simply verbal pronouncements, there is also tangible back-up associated with the President's words, then the stated policy is probably more than propaganda. Professions of interest in arms control and disarmament achieved tangible backing during the late 1960s and early 1970s. The actions at SALT suggested that some key American officials had come to regard arms limitations as offering greater potential dividends than simply those derivable from propaganda.

Characteristics of Contemporary American Foreign Policy

1. *The requirements of modern diplomacy are demanding and diverse.* At SALT the traditional tasks of diplomacy were clearly evident, tasks such as attention to ceremonial and social functions, matters of protocol, and the drafting of interim and final agreements—each involving the familiar language, ritual, and form of international exchanges. All of these time-consuming and frequently complicated activities were modern extensions of the traditions of formal diplomacy. However, at SALT, as has become generally true of diplomacy in the nuclear area, additional special skills were demanded of the career diplomat. First, modern diplomatic bargaining required sophistication concerning the technical aspects of nuclear weaponry. For example, it was necessary for the diplomat at SALT to be familiar with the technical capabilities available for detecting, identifying, and monitoring arms developments conducted by other nations; to be able to assess his own nation's weapons capabilities and potentialities in comparison to those of another nation; to be able to relate standards of missile silo hardening to enemy offensive weapons capabilities and to then draw conclusions pertaining to the continued existence or non-existence of a second strike, i.e., retaliatory, capability, etc. A new level of technical professionalism was required of the modern diplomat because nuclear weaponry, as the basis for deterrence, had assumed such broad political significance in America's foreign relations.[56]

Second, the diplomat also required the skills of a military strategist. He needed a sense of how military capabilities might be applied, deployed, or displayed for purposes of achieving political advantage. He needed to know how and when to bargain from a position of military strength or weakness to maximize his negotiating advantage. Once again, the per-

---

[56] American negotiators at SALT commented on the relative lack of technical knowledge on the part of Soviet negotiators early in SALT. One American said that Deputy Foreign Minister Semyonov knew "zilch" at first, but was "wise enough to move cautiously until he learned what was going on." (*New York Times*, June 18, 1972, p. 16.)

vasiveness of the concept of deterrence in policy circles made such skills mandatory.

Third, more rigorous demands were imposed upon the diplomat for a familiarity with the social science disciplines, particularly political science and economics. He needed to know the political experience and attitudes of those with whom he was negotiating and to comprehend the political constraints and social conditioning to which his diplomatic counterpart had been subjected. The diplomat, as an economist, had to grasp the economic strains at play within the society of his counterpart. With regard to SALT, such knowledge, together with relevant political data, enabled American diplomats to reach informed judgements concerning the probable inclination of Soviet officials to make specific bargaining concessions to achieve an arms agreement.

Finally, the diplomat was subject to unprecendented administrative demands. Reporting chores have always been a burden and these have increased with America's tremendously expanded world role. The most challenging administrative task, however, was that of integrating the international activities of the numerous participating United States government agencies. (This issue was discussed in Chapter 3). The requirement for administrative integration was strikingly evident in the arms control area since related negotiations involved personnel from a large number of executive agencies, particularly the State Department, ACDA, army, navy, air force, Atomic Energy Commission, CIA, USIA, and NASA. A deluge of paper passed between every embassy and Washington and simply processing this vast flow of words frequently demanded full-time attention.

2. *There is an increased need for a technologically based intelligence capability.* Intelligence has always been a requirement for the formulation of foreign policy. Modern technology introduced intelligence collection methods that exceeded, by a wide margin, the collection capabilities and reliability of human agents. The SALT agreements included no provisions for on-site inspection and thus, from America's standpoint, required some other means of monitoring Soviet compliance with arms commitments. This specific requirement was representative of the general need for strategic intelligence in the age of strategic threats.

Compliance with the terms of SALT was to be monitored largely by reconnaissance satellites, seismic, and electronic sensors.[57] Such modern collection capabilities offered a number of advantages. In addition to producing more reliable intelligence concerning potential enemy capabili-

---

[57] Richard Helms, Director of CIA, testified before the Senate Foreign Relations Committee three weeks after the signing of the SALT accords and stated that the United States would verify Soviet adherence to the terms of the agreements primarily by photographic and electronic satellites and through stations near the borders of the USSR.

ties that would otherwise be unobtainable, technical collection capabilities seemed less blatant and less offensive to national sovereignty than many of the interventionist practices of covert agents sponsored by American intelligence collection agencies. National sensitivity was less likely to be irritated by collection devices operated from remote positions, and about which little could be done.

3. *The Presidential-Congressional relationship in foreign affairs is that of initiator-respondent.* The initiator-respondent foreign affairs relationship between the President and Congress that had become most sharply defined during the years following World War II was again evident during and immediately following the agreements at SALT. Presidential initiative was responsible for SALT, Presidential backing brought the arms agreement to completion, and strong statements by the President to Congress and the nation in support of the agreements were designed to set the stage for Congressional approval. Thus Congress was again placed in the role that legislators found more and more familiar and, for some, distasteful—that of considering, assessing, discussing, and then either approving or disapproving, "after the fact," international commitments already made by the President.

4. *The foreign policy center has shifted more and more toward the White House staff.* The trend that has moved many of the tasks associated with foreign policy planning and the monitoring of on-going foreign programs into the White House and away from the State Department was visible in all of the activities that were associated with SALT. The personnel of the State Department were certainly involved in the daily sessions of SALT but State operated in a supportive junior-partner role. The planning and directing appeared to be a Kissinger staff function tied to the NSC's Verification Panel.

An event related to SALT that illustrates this point and the preceding point concerning the foreign policy relationship of the President and Congress took place two weeks after the Nixon-Brezhnev summit meeting. On June 15, 1972, over 100 Congressmen were invited to the White House to attend an "in-depth discussion" on the SALT accords to generate support for both the arms agreements and the administration's request for a $1.3 billion increase in the defense budget of FY 1973.[58] President Nixon and Dr. Kissinger were the only two speakers. Secretary Rogers and Ambassador Smith were to go to Congress the following week to answer further questions. President Nixon spoke to the assembled Congressmen for 12 minutes, concluding with the expressed hope that the two arms agreements would enjoy rapid approval by Congress so that Phase II of

---

[58] The key Congressmen invited were from the five important (from the standpoint of SALT and defense funds) Congressional committees: the Senate Foreign Relations and Armed Services Committees; the House Foreign Affairs and Armed Services Committees; and the Joint Committee on Atomic Energy.

the SALT talks, aiming at a more comprehensive arms treaty, could begin as soon as possible. Then Dr. Kissinger spoke for one and one half hours, giving Congressmen the details of the SALT negotiations. This event was revealing in several ways. First, the White House staff had assumed a central role in foreign policy matters, with the secretary of State, who was absent from the briefing, relegated to a subordinate position. Second, the "respondent" role of Congress in foreign affairs, mentioned above, was suggested by the visit to the White House in order that they might be informed of decisions already acted upon by the President. Third, the request for increased defense funds for new bombers and submarines, necessary (according to the President) to motivate the USSR to negotiate a more comprehensive arms limitation agreement, suggested a reliance on the President's "bargaining chip" notion and the continued dependence on arms for political as well as military ends.[59]

Characteristics of American Foreign Policy Which Impede Change

1. *The President leads but is not always followed.* It has already been indicated that postwar Presidents have been outspoken in stating their support of arms control and disarmament as a major foreign policy objective. It was also pointed out that they have not been consistently effective in rallying support within their administration for the realization of this objective. Arms control negotiations offered a vivid revelation of the distance that could separate the policy position of the President and the disposition of the President's administrators to implement that policy. It was mentioned in Chapter 4 that departmental secretaries have the interests of their departmental constituencies to serve, and this commitment may tend to separate them from the President and his broader responsibilities of national, as distinct from departmental, scope. Also, the career civil servant, usually, having come to his job long before the President assumed his executive position, and hoping to be in his job long after the President is replaced by a successor, may be more cautious, more resistant to change than is a new President. These conditions provided a basis for a President-administrator gap. A sense of the competing agency interests and the need for administrative integration, referred to earlier, is suggested by the following statement by Secretary of State Rogers:

The work of the National Security Council is, of course, essential to the success of the President's foreign policy, and Henry and his staff deserve much

---

[59] The "bargaining chip" notion that through more and better American arms the USSR would be drawn into extended future arms limitation negotiations was challenged by some arms control specialists who expressed the view that qualitative improvements in arms, rather than providing a bargaining incentive to the USSR through intimidating them, required Soviet officials to follow the American lead and improve their own weapons, thus accelerating the arms race.

of the credit. Take the SALT talks as an example. The State Department is in charge of negotiations. But the issue encompasses the interests of the Defense Department, the Atomic Energy Commission, the arms-control agency and the CIA. Henry coordinates these interests in the President's behalf. The President has to consider each of them in his deliberations. After all, he's got to make his decisions in orderly fashion.[60]

As an expression of a Defense Department view, one that could suggest differences "within the family" to a President interested in achieving progress toward arms limitations, the following statement by Secretary of Defense Laird is appropriate:

Our strategic forces—both offensive and defensive—account for about 12 per cent of the total FY 1971 Defense budget, but their vital importance to our security, and, indeed, the security of the entire Free World, far transcends their relative cost. These forces unquestionably provide the basic foundation of our deterrent.[61]

Secretary Laird, three weeks following the signing of the SALT accords, stated that he would recommend scrapping the arms limitation agreements if Congress refused to provide additional funds to strengthen America's offensive strategic forces.[62] Secretary Laird's position was supported by the Joint Chiefs of Staff whose chairman, Admiral Thomas H. Moorer, said that he supported SALT so long as "we press forward vigorously" with programs "designed to protect against a degradation in national security posture." [63]

President Nixon's stand on SALT differed from that of his Defense Secretary and the Chairman of the Joint Chiefs. He believed that the arms agreements and the defense spending program should be considered separately by Congress, each on its own merits. Congress should first approve the arms agreements and then, as a separate action, consider the issue of new military requirements. The President stated that "I would not have signed those agreements unless I had believed that, standing

---

[60] *New York Times Magazine,* February 27, 1972, p. 38.

[61] Statement by Secretary of Defense Melvin Laird to the Senate Armed Services Committee, February 20, 1970. *Documents on Disarmament, 1970* (Washington, D.C.: U.S. Arms Control and Disarmament Agency, December 1971), p. 40.

[62] Secretary Laird was seeking additional defense funds for FY 1973 with which to develop the B-1 long-range strategic bomber and the Trident long-range nuclear submarine. These two items were estimated to cost $20 billion over the five-year period covered by the SALT offensive arms agreement. In an effort to gain Congressional support for Trident, Secretary Laird asserted that the USSR was building new Trident-type submarines. In response to this statement, Sen. Fulbright stated that the USSR was not even close to building such a submarine and then confronted Secretary Laird with the statement, "I am hopeful Senators will be able to vote on the weapons without being scared to death by your misinformation." (*New York Times,* June 22, 1972, p. 10.)

[63] Ibid., June 21, 1972, p. 12.

alone, they were in the interest of the United States." [64] Differences between the President and executive branch officials over the issue of arms persisted before, during, and after SALT.

2. *The Defense Department is the center of resistance.* From the administration of President Eisenhower to the administration of President Nixon, the Department of Defense, the military services, and the Joint Chiefs of Staff have stood as the constant source of resistance to arms control and disarmament. While there have appeared differences over arms control between the Defense Department and other executive agencies, as well as differences between the department and the President, a unified position has usually been maintained among the agencies of the so-called defense establishment. The Defense Department's reactions to SALT conformed to the department's traditional position of resistance. Numerous examples could be cited in support of this assertion. One example, which also provides an additional illustration of the point previously made concerning interagency differences over arms control, occurred less than two weeks following President Nixon's signing the SALT agreements in Moscow. Secretary of Defense Laird, during a closed session with the Senate Armed Services Committee, mentioned that intelligence reports had revealed Soviet flight tests of a missile that was capable of firing several warheads at several targets. [65] This statement was significant because it suggested an important Soviet advance in nuclear weaponry, but it was also significant because it weakened the position held by President Nixon, Dr. Kissinger, and Ambassador Smith that, although the USSR was permitted superiority in offensive missile launchers, the United States had and would maintain a technical advantage over the USSR, a prime example being its MIRV capability. Secretary Laird challenged the SALT agreement by suggesting that this was, at best, a fleeting advantage.

In response to Secretary Laird's statement, Ambassador Smith said that the USSR was so far behind the United States that it had not yet even tested a multiple warhead system. [66] The State Department supported Ambassador Smith in his retort to Secretary Laird by agreeing that while the USSR may have tested a missile capable of carrying several independently targeted warheads, it had not yet tested the warhead system itself. [67]

3. *Arms continue to constitute a central theme in America's national security thinking.* It is ironic in a sense that the process of attempting to limit arms at SALT reflected the extent to which nuclear arms continued to be intimately tied to America's concept of security. The close relationship between arms and security could not be altered overnight. The priority

---

[64] Presidential news conference, June 22, 1972, in *New York Times*, June 23, 1972, p. 14.

[65] *New York Times*, June 9, 1972, p. 1.

[66] Ibid., p. 4.

[67] *New York Times*, June 10, 1972, p. 5.

status assigned to nuclear weapons was suggested by the guarded behavior of negotiators, the caution with which concessions were made, the
emphasis given to arms in Presidential pronouncements, the President's
conviction that negotiating success demanded the availability of a
"bargaining chip" which itself was in the form of arms, and the synchron-
ized timing that brought the completed SALT agreements to center stage
as the culminating pronouncement of the Nixon-Brezhnev summit conference.[68] For 25 years nuclear arms had been a primary preoccupation of
American statesmen and SALT stood as a vivid testimony to the continued
validity of this fact.

SALT: Part of the Beginning of Change

As American foreign policy officials began to anticipate SALT II, the
considerations mentioned that tended to impede foreign policy change
assumed a slightly diminished significance. Arms, which for decades had
constituted the central theme in America's national security thinking, were
being reassessed with a much more critical eye than had been the case at
any previous time since the end of World War II. If the role of arms in
American foreign policy was to be reduced, this would affect the Defense
Department's ability to resist change and also provide an opportunity for
the President to move toward further arms limitations with less bureaucratic divisiveness obstructing the way. SALT suggested a new direction.
It also suggested that behind SALT was a more broadly based effort to
adapt America's foreign policy to the realities of international relations in
the decade of the '70s. Developments that make a new emphasis apparent
in foreign policy may now be considered.

---

[68] See Appendix C, *Selected Chronology, Strategic Arms Limitation Talks,* for an
indication of the use made of the "bargaining chips" notion as a negotiating technique.
Following SALT, when the President was seeking Congressional support for additional
defense funds for FY 1973, Sen. Fulbright asked Dr. Kissinger if a concentration on
extended offensive missile programs might not lead to distrust by the USSR. Dr.
Kissinger replied that, on the contrary, "our experience is that an on-going program is
no obstacle to any agreement," and stated that in some cases it might facilitate agreement. He cited the SALT ABM agreement as possible only because the United States
had begun to deploy Safeguard missiles. (*New York Times,* June 16, 1972, p. 8.)

chapter 7

The New Direction of American Foreign Policy

We are attempting to shape our future policies realistically in the light of the world situation and in the light of our capabilities. . . . We have been in what has been described as a cold-war period for about 25 years, and I believe we are leaving that period. . . . Things do change.[1]

Containment: A Quarter Century Later

Ambassador George F. Kennan, the author of the containment policy discussed in Chapter 1, came to resent the use that had been made of this policy during the years of the Cold War. Twenty years after the 1947 publication of his "X-Article" in *Foreign Affairs,* the author wrote that perhaps his essay's most serious defiiciency "was the failure to make clear that what I was talking about when I mentioned the containment of Soviet power was not the containment by military means of a military threat, but the political containment of a political threat." [2] Another deficiency pointed to by Ambassador Kennan was the failure ". . . to make clear that the 'containment' of which I was speaking was not something that I thought we could, necessarily, do everywhere successfully, or even needed to do everywhere successfully. . . ." [3] Ambassador Kennan was

---

[1] Interview with Secretary of State William Rogers, *U.S. News and World Report,* January 26, 1970, pp. 29–30.
[2] George F. Kennan, *Memoirs, 1925–1950* (Boston: Little, Brown and Co., 1967), p. 358.
[3] Ibid., p. 359.

"deeply embarrassed" by the fact that his concept of containment was improperly interpreted and used as a justification for America's military alliances, the rearming of Western Germany and creating "unreal blocs" such as SEATO, CENTO, and NATO.[4]

SEATO, the Southeast Asia Treaty Organization, was an "unreal bloc" that reflected the approach of American officials to the task of containing communism which Ambassador Kennan found ill-conceived and therefore disturbing. In the early 1950s President Eisenhower and Secretary Dulles saw the influence of the West threatened in Asia. What had appeared to threaten Europe and the United States in the late 1940s appeared to threaten the United States and Asia in the mid-1950s. The Communist party had assumed power in China in 1949; in 1951 China absorbed Tibet; British and Dutch colonial power in Asia had dissolved; there had been civil disturbances in Burma, Malaya, Indonesia, and the Philippines; the Communists had attempted to force the West to abandon Korea; and, by 1954, the feeling in Washington of losing Asia to communism was strong enough to lend crisis proportions to the Communist offensive against the French in Indochina. State and Defense officials concluded that what was needed was an Asian NATO—simply to move to Asia what was viewed as having been effective in stopping the threat of communism in Europe. If he had been asked, Ambassador Kennan would probably have advised Secretary Dulles and other officials that containment was not possible everywhere in the world, that what "worked" at one time with one group of nations would not necessarily be appropriate elsewhere under different conditions.

The Southeast Asia Collective Defense Treaty was signed in Manila on September 8, 1954, as a means of promoting security (i.e., containing, communism) in Asia through SEATO.[5] Eight nations agreed to participate: the United States, Britain, France, Australia, New Zealand, the Philippines, Thailand, and Pakistan. A separate protocol was drawn up to include Laos, Cambodia, and Vietnam within the geographic area covered by the treaty. The core of SEATO was Article Four of the treaty which stated that in case of enemy *aggression*, each treaty participant would "act to meet the common danger in accordance with its constitutional processes." An attack against one SEATO member was considered an attack against all. With regard to enemy *subversion*, treaty members were to "consult immediately" to determine the most effective response to such

---

[4] Marvin Kalb, "The Vital Interests of Mr. Kennan," *New York Times*, March 27, 1966, p. 75.

[5] On April 14, 1954, Secretary of State Dulles was reported to have stated, "The Communists must be made to realize that they are up against something strong enough to force them to abandon plans to extend their rule over Southeast Asia." (C. L. Sulzberger, "Foreign Affairs: An Alliance That Never Was," *New York Times*, January 9, 1970, p. 32.)

a threat. It should be noted that, because of American air and sea power, overt Communist aggression was the form of enemy action with which SEATO was best equipped and organized to contend. Overt aggression was also the least probable form of action that an enemy might initiate in Southeast Asia. Subversion—antigovernment, guerrilla-type action— given the limited material resources of insurrectionist groups in Asia, was the most likely enemy tactic and yet, ironically, SEATO was least well organized, trained, and supported to contend with this form of threat.

There were other defects related to SEATO. It was an Asian defense organization but most Asian nations did not choose to join. India, Burma, Indonesia, and Malaysia did not participate, except to the extent of criticizing the idea of a Western, neocolonialist-sponsored military pact in Asia. Of the Asian nations that did participate, Pakistan joined as a means of gaining support against India, and Thailand and the Philippines participated as loyal allies of the United States. Britain had deep reservations about supporting the United States in this Asian venture and France, after its defeat in Indochina, openly expressed its advocacy of noninvolvement in Southeast Asia.

SEATO, inspired by the Communist assault against the French Indochinese fortress at Dienbienphu, stood as a profession of America's determination to contain communism in Asia. It gave the President authorization to act to do so.[6] In reality, SEATO remained little more than a statement of intention. While it brought Americans into Southeast Asia it did not keep Communists out. SEATO never acquired a capability to contend effectively with guerrilla forces. It had no unifying command structure, and its presence in Asia conflicted with the nationalistic aspirations of the newly independent nations of the area. As indicated by Carlos P. Romulo, Philippine Foreign Secretary:

[SEATO] needs to redefine its purposes in the light of the rapidly evolving times. . . .

It needs to change its orientation to meet the new requirements of Southeast Asia. It needs to take full account of the popular aspiration to be free from all kinds of interference in international affairs. It may be that in refashioning SEATO in accordance with that prescription the old SEATO will cease to be.[7]

CENTO, the Central Treaty Organization for the Middle East, was no more effective in supporting American interests in Northern Africa. This American-sponsored alliance to prevent Soviet communism from moving southward generated considerable Arab opposition. The only Arab par-

---

[6] The Senate strongly approved the Southeast Asia Collective Defense Treaty by a vote of 86–1.

[7] Address by Carlos P. Romulo, Foreign Secretary of the Philippines, at the annual meeting of the Southeast Asia Treaty Organization in Canberra, Australia. (*New York Times,* June 28, 1972, p. 9.)

ticipant, Iraq, withdrew in 1959, and in the Arab mind, such a non-Arab organization revived recent memories of Western colonialism in Arab territory.

In Western Europe, divisiveness grew among members of NATO. American leadership and nuclear dominance was resented. European nations sought ways of dealing with the United States as equals rather than from within the structure of the NATO alliance where their relations with American officials were tinged with the demeaning sense of an inferior seeking favors from a superior.[8] European nations, economically developed and politically stable, wished to define their own foreign policies. In European eyes, the prospect of Soviet aggression was significantly diminished and it was extremely difficult for them to justify the need for allied cohesiveness and the expense of military preparedness. The move toward economic integration, which the United States had encouraged in the late 1940s, had begun to take hold. European nations thought more in terms of European interests, as opposed to broader North Atlantic interests, and this orientation of the 1960s and '70s frequently clashed with America's efforts to maintain military and political influence in Europe.

Communism in Asia

As America moved into the 1970s, disillusionment increased with regard to formal alliances as a means of containing communism or securing American interests abroad. This sense of disillusionment was also associated with the political utility of foreign aid programs. Since the end of World War II, America had spent over $140 billion on foreign aid and, by the 1970s, had concluded that there was no significant relationship between extending aid and winning, or even retaining, allies. The question asked by most Americans, within and outside the government, was, "What has it bought us?" It appeared that both alliances and foreign aid programs were ineffective as means of promoting an acceptance abroad of America's political values or foreign policy objectives. A sense of new nationalism affected the leaders of the developing nations of Africa and Asia, as well as officials in the developed nations of Europe. Developing nations sought a condition of nonalignment that made them suspicious of American economic overtures and promises of military support—especially with the graphic example of South Vietnam as a model of what a recipient of American "aid" might be forced to endure. An American-sponsored war

---

[8] An American attempt to adjust to the resentment of European statesmen concerning their "junior-partner" alliance status was reflected by President Nixon's statement that, "In Western Europe, we have shifted from predominance to partnership with our allies." (Address by President Nixon, February 25, 1971, "A Redefinition of the United States Roles in the World," *United States Foreign Policy, 1971* (Washington, D.C.: Department of State, March 1972), p. 423.)

in support of American objectives within the borders of a developing nation suggested a threat to the independence, and even the existence, of such nations. The presence of American arms and men altered the social characteristics and values of the "host" nation, just as American-style combat changed the terrain, weather, and ecology of the nation. An awareness of the negative consequences that could follow from alignment with the United States prompted national leaders of developing nations to exercise caution and restraint in their relations with America.[9]

Not only did alliances and foreign aid fail to work for what was clearly America's national advantage but, by the early 1970s, even the utility of military capabilities had come to be questioned as a means of exerting American influence abroad. Some of the concerns that were associated with strategic military power—the cost and the threats to national security associated with the arms race—were discussed in the preceding chapter. With regard to tactical military power, deep, and deepening, reservations grew from a decade of combat in Vietnam.

America's involvement in the Vietnam war was a logical extension of the principles embodied in the Truman Doctrine, the policy of containment, the obsessive preoccupation with the threat of communism, and the persistent faith in military power as the means for resolving America's perceived threats. All of these "principles" of the Cold War were brought together in the so-called Domino Theory that was used to justify America's long involvement in the Vietnam war. There is a striking parallel between the approach to communism by President Truman and Secretary Acheson in early 1947 and the approach to communism supported by Presidents Johnson and Nixon a quarter century later. In 1947 Secretary Acheson had stressed that if Greece were lost, Turkey would also fall.

---

[9] Leaders of developing nations have observed that even without actual combat within a nation, the American presence could subvert a nation's culture. In Thailand, for example, the United States constructed one of its six large B-52 bases near the Thai village of Sattahip. The hills were leveled, marshes filled, and the bay dredged to accommodate the requirements of this air base. The village population tripled in size, almost all the men becoming American employees. It was reported that the new residents of Sattahip lived in shanties behind a garish strip of bars and dance halls that were strung along the highway to the base. The report from Sattahip continued, "Directly across the road from the main gate to the air base is a sign advertising the Doll Court, an establishment that offers all the pleasures of the area under one roof: 'Mexican-American food, massage parlor, charming girls, and bungalows.'

"Scores of gaudily painted panel trucks that serve as taxis rattle back and forth along the length of the strip at night, carting soldiers and airmen from the G.I. Blues beer hall to the Latin Quarter, or the Darling Nightclub. The soldiers bring their own bottles, bought at duty-free prices at the Post Exchange, and dance with hostesses dressed in tight silk dresses slit to the hip on the side. It's known that there probably were some prostitutes in the days before the base, but now some 300 girls work the area. Despite weekly medical checks, venereal disease is rampant.

"The Thai Government last week formed a committee to investigate the possibility of putting the 'recreation areas,' as they are officially called, inside the American base." (*New York Times*, April 23, 1968, p. 15.)

The USSR would then occupy the Dardanelles and thereby threaten the security of the entire Middle East. This would bring on a serious weakening of the political stability of Italy, Germany, and France, and a Communist triumph in Europe would result.[10] Here was the Domino Theory but instead of the metaphor of falling dominoes Secretary Acheson employed rotting apples, suggesting that one rotten apple would infect the entire barrel. Twenty years later it was said that America must fight in Vietnam because if South Vietnam fell to communism, Southeast Asia would also soon succumb. Communism in Southeast Asia would lead to communism in all of Asia. India and then the Middle East would become victims of a Communist take-over. Again, in the late 1960s and early 1970s, as in 1947, the falling dominoes would leave Europe vulnerable to expanding communism. The United States would then be left standing alone, the bastion of democracy surrounded by a Communist world.

The use of the Domino Theory as the rationale for America's approach to Asia suggests several basic policy assumptions on the part of American statesmen. Communism in Asia, regardless of the nation in which it appeared, was tied to and directed from one center—Peking. The concept of national communism or, for example, the belief that North Vietnamese communism was different from, and would conflict with, Chinese Communism, was discounted. What Moscow had represented as the source of all Communist threats to Europe and America during the 1950s, Peking had come to represent as the source of all threats to Asia and America in the late 1960s. Because, as stressed by Secretary Rusk, ". . . Aggression feeds on success," it followed that ". . . appeasement of powerful aggressors leads either to surrender or to a larger war." [11] The United States, in support of American national security and world security in general, had no responsible choice but to accept the burden of containing communism in Asia. In President Nixon's words, " . . . the mantle of leadership fell on American shoulders not by our desire and not for the purposes of conquest." [12] The official conviction was that there simply was no other nation with the resources to do the job.

A New Realism

America's approach to containing communism in Asia was initiated and supported by successive groups of officials under successive Cold War Presidents who were motivated by a sense of purpose and responsibility,

---

[10] See Chapter 1, Figure 1, *A Quarter Century of Policy Consistency*.

[11] For a vivid reflection of Secretary Rusk's views toward communism in Asia and how to respond to it, see Dean Rusk, "Guidelines of U.S. Foreign Policy," *The Department of State Bulletin*, June 28, 1965, pp. 1030–34. The above quotations (p. 1032) suggest the rigidity of America's approach to communism.

[12] C. L. Sulzberger, interview with President Richard M. Nixon, *New York Times*, March 10, 1971, p. 14.

a sincere desire to preserve the status quo in Asia, and a dedicated interest in extending American political values to Asia. These were America's preoccupations and desires and America's desires became America's foreign policy objectives. The burden of the war in Vietnam caused a narrowing of America's policy focus to the exigencies of the day-to-day process of waging that war. This focus was considered justifiable because success in Vietnam was mandatory if America's objectives were to be fulfilled in the rest of Asia.

As a military "victory" and an "honorable" peace in Vietnam became more and more remote, there began a gradual questioning of America's foreign policy objectives in Asia. In the past, American officials, military and civilian, had been consistently unwilling to engage in the relatively deflating process of distinguishing the desirable from the feasible. After all, for the Number One nation, the desirable and the feasible should have been synonymous. However, America's objectives in Asia, although clearly desirable from an official point of view, were simply not feasible. Almost 20 years of containment efforts in Asia, from the creation of SEATO to the Vietnam war, had failed to bring America closer to fulfilling its objectives. There were many reasons for the infeasibility of America's Asian objectives. These have been described by numerous authors.[13] The basic reason why America's objectives in Asia were not feasible was that they were politically unacceptable at home. As the Vietnam war ground on, public and Congressional opposition grew, month by month, year by year, because the burden of containing communism was simply too expensive— too costly in money, world opinion, and especially in American lives.[14]

As the Vietnam war continued into the 1970s, American foreign policy officials were forced to play down and qualify their commitment to what was desirable and shift more emphasis to what appeared feasible when attempting to arrive at policy decisions. The tempering influence of feasibility did not make a sudden appearance in foreign policy with the 1970s. Feasibility had affected decision making from time to time in specific cases during the Cold War, but in a relative sense, it exerted

---

[13] Of the numerous books available concerning America's involvement in the Vietnam war, four provide useful insights into factors that determined America's foreign policy perceptions in Asia: (1) American Friends Service Committee, *Peace in Vietnam* (New York: Hall and Wang, 1966); (2) Marcus G. Raskin and Bernard G. Fall (eds.), *The Viet-Nam Reader* (New York: Vintage Books, 1965); (3) *The Pentagon Papers* (New York: Bantam Books, Inc., 1971); and (4) Richard M. Pfeffer (ed.), *No More Vietnams?* (New York: Harper and Row, 1968).

[14] In January 1969, there were 550,000 American troops in Vietnam, 30,000 men were being drafted every month, and combat casualties were as high as 300 a week. By 1972 there had been 46,000 American soldiers killed in combat plus over 300,000 Americans wounded. The United States, during the late 1960s and early 1970s was spending $2½ billion a month in support of the Vietnam war. In contrast to the enormity of the American war effort, the French in the early 1950s, when they were at their greatest strength, had only 70,000 men assigned to the war in Vietnam.

less general emphasis than did the lure of the desired. For example, in the mid-1950s, although America was deeply committed to the task of containing communism and although it was clearly desirable from the American point of view to "liberate" the Communist nations of Eastern Europe, the United States refrained from military intervention in any Eastern European Communist nation. This restraint was adhered to even in 1956 when overt resistance to Communist party control broke out in Poland and Hungary. The costs of the anticipated consequences were simply too high. In 1949, immediately following the Communist party's assumption of political control in China, America could have intervened to contain communism. However, an undertaking of this magnitude would have required American military forces to assume command of the Nationalist Chinese forces, American men and arms would have been required to wage a large air and ground war in China, and America would have had to spend considerably more than the $2 billion in aid that, by 1948, had already been extended to Chiang Kai-shek. Although it was desirable to contain communism in Asia, such an objective did not seem feasible, from the standpoint of the American people, so soon after World War II's demobilization.[15] Another instance of restraint, based on considerations of feasibility, occurred in 1954 when, despite encouragement from Vice-President Nixon and Admiral Radford, Chairman of the Joint Chiefs of Staff, America refrained from intervening to assist French forces in Vietnam when their defeat appeared imminent.

By the 1970s America had learned to "live with" Soviet and Eastern European communism. A broad set of contacts with European Communist nations had developed on diplomatic, cultural, commercial, and scientific levels. The varied American-Soviet agreements that emerged from the Moscow summit meeting of 1972, described in the preceding chapter, reflected this trend. In fact, six weeks following the 1972 Moscow summit talks, President Nixon's science adviser, Dr. Edward E. David, Jr., acted upon the promise of American-Soviet cooperation in research by signing an agreement for joint efforts in the fields of science and technology. An additional follow-up of the Moscow talks was the official visit by Secretary of State Rogers to Rumania and Hungary (the first time an American Secretary of State had visited either country) to establish more extensive consular, diplomatic, and economic contact.[16] With regard to Communist China, President Nixon's visit to Peking in early 1972 sug-

---

[15] For a concise discussion of communism in China and its American foreign policy significance, see John W. Spanier, *American Foreign Policy Since World War II* (3rd rev. ed.; New York: Frederick A. Praeger, 1968), especially pp. 86–87.

[16] This action was in line with an earlier statement made by President Nixon during his visit to Rumania in the summer of 1969. At that time President Nixon indicated that he recognized the national differences between the United States and Communist nations but "nations can have widely different internal orders and live in peace." (*New York Times*, August 3, 1969, p. 1.)

gested the beginning of America's willingness to accept the existence of China and the abandonment of the determined effort to contain China primarily through the application of military force.

Why would American foreign policy have begun to change? American officials of the 1970s were no more disposed to approve of Communist practices and objectives than had been the officials of the 1950s and 1960s. American statesmen were no more disposed to be "soft on communism," than they had been in the past. It seems most likely that American officials in the 1970s were more disposed to change, were more willing to accept the existence of communism, because it had become more evident that there was no acceptable alternative. The mutually devastating implications of a general strategic war were seen to be completely unacceptable.[17] Also, following Vietnam, situations that could again involve United States forces in a limited war—other Vietnams—had to be avoided if at all possible. It was difficult and disquieting for American officials to reconcile themselves to the realization that the United States could be the most powerful and affluent nation in the world and yet be thwarted in the fulfillment of the goals to which it had applied so much time and money. In a more general sense, it is frequently difficult for the rich and strong to curb their desires. However, if they can, and when they do, it suggests a new realism.

The Nixon Doctrine

On July 26, 1969, President Nixon, during a stopover on Guam on his way to visit Rumania, discussed the question of what the American role in Asia and the Pacific area would be following the end of the Vietnam war.[18] He first stated that he thought one of the weaknesses of American foreign policy was that the United States too often reacted precipitously to events. America failed to have the perspective and long-range view required for an effective foreign policy.

---

[17] The conclusion in official circles that it was necessary, somehow, to learn to adjust to the existence of Soviet communism was probably made most apparent through United States involvement in the Cuban missile crisis in October 1962. Confrontation with the USSR, following the Soviet deployment of medium-range offensive missiles to Cuba, had brought America and the USSR to what appeared to be the brink of nuclear war. This sobering experience motivated American officials to seek methods other than military confrontation in dealing with the USSR. Two excellent articles analyzing this extremely important event are Albert and Roberta Wohlstetter, "Controlling the Risks in Cuba," in Linda B. Miller, *Dynamics of World Politics* (Englewood Cliffs, New Jersey: Prentice-Hall, 1968), chap. 4; and Arnold L. Horelick, "The Cuban Missile Crisis: An Analysis of Soviet Calculations and Behavior," *World Politics,* April 1964, pp. 363–89.

[18] Informal news conference with President Nixon, July 25, 1969. The President spoke for publication but stipulated that he not be quoted directly. *New York Times,* July 26, 1969, p. 8.

A second point made by the President was that America was a Pacific power. Because the President believed that the greatest threat to world peace during the next ten to twenty years was in the Pacific area, it was important that America continue to play a significant role in Asia.[19] However, the President was impressed by the growth of nationalism in Asia and noted that Asians were wary of control that might be imposed upon them by an external power. Asia for Asians was their guiding principle. The President's observations concerning Asian nationalism and attitudes of neutralism toward the major powers led him to a third point which, during subsequent months, was to be given additional emphasis. If America were to play a role in Asia, what should this role be? The President indicated that America supported the idea of Asia for the Asians and that America should act to assist Asia in fulfilling this objective but, in doing this, the United States should not so encourage the dependence of Asian nations that America would again be drawn into conflicts such as Vietnam.[20] America would continue to honor treaty commitments but American policy should be designed to encourage Asian nations to assume gradually increased responsibility for their own security and defense.[21] Where American interests and treaty commitments were not involved, America's role would be limited and would not include military intervention.

Three months later the President spoke again to elaborate on his Guam statement. Then, over one year later, the President expressed similar points in a broader policy context and conveyed these to the American people in a nationwide Presidential address as follows:

The world has changed. Our foreign policy must change with it.

We have learned in recent years the dangers of overinvolvement. The other danger—a grave risk we are equally determined to avoid—is underinvolvement. After a long and unpopular war, there is temptation to turn inward—to withdraw from the world, to back away from our commitments. That deceptively smooth road of the new isolationism is surely the road to war.

Our foreign policy today steers a steady course between the past danger of overinvolvement and the new temptation of underinvolvement.

That policy, which I first enunciated in Guam 19 months ago, represents our basic approach to the world:

—We will maintain our commitments, but we will make sure our own troop levels or any financial support to other nations is appropriate to current threats and needs.

—We shall provide a shield if a nuclear power threatens the freedom of a nation allied with us or of a nation whose survival we consider vital to our security.

---

[19] Ibid., p. 8.
[20] Ibid., p. 8.
[21] Ibid., p. 8.

—But we will look to threatened countries and their neighbors to assume primary responsibility for their own defense, and we will provide support where our interests call for that support and where it can make a difference.

These principles are not limited to security matters.

We shall pursue economic policies at home and abroad that encourage trade wherever possible and that strengthen the political ties between nations. As we actively seek to help other nations expand their economies, we can legitimately expect them to work with us in averting economic problems of our own.

As we continue to send economic aid to developing nations, we will expect countries on the receiving end to mobilize their resources, we will look to other developed nations to do more in furnishing assistance, and we will channel our aid increasingly through groups of nations banded together for mutual support. . . .

In carrying out what is referred to as the Nixon doctrine, we recognize that we cannot transfer burdens too swiftly. We must strike a balance between doing too much and preventing self-reliance, and suddenly doing too little and undermining self-confidence. We intend to give our friends the time and the means to adjust, materially and psychologically, to a new form of American participation in the world.[22]

Two weeks later, in an informal interview with *New York Times* correspondent C. L. Sulzberger, President Nixon summarized the Nixon doctrine in somewhat more casual language:

As I stated in first explaining the Nixon doctrine, our idea is to create a situation in which those lands to which we have obligations or in which we have interests, if they are ready to fight a fire, should be able to count on us to furnish the hose and water.[23]

Despite the vagueness of a number of statements contained in the Nixon doctrine, and the contradictions between statements and actions (discussed further below), this doctrine provided an indication of the general direction, the new direction, of American foreign policy in the 1970s. The basic elements of the new direction set by the Nixon doctrine were:

(1) A determination to avoid more Vietnams. This, it was hoped, would be possible through a reduced American voice and presence abroad, and through encouragement to the developing nations to do more for themselves. When support was extended to other nations, the amount of aid would be determined by existing needs of the recipients.

(2) A realistic acknowledgement of the existence of a multipolar world.

(3) Emphasis on multilateral, rather than bilateral, aid as the most appropriate, i.e., feasible, means for supporting America's interests abroad.

---

[22] Address by President Nixon, "A Redefinition of the United States Role in the World," February 25, 1971, *United States Foreign Policy—1971* (Washington, D.C.: Department of State, March 1972), pp. 422–23.

[23] Sulzberger interview with President Nixon, p. 14.

(4) The pursuit of national advantage through diplomatic negotiation rather than military confrontation. American military power was viewed as having passed the point of maximum political (and perhaps even military) usefulness.

(5) The emphasis on a gradual movement toward change to minimize political and economic dislocations at home and abroad.

(6) An indication that although America was not withdrawing from the international scene, the form of its involvement would be different— basically, more restrained.

The Nixon doctrine was a general and ambiguous statement of policy and, as such, may prove to be of questionable utility in designing approaches to those nations in which social and political change are a perpetual phenomenon. For example, the President indicated that the United States would provide a "shield if a nuclear power threatens the freedom of a nation allied with us or of a nation whose survival we consider vital to our security." This statement suggests at least four unanswered questions: What would constitute the "shield" provided by the United States? What actions taken by a "nuclear power" would actually threaten the freedom of an ally? Which nations were "vital to our security"? How was another nation's "survival" defined? The overall unanswered question was how it might be possible to furnish the "hose and water" without having American firemen drawn into the fire.

Doctrinal ambiguity was accompanied by what appeared to be official ambivalence in the early implementation of the Nixon doctrine's directive that called for decreased American involvement, particularly military involvement, in the internal affairs of other nations. Interventionist behavior continued in the form of the military invasion of Cambodia and Laos, the intensification during 1972 of American B-52 raids against military and civilian targets in Vietnam, the continued build-up of American military bases in Thailand, the CIA's counterinsurgency efforts in Southeast Asia, and in a broader sense, the "military trappings now maintained from Taiwan to Spain." [24]

Also, on a verbal level, the President's statements appeared contradictory. In the interview cited where President Nixon expressed the "hose and water" approach to aid, he also conveyed a detailed sense of the global scope of America's foreign policy responsibilities, indicating that America's responsibilities extended to all areas of the world, that the "400 million people in non-Communist Asia rely ever more on us," and that the "mantle of leadership" had fallen on American shoulders.[25] One year later, in speaking about the war in Vietnam, the President reminded the American people that, "No man who sits here [in the President's office]

[24] Merlo J. Pusey, *The U.S.A. Astride the Globe* (Boston: Houghton Mifflin, 1971), p. 34.

[25] Sulzberger interview with President Nixon, p. 14.

has the right to take any action which would abdicate America's great tradition of world leadership." [26]

It is probable, however, that the vagueness and apparent contradictions that are associated with the Nixon doctrine would be a part of any effort to initiate policy change. In discussing SALT in the preceding chapter, it was indicated that unprecedented arms limitation agreements evoked intra-administration contradictions as well as efforts to move in opposite directions at once, i.e., developing more advanced weaponry while, at the same time, limiting existing arms. The same phenomenon may be reflected in the Nixon doctrine in the sense that the doctrine's generalizations and contradictions do not reflect a lack of serious intent but, instead, are indications of the caution and uncertainty that accompany the process of beginning to act on a different set of perceptions.

An important observation concerning the process of policy change is suggested by the conflict between the six basic elements of the Nixon doctrine enumerated above and the recurring manifestations of America's interventionist behavior. In Chapter 1 the immediate postwar change was described under which American officials shifted from confidence in future United States-Soviet cooperation to a perception of the USSR as an aggressive power committed to the destruction of American life and values. The policy alterations that accompanied perceptual changes occurred rapidly, with a minimum of ambivalence or doctrinal contradiction. The achievement of policy consistency was facilitated by the fact that America felt threatened. A crisis was at hand, no time could be wasted, no expense was too great since America's survival was at stake. What is more, the means of survival was defined—that of military power—and this enabled Washington to know what resources needed to be rapidly marshaled for the nation's security. Policy and action meshed and there was little backtracking or second thoughts.

The movement from crisis policies to policies oriented toward coexistence, negotiation, and cooperation is of a very different sort. It is in this policy process that uncertainties and caution lead to inconsistencies and reversals. Former doubts and suspicions linger on, especially after a quarter century of Cold War conditioning. Fears are slow to disappear, relaxation suggests vulnerability, and the possibility of being taken advantage of inhibits change to a "softer" line. For foreign policy officials of the Cold War era, a change toward conciliation seemed less safe and thus less responsible than were policies geared to the "worse case" situation.

It is difficult to ascertain, at this time, the extent to which the Nixon doctrine was a statement of serious intent. The main reason for attributing credibility to the doctrine is that its expressed perceptions were consistent with the most recent trends in America's foreign pol-

---

[26] *New York Times,* April 27, 1972, p. 20.

icy—such developments as more frequent and broadened negotiations with Communist nations, limitations on arms, intensified efforts to achieve a settlement of the Vietnam war, and a general, openly expressed disenchantment in the United States with the possibility of other Vietnams. The direction of globalism and military intervention had been followed and, by the early 1970s, was possibly being abandoned. The Nixon doctrine suggested a logical and understandable alternative to what had become unacceptable. If change was necessary, and it seemed that it was, then the Nixon doctrine offered a reasonable and realistic approach to strengthened national security. As suggested by Secretary Rogers in his statement quoted at the beginning of this chapter, after "about 25 years" American policy was changing in that efforts were evident to have it "realistically" shaped "in the light of the world situation and in the light of our capabilities . . . . "

Changes for the Future

Just as America's unsurpassed weapons capability had lent definition to the nation's foreign policy, the realization of the limitations of physical power began to stimulate new approaches to foreign affairs. It was necessary, however, if new approaches were to become more than simply "approaches," that new or revived resources be available within the government to support the tentative moves toward change discussed above. Foreign policy change required a reordering of certain functions and operations within the government to transform cautious policy pronouncements and restrained gestures toward a new approach to foreign relations into a basic and consistent policy shift away from confrontation and toward negotiation. The discussion that follows identifies specific institutions and practices within the government that have had a significant impact on the shape of America's foreign policy since the 1940s. Each of these institutions and practices was discussed earlier. However, they are considered at this point from the standpoint of how they are already changing, or how they must change, if American foreign policy is to achieve a new orientation.

1. Decreased Dependence on the Military for the Implementation of Foreign Policy

There must be a reduced reliance on military strength if there is to be a decreased influence of militiary opinion in decision-making circles. The Nixon doctrine, SALT, efforts toward coexistence with Communist nations, and Congressional reservations regarding defense spending reflected an official disposition to place restraints on the development of military capabilities.[27] A possible additional reflection of this disposition was the composition of the groups and committees within the NSC system developed under President Nixon and Dr. Kissinger. These groups, because of their membership, required military opinion and advice to be coordinated with advice from other participating nonmilitary agencies. Military advice concerning military force requirements and possible force reductions, of relevance to arms limitation negotiations at SALT II, for example, was forced to contend with the nonmilitary participants in Verification Panel discussions. Defense budget requests were reviewed by representatives of the Office of Management and Budget, the Council of Economic Advisers, and the State Department as they passed through the Defense Programs Review Committee. The Washington Special Actions Group brought military planning and proposals for the deployment of forces before nonmilitary officials.

The mood of the 1970s was different from that of the preceding two decades when military resources steadily became more plentiful and diverse, and as a consequence, foreign policy officials were disposed to allow their first reaction to be a military reaction. If the developments of the late '60s and early '70s that suggest the imposition of restraints on military responses continue to enjoy official support, military capabilities will become less accessible, and by necessity, more nonmilitary responses will begin to characterize America's initial response to conflict situations. Under such circumstances, military advice will assume less significance, thus bringing about a lowered profile of the military bureaucracy within decision-making circles in Washington as well as in areas abroad.

2. Restricted Role for Intelligence Collection

A reduced sense of threat and efforts toward coexistence go hand in hand. A less threatening world and efforts to coexist made it more difficult to justify the urgency that has been associated with intelligence collection requirements. The pace, volume, scope, and method of intelligence collection can be more restrained and, in the setting of greater international contact, it is not likely to seem that the President, by imposing such restraints, is acting irresponsibly with regard to the nation's security.

---

[27] Symptomatic of Congress' increasing skepticism regarding Defense Department requests for funds was the response of Sen. John C. Stennis, Chairman of the Senate Armed Services Committee and a senior member of the Appropriations Committee, to an "emergency request" in mid-1972 for money to acquire more nuclear submarines and bombers. Sen. Stennis indicated that a critical attitude had been adopted by his committee toward Pentagon requests for major new weapons systems. This development was one of numerous steps by Congressmen that reflected reservations concerning defense spending. This development stood in striking contrast to the situation from the Korean War to the mid-1960s when Congress tended to appropriate *more* than the President had requested for defense.

Covert intervention in the domestic affairs of other nations was justified by the immediacy of the threat to America's security. As suggested in the discussion of the Central Intelligence Agency in Chapter 5, official stress on the immediacy of the threat endowed intelligence agencies with certain prerogatives that enhanced their authority and foreign policy influence.

In the 1970s, as the sense of threat receded and coexistence efforts gained stronger official support, the President and other foreign policy officials became more sensitive to the potentially disruptive political risks associated with interventionist behavior. What had appeared to some observers as an "anything goes" attitude regarding intelligence practices, began to be viewed with deep reservation in official circles. Considerably greater stress was placed on collection techniques that were less obviously interventionist, less potentially offensive, more obviously discreet. Emphasis shifted toward practices that permitted the monitoring of Communist activity from positions outside national boundaries. Strengthening the impersonal and invisible aspects of the intelligence community's technological collection capabilities seemed compatible with efforts to lower America's international profile. This emphasis on technological collection techniques suggested a more routinized set of operating procedures, less subject to alteration by human impetuousness, and less conducive to the development of situations in which collection personnel might begin to perform in activitist capacities to serve, in their own way, the objectives of American foreign policy.

To strengthen the ability of the President to manage his intelligence service, the Kissinger NSC system includes three review and control groups: the NSC Intelligence Committee, the Net Assessment Group, and the Forty Committee, each discussed in Chapter 5. Through the work of these groups, bringing CIA into closer contact with the White House, and with the expanded use of technological collection methods, there is a basis for reinforcing the President's efforts to eliminate what sometimes suggested a discrepancy between publicly declared foreign policy objectives and the overseas operations of CIA.

3. Increased Foreign Policy Participation by Congress

Congressional advice and approval is an important element of a sound foreign policy. From the point of view of most Congressmen in 1972, this element has been largely absent from the foreign policy decision-making process. As indicated in earlier references to the foreign policy role of Congress, the trend in postwar years was toward less participation by the legislative branch. The President had acquired the essential power of war and foreign policy, and Congress was left with only an appropriations or confirmatory role. The importance of this development was expressed by McGeorge Bundy, national security affairs adviser to Presidents Kennedy and Johnson, when he indicated that the most serious difficulty in 1972 in the framing of American foreign policy was "the almost complete breakdown of effective relations" between the executive and legislative branches.[28]

The basic complaint of Congress concerning its marginal role in the formulation of foreign policy was that Congress was not getting the facts. Many Congressmen believed that the President was intentionally withholding national security information from Congress. This feeling became more and more pronounced in the years following the near-unanimous support by Congress of the Gulf of Tonkin Resolution in August 1964.[29] Congressional resentment toward the President did not subside following the election of President Nixon. Sen. Fulbright, during 1971 and 1972, in speeches, testimony, and private comments, criticized the members of the President's White House staff who, in the words of Representative Wayne L. Hays (Democrat, Ohio) had "taken over the policymaking functions of the State Department."[30] The President's White House advisers were attacked for their persistent unwillingness to appear before Congressional committees responsible for formulating legislation affecting foreign policy. Presidential adviser Henry Kissinger was the focus of Congressional criticism because, on the grounds of executive privilege, he had remained largely inaccessible to Congressmen. Congress attempted to use resolutions, legislative amendments, and votes to deny support to the President in foreign policy matters and thereby force the executive branch to consult with Congress before entering international agreements committing American resources to foreign areas. In the words of Sen. Ernest F. Hollings (Democrat, South Carolina),

> The conduct of the Executive branch in recent years has almost nothing in common with what representative government is supposed to be all about. The decisions are made in secret. No one is consulted. Then time is set aside on TV while the nation plays a guessing game called "What's up the President's sleeve tonight?" Finally comes the dramatic announcement, and then the President moves on to something else. It is the theatre of the absurd. Meanwhile the people, their elected representatives in Congress, and even officers of the Cabinet have no idea of the reasons behind the President's frequent policy reversals. That . . . is the worst kind of courthouse politics.[31]

---

[28] *New York Times*, May 25, 1972, p. 4.

[29] On August 2 and 3, 1964, President Johnson was informed that American destroyers had been attacked by North Vietnamese torpedo boats in the Gulf of Tonkin. The President, seeking authority to expand the war as he felt necessary without having to consult Congress, asked Congress for permission to use "all necessary measures" to "repel any armed attack" against American forces. The so-called Gulf of Tonkin Resolution, granting the President this authority was unanimously approved by the House and was passed in the Senate by an 88–2 vote.

[30] *New York Times*, March 1, 1972, p. 16.

[31] Editorial, "The Worrying Post," *Nation* (January 24, 1972), p. 98.

If Congress is to become more actively involved in foreign policy matters, it is the President who is required to bring this about. The President in his attempts to achieve innovation in American foreign policy must initiate efforts to solicit advice from Congress. The continuation or intensification of Congressional resistance to Presidential "unilateralism" in designing American foreign policy is seriously detrimental to the security interests of the nation.

4. Strengthening of the State Department

Near the end of the discussion of the State Department in Chapter 3 the observation was made that if there were a strong conviction within the executive branch that State had an important contribution to make to national security, then there would be an effective effort to strengthen the department. Official perceptions of foreign affairs in the 1970s, with stress on coexistence, multipolarity, avoidance of military involvement, and, as urged by President Nixon, the need for the nation to maneuver between the dangers of "overinvolvement" and "underinvolvement," suggest that the time is at hand when the State Department can be the source of the most significant contributions to America's security.

As mentioned above, greater emphasis on efforts to ascertain the feasibility of foreign policy objectives has been seen as necessary to America's national security interests. Foreign affairs specialists are needed on the working level of policy making to help specify what is ultimately desirable and then to determine how far short of the ideal it is necessary to set policy goals to be realistic, i.e., to have the concept of feasibility actually determine national goals. Beyond this, with feasibility as the guide to policy formulation, familiar platitudes so often used to describe ideal goals can be replaced by a level of specificity that will provide the clarity and detail needed for effective policy implementation. This contribution has the potential of considerable utility in the process redirecting American foreign policy.

The competence of foreign affairs specialists is necessary to carry out the Nixon doctrine's directive that American assistance to other nations should be "appropriate to current threats and needs." The task of matching aid to needs, assigning priorities to requests for foreign assistance, ascertaining the political implications of granting or denying aid, and, in a more fundamental sense, defining and avoiding "underinvolvement" and "overinvolvement" all require the professional skills of the specialist in foreign affairs.

A recognition of multipolarity carries with it the responsibility of developing more extended and regular diplomatic contact with an increasing number of nations. While this requirement applies to nations that are Communist, neutralist, or allied with the United States, it was America's allies that during the '60s and into the '70s expressed their concern over the extent to which American Presidents had failed to consult them before embarking on foreign policy initiatives. Examples of United States unilateralism included America's sudden imposition, in August 1971, of protectionist trading measures of benefit to American business but detrimental to Europeans, and, in 1972, the official and highly significant visits by President Nixon to Communist China and the Soviet Union. By 1972, there was a marked need to restore the practice of diplomatic consultation, if only to convey a sense of respect for the judgment and advice of America's allies. As European nations moved toward economic union and diplomatic innovation of their own, the initial task of American diplomacy was to dispel impressions of America's arrogance and superiority and replace these in the European mind with an appreciation of America's interest in reestablishing ties with its allies on the basis of relations among equals. Again, this was a task for the State Department.

Despite the requirements for diplomatic experience, policy judgment, and regional expertise. the status of the Department of State within the foreign affairs bureaucracy in the early 1970s was unimpressive. Despite the need for skills traditionally associated with the State Department, the center of foreign policy advice and support for the President was occupied by the White House National Security Council system. However, because of the diverse diplomatic responsibilities suggested by a new direction in American foreign policy, a strengthened Department of State appears to be a more suitable focus for foreign policy responsibility than does the National Security Council system. Some reasons for this conclusion include the following.

A regular career corps of foreign affairs specialists, operating under conditions conducive to the maintenance of professionalism in diplomacy and research, is more likely to be achieved within the context of an executive department than within the atmosphere of the White House. As described in Chapter 4, all White House aides serve the President. They hold their jobs as long as the President finds them useful. A number of White House observers have suggested that this fact, combined with the disconcerting experience of directly confronting the President, prompts Presidential aides to say what the President wants to hear.[32] From the

---

[32] George Reedy, Press Secretary to President Johnson, mentioned that at meetings between the President and his White House aides, "The first strong observations to attract the favor of the president become subconsciously the thoughts of everyone in the room. . . . A thesis which could not survive an undergraduate seminar in a liberal arts college becomes accepted doctrine, and the only question is not *whether* it should be done but *how* it should be done." Reedy, to stress the point that members of the President's staff attempt to tell the President what they think he wants to hear, writes that "the concept that 'even your best friends won't tell you' about unpleasant things applies with tremendous force to the President." (George E. Reedy, *The Twilight of the Presidency* (New York: World Publishing Co., 1970), pp. 12 and 97.

President's point of view, as he seeks help in coping with the pressure of the day-to-day demands of his office, the relationship between himself and his aides, one in which he is *served* by them, holds definite advantages. However, it is not a setting conducive to professional objectivity nor is it a setting designed to elicit the straightforward expression of conclusions that are clearly at odds with views held by the President. The foreign policy specialist, working to implement a policy that is in the process of change, requires a setting, a place of work, that will allow him to develop informed, independent views for Presidential consumption. The State Department has the strongest potential as a base from which to derive a more substantive and fully developed set of options for foreign policy action.

White House personnel working on national security problems were characterized by a high rate of turnover under the administrations of Presidents Johnson and Nixon.[33] This situation is likely to persist. Frequently the type of individual drawn into White House service is brought to the President's attention because of outstanding individual achievement. Such an individual is frequently unable to sacrifice his professional independence in service to the President for more than a limited period of time. The State Department is comprised of a career corps of long-term foreign affairs specialists who, because they are less prone to seek different professional opportunities during or following each President's term of office, can offer a foreign policy perspective and an understanding of bureaucratic reality that could significantly strengthen the implementation of foreign policy.

Keeping the personnel of the NSC staff in mind, it is also important to question the scope and depth of the foreign policy activities that a limited number (50 to 70) of staff members could sustain. Under Dr. Kissinger, the NSC staff performed with apparent effectiveness in supporting the President in his visits to the USSR, China, and in developments at SALT. Foreign policy responsibilities, however, extend beyond a limited number of dramatic events and demand that the continuous attention and thought of career officers be directed toward a wide range of diverse regional problems in all areas of the world. The NSC system might be able to confront critical issues in limited areas on a "crash project" basis after an issue had assumed crisis proportions. State, on the other hand, suggested the potential for a resource with which to deal with the same issues and more, on a regular continuing basis, thereby providing improved opportunities to prevent conflicts from developing to crisis proportions.

Another consideration that favors more foreign affairs authority being reinvested in the State Department is the fact that, because of the concept

---

[33] It was reported that approximately 75 percent of Dr. Kissinger's professional staff had departed during the course of the first three years of the Nixon administration. "Mr. Nixon's Secret Agent," *Newsweek*, February 7, 1972, p. 15.

of executive privilege, State's personnel are more accessible to Congress than are the personnel of the White House. A prerequisite for Congressional participation in foreign policy is contact with the center of foreign policy affairs, but as was indicated above in discussing the need to involve Congress more fully in foreign policy matters, the personnel of the NSC system, particularly Dr. Henry Kissinger, have been generally inaccessible to Congress. To move toward reestablishing a more cooperative foreign policy relationship between the President and Congress, a relationship that can make their collective judgment available to decision makers, it is first necessary to establish sustained, in-depth contact. State is the only organization within the executive branch through which it is possible to rebuild such a relationship.

With the increased sensitivity of Congress to the possibility of future unilateral foreign policy actions by the President, the President may begin to increase his use of treaties for international agreements and decrease the frequency with which he has resorted to the use of executive agreements. The arrangement at SALT, where both the treaty and executive agreement were submitted to Congress, may reflect a trend toward a conscious effort on the part of the President to involve Congress in more international agreements. If, as the President moves toward foreign policy innovation, he also seeks ways to involve Congress more fully than was the case during the past decade, there is an additional justification for a strengthened role for State since the department would have a special contribution to make through efforts to keep Congress informed. The constraints of executive privilege have not permitted the personnel of the National Security Council system to perform this function.

In the same way that the State Department could be useful in "building bridges" to Congress, so State could establish necessary centers of support and day-to-day working relationships with other agencies in the government's foreign policy bureaucracy. The orientation of Dr. Kissinger's NSC system is toward serving the President, and the demands of this task leave little opportunity or patience for the corollary of this effort, i.e., establishing working contacts in the bureaucracy that will facilitate the implementation of the President's policies. One writer discussing the need for foreign policy support outside the White House wrote:

. . . If a large part of foreign policy inevitably grows out of day-to-day actions taken and commitments made by officials outside the White House, a foreign affairs control system must build centers of strength responsive to the President around key officials in the larger bureaucracy, or much of what the government does will fall outside of Presidential influence.[34]

---

[34] I. M. Destler, "Can One Man Do?", *Foreign Policy*, Winter 1971–72, p. 39.

5. A New Approach to Foreign Aid

". . . A predominantly bilateral United States program is no longer politically feasible . . ." and the greatest hope for economic development abroad is through cooperative international programs. This was the underlying theme of the recommendations included in the Peterson Report, an analysis of America's foreign aid program by a task force chosen by President Nixon.[35] The Peterson Report urged a new focus for America's aid programs, a new emphasis on multilateral organizations and a new institutional framework for administering aid. All recommendations were consistent with what appeared to be the prevalent attitudes of nations seeking economic assistance. Some of the foreign aid recommendations made by the Peterson Report included the following:

(1) America should help make aid an international effort. America's aid program should be designed so that the developing nations "stand at the center of the international development effort." The developing nations should establish their own priorities and receive assistance in relation to their own efforts. International lending institutions (such as the World Bank) should become the major channel through which American aid was made available. American bilateral aid should be provided within a framework defined by international lending institutions. America should increase its support of international lending institutions.[36] Over the long term, American assistance for development abroad should be small in relation to expenditures for development at home and, moreover, these two development programs (domestic and foreign) should become mutually reinforcing.

(2) In granting aid, Americans should not look for a political "pay-off" for the United States:

This country should not look for gratitude or votes, or any specific short-term foreign policy gains from our participation in international development. Nor should it expect to influence others to adopt U.S. cultural values or institutions. Neither can it assume that development will necessarily bring political stability.

---

[35] The Peterson Report was prepared by a panel of 16 private citizens, headed by Rudolph A. Peterson, retired president of the Bank of America. It was presented to President Nixon on March 8, 1970. The President stated that he found the ideas suggested in the report to be "fresh and exciting," and, in a message to Congress on April 21, 1971, he indicated that he supported its principal recommendations. See "Reform of the U.S. Foreign Assistance Program," *Department of State Bulletin,* May 10, 1971, pp. 614–25.

[36] Although the United States was, in 1972, the largest contributor in absolute terms to overseas development programs, its contribution measured in terms of ability to pay, i.e., aid as a percentage of gross national product, ranked 12 among the 16 aid-donor nations.

Development implies change—political and social, as well as economic—and such change, for a time, may be disruptive.[37]

(3) America's international development programs should be clearly separate from its military and economic programs that provide aid for security purposes.

(4) The State Department's authority over foreign aid programs should be strengthened and extended. The Secretary of State should provide overall policy guidance for all foreign aid. This would mean that the State Department would exercise firm policy direction over all types of security assistance (military assistance grants, use of surplus military supplies, military credits, etc.). Also, to the extent that bilateral American aid programs continued, they should be administered under the direction of American ambassadors.

(5) Military aid should strengthen military security only to the extent that a country was helped to move toward greater self-reliance. In line with the Nixon doctrine, American military aid should be geared to the resources that the recipient nation ultimately will be able to provide for its own security. With developing nations, the United States should reduce its supervision and advice to a minimum, thus encouraging progress toward economic independence. American aid policies should attempt to use individual initiative and private skills and resources in the developing nations.[38]

(6) Institutional changes for the implementation of aid should include:

(a) Creation of a United States international development bank to make capital and related technical assistance loans to selected developing nations.

(b) Creation of a United States international development institute in which research would be conducted to apply science and technology to the development of resources and processes of critical importance to the economies of the developing nations.

(c) Use of the Overseas Private Investment Corporation to mobilize and facilitate the participation of American private capital and skills in foreign development programs.

(d) Creation of a United States international development council to emphasize international development in the formulation of policies pertaining to American overseas trade, investment, agricultural, and export promotion programs.

The changes recommended above would involve the dissolution of the Agency for International Development and the recall of most of its over-

---

[37] Letter to President Nixon, March 8, 1970, from Peterson Report task force, summarizing report's recommendations. *New York Times,* March 9, 1970, p. 12.

[38] The report suggests that as the United States reduces its involvement in Vietnam, cuts back its military forces abroad, and seeks to restrict the arms race, it will be more able to respond to the initiatives taken by the developing nations.

seas personnel since the recommended new institutional framework would require fewer American advisers and other personnel abroad. America would assume a supporting rather than a directing role in administering aid. All of the changes were consistent with the foreign policy implications of the Nixon doctrine and, in themselves, suggested an innovative turn in foreign policy.

6. Consciousness Raising Among the Electorate

The American people have been largely uninformed and generally disinterested in matters of foreign policy—except when American intervention began to cost too much in American lives. Although Americans were told of the need to resist communism everywhere if America was to be secure, no corresponding effort was made by the government to enlighten them concerning the cost, in money and human life, that an undertaking as ambitious as global containment would entail.

During the Cold War, indifference to the complications in international relations, combined with the government's simplistic pronouncements concerning the threat of communism, left Americans resigned to an acceptance of their burden of taxes for defense. Government officials, through their access to restricted security information, periodically conveyed to the public what the "enemy" was capable of doing. The stressing of enemy potential, as distinct from enemy intentions, offered an opportunity to suggest, but not substantiate, a high level of threat. Estimates of enemy capabilities were emphasized to the extent necessary to justify continuing demands by the government for increased defense funds. Few Americans made the effort to acquire sufficient information to challenge official assertions of impending doom. Instead most Americans acquiesced to the sacrifices asked of them.

America's experience in Vietnam changed this. By early 1968 the level of opposition to the government's involvement in the war was sufficiently high to force President Johnson to withdraw from consideration as a Presidential candidate. The credibility of official statements had become eroded by empty promises of "victory soon" and the intolerably high casualty rates among American forces. Public disenchantment was intensified by unofficial disclosures of policies that indicated that government officials had consciously distorted facts concerning America's involvement in the war. The growing sense of the purposeless cost of a war in a small, remote Asian country, combined with a sense of deception at the highest levels of government, provoked deep divisiveness both among groups of Americans and between many Americans and their government.

The detrimental effects of the heritage of the Vietnam war can be overcome, at least in part, through a conscious, patient, protracted effort to bring more foreign policy facts to the American people and, as mentioned above, to Congress. Educating the public in foreign policy matters presents a difficult challenge to official imagination and persistence. With the government's intention of lowering America's profile abroad and attempting to adhere to a course of action somewhere between the recommendations of those who continue to seek "victory" in the Cold War (overinvolvement) and the recommendations of those who wish to withdraw completely from foreign relations (underinvolvement), America's foreign relations will assume a less dramatic, less emotional quality than that which characterized global anticommunism. The fact that America's actions abroad will be less "newsworthy" at home will make public interest more difficult than ever to hold.

As difficult as the task may be, efforts must be initiated to narrow the gap between official pronouncements concerning foreign policy and the level of public comprehension concerning the implications, i.e., probable cost, of efforts to implement policy decisions. To fail to do this can mean that when the call for greater public support is again issued, there will be a resurgence of divisiveness, separating the people from their government, a development that threatens the perpetuation of representative government.

Consciousness raising has occurred among groups such as labor unions, blacks, and women when the members of such groups have become sensitive to the fact that they have been treated in a discriminatory manner and that advantage has been taken of them. The mood of the American people suggests a greater sensitivity to foreign affairs during "peacetime" than has ever before been the case in American history. How might this concern, this consciousness, be constructively extended?

Present on-going international programs for the cultural, professional and educational exchange of persons often yield constructive results and should be continued. These programs, however, in terms of general interest and total number of participants involve only a limited segment of American society. Additional government programs that have the potential for stimulating broader public interest in foreign affairs include the following:

First, increased attention to foreign affairs may develop "naturally" as private domestic economic interests become more involved in foreign areas. The governments of the USSR and Eastern Europe have expressed interest in American agricultural products, automobiles, and computer and electronic equipment. Western Europe is interested in many of the products of America's technological society. As the American business community expands its commercial relations with foreign nations, both Communist and non-Communist, and as profits and individual salaries become tied to foreign commercial ventures, the basis for public interest in foreign affairs will expand.

Second, East-West programs for cooperation already publicly announced should be vigorously supported and publicized broadly within the United States. The 1972 American-Soviet Moscow summit meeting provided a forum for the announcements of programs for research cooperation in science, medicine, space, and environmental pollution control. Imaginatively conceived domestic publicity related to American participation in these, and future, programs would generate increased public interest in America's involvement in world affairs.

Third, the activities of the government's nonmilitary agencies (ACDA, USIA, Peace Corps, and AID—or AID's successor) should be expanded and publicized domestically. At the present time these agencies are prohibited by law from using their funds for publicity within the United States that would describe agency objectives, activities, and accomplishments abroad. This prohibition must be changed so that these nonmilitary agencies can convey to the American public an understanding of how public money is being used. There is no such restriction that limits Defense Department "public relations" activities, and there should be none imposed on these agencies.[39] Domestic publicity describing America's nonmilitary foreign activities would not only offer a refreshing, and possibly uplifting, change for the American public; it would also make it possible for Americans to begin to identify with the agencies using their tax money and, hopefully, begin to develop a sense of participation in and support for foreign programs. It is interesting to note that in the USSR considerable attention is devoted to publicizing the government's foreign aid programs. Leading party and government officials visit aid projects in Africa and Asia, and official recognition and attention is focused on Soviet industries and employees supporting foreign aid programs. These efforts attract both domestic and foreign attention to Soviet aid projects.

Finally, the executive branch should initiate a reevaluation of the criteria employed in establishing various levels of security classification for information concerning matters of national defense. In a number of cases, the standards established for the restriction of information for security purposes were defined decades ago in the early years of the Cold War. International conditions have changed, as has America's sense of its world role. The handling of information by the government should reflect these changes, and accordingly, a broad reassessment of security policy should be undertaken in the light of current foreign policy perspectives

---

[39] It has been estimated that more than 200 military and civilian personnel were attached to the Defense Department's Public Affairs office and that "hundreds more performed similar functions for the military services. In all, the various arms of the Pentagon are spending [in FY 1969] at least $27.9 million a year on public relations activities." See Adam Yarmolinsky, *The Military Establishment* (New York: Harper and Row, 1971), p. 200.

and objectives to differentiate information that must remain classified because it would threaten America's security if it were accessible to a potential enemy from information that can be made available to the public and Congress. The availability of as many facts as possible concerning foreign affairs does not assure public interest or participation, but if public involvement is to develop, access to facts is a prerequisite.

7. Assertive Leadership by the President

There will be no new direction in American foreign policy without strong Presidential leadership. A new emphasis in America's methods of conducting foreign relations can shape the functions of all the foreign policy related institutions of government if the President acts to bring about this change.

All of the changes suggested above that affect the Defense Department, CIA, State Department, AID, Congress, and the American electorate can only be realized as a result of the President's first becoming convinced that America's foreign policy requires these changes, and then acting on this conviction. Limitation of the impact of the Defense Department on foreign policy in line with what the Nixon doctrine seems to advocate can only be achieved through the President's implementation. To insure that CIA and other members of the intelligence community will not engage in actions detrimental to his policy, the President must be firmly determined to assert his executive authority. The State Department can be strengthened to the point of being capable of providing the President with his *first* line of foreign policy advice and support only if the President acts to make this happen. If the nation's organization for administering foreign aid is to be strengthened and redesigned along the lines suggested above, the President will have to be the central figure in the major effort to "sell" this change to Congress and the electorate. Finally, improving channels of communication with Congress and the electorate is obviously dependent on Presidential initiative, imagination, and persistence.

If the foreign policy role of the State Department were strengthened, the authority in this field exercised by the National Security Council system would have to be both curtailed and redirected. This should occur as State reassumes critical foreign policy responsibilities. Also, as State reassumes former responsibilities, the NSC should do the same, i.e., function as a coordinating body in the broad area of national security affairs. For example, the NSC would provide coordination of State and Defense policies, the diverse contributions to foreign aid from within and outside the government would be integrated by the NSC, and control of intelligence community plans and monitoring of intelligence operations would be a NSC staff responsibility. Coordinating the activities of the government's agencies concerned with national security affairs is a task of enormous scope, as is evident from the discussion in Chapters 2 through 5, and demands the authority that can come only from the direct and clearly visible backing of the President. This being the case, the White House National Security Council staff appears as the logical channel through which this coordinating authority can be most effectively expressed.

The President has acknowledged the need for change. Pursuing the actions recommended above, all of which are consistent with the general guidelines for change suggested by executive statements, will set in motion institutional changes and thereby more firmly commit the resources of the government to new directions in foreign policy.

The seven recommendations set forth above focus upon the traditional centers of American foreign affairs—the President and the Department of State. The history of the Cold War reflects a strengthening of one element of this relationship, the President, while the other, the State Department, became increasingly less influential in shaping policy. This imbalance between the two fundamental components of the nation's ability to define and implement its foreign policy must be corrected if there is to be a new direction in America's foreign relations.

Conclusion

American foreign policy is at a crossroads. This rather trite figure of speech suggests that policy can move in two directions. "Old" Cold War institutions and thought remain sufficiently strong so that, with the emergence of new or unanticipated threats, the reflexes of the Cold War could again come into play. For example, consider once again SALT. Assume that at some time in the near future the United States discovered that the USSR had secretly violated the agreement to limit offensive strategic weapons by surreptitiously deploying "up to 100" additional ICBM's to newly constructed missile silos in eastern USSR. Despite Soviet explanations, American officials would probably experience a deep sense of betrayal and many of the feelings toward the USSR described in Chapter 1 would be quickly reactivated. Why, Americans would ask themselves, would the USSR violate the SALT agreement by cheating if it did not have some aggressive intention in mind? A renewed feeling of threat would reactivate the arms race, probably lending to it a rate of acceleration greater than that of the 1960s.

The other direction that American foreign policy can take is that suggested at the beginning of this chapter—away from the perceptions and actions of the Cold War and toward coexistence. Each step that is taken in this direction makes it less probable that the Cold War will return. As money and personnel become committed to the development of resources that support coexistence, a momentum is given to the process of change and it becomes more difficult to revert to old ways.

However, as mentioned above, change in the American political system requires time. It was also mentioned that the process of change will probably, from time to time, include relapses into Cold War forms of behavior. During the time required for change to congeal into a new foreign policy, it is always possible that such relapses could assume proportions that would preclude changes. To prevent this from happening, the forceful and steady leadership of the President is essential. The enormity of the task cannot be overstated. But the security of the nation demands that it be carried out.

appendix A

The Truman Doctrine:
Recommendations on
Greece and Turkey[1]

Mr. President, Mr. Speaker, Members of Congress of the United States:

The gravity of the situation which confronts the world today necessitates my appearance before a joint session of the Congress.

The foreign policy and the national security of this country are involved.

One aspect of the present situation, which I wish to present to you at

---

[1] Delivered by the President before a joint session of Congress on March 12, 1947, and released to the press by the White House on the same date. This message was also printed as Department of State publication 2785. The full text of the President's speech was translated into eight languages and broadcast at differing times to Europe, the Soviet Union, and the Far East. Summaries of the speech were broadcast several times in all the 25 languages of the "Voice of the United States of America."

As the President was speaking at the Capitol, a "live" broadcast of his voice was transmitted to Europe and to the Middle East through relay at Algiers. A recording of the President's voice was broadcast to Latin America at 5:30 and 9:25 P.M. on March 12; to the Far East at 5:30 P.M. on March 12, and at 5 and 8.30 A.M. on March 13; and to Europe and the Middle East at 5:30 A.M. on March 13. With the time changes around the world, the rebroadcasts carried the President's voice to all parts of the world at the most favorable listening hours during the morning, afternoon, and evening.

Since the "Voice of the United States of America" does not include the Greek and Arabic languages, the President's message was heard in Greece and Turkey only in the English language.

this time for your consideration and decision, concerns Greece and Turkey.

The United States has received from the Greek Government an urgent appeal for financial and economic assistance. Preliminary reports from the American Economic Mission now in Greece and reports from the American Ambassador in Greece corroborate the statement of the Greek Government that assistance is imperative if Greece is to survive as a free nation.

I do not believe that the American people and the Congress wish to turn a deaf ear to the appeal of the Greek Government.

Greece is not a rich country. Lack of sufficient natural resources has always forced the Greek people to work hard to make both ends meet. Since 1940 this industrious and peace-loving country has suffered invasion, four years of cruel enemy occupation, and bitter internal strife.

When forces of liberation entered Greece they found that the retreating Germans had destroyed virtually all the railways, roads, port facilities, communications, and merchant marine. More than a thousand villages had been burned. Eighty-five percent of the children were tubercular. Livestock, poultry, and draft animals had almost disappeared. Inflation had wiped out practically all savings.

As a result of these tragic conditions, a militant minority, exploiting human want and misery, was able to create political chaos which, until now, has made economic recovery impossible.

Greece is today without funds to finance the importation of those goods which are essential to bare subsistence. Under these circumstances the people of Greece cannot make progress in solving their problems of reconstruction. Greece is in desperate need of financial and economic assistance to enable it to resume purchases of food, clothing, fuel, and seeds. These are indispensable for the subsistence of its people and are obtainable only from abroad. Greece must have help to import the goods necessary to restore internal order and security so essential for economic and political recovery.

The Greek Government has also asked for the assistance of experienced American administrators, economists, and technicians to insure that the financial and other aid given to Greece shall be used effectively in creating a stable and self-sustaining economy and in improving its public administration.

The very existence of the Greek state is today threatened by the terrorist activities of several thousand armed men, led by Communists, who defy the Government's authority at a number of points, particularly along the northern boundaries. A commission appointed by the United States Security Council is at present investigating disturbed conditions in northern Greece and alleged border violations along the frontier between Greece on the one hand and Albania, Bulgaria, and Yugoslavia on the other.

Meanwhile, the Greek Government is unable to cope with the situation. The Greek Army is small and poorly equipped. It needs supplies and equipment if it is to restore authority to the Government throughout Greek territory.

Greece must have assistance if it is to become a self-supporting and self-respecting democracy.

The United States must supply that assistance. We have already extended to Greece certain types of relief and economic aid, but these are inadequate.

There is no other country to which democratic Greece can turn.

No other nation is willing and able to provide the necessary support for a democratic Greek Government.

The British Government, which has been helping Greece, can give no further financial or economic aid after March 31. Great Britain finds itself under the necessity of reducing or liquidating its commitments in several parts of the world, including Greece.

We have considered how the United Nations might assist in this crisis. But the situation is an urgent one requiring immediate action, and the United Nations and its related organizations are not in a position to extend help of the kind that is required.

It is important to note that the Greek Government has asked for our aid in utilizing effectively the financial and other assistance we may give to Greece, and in improving its public administration. It is of the utmost importance that we supervise the use of any funds made available to Greece, in such a manner that each dollar spent will count toward making Greece self-supporting, and will help to build an economy in which a healthy democracy can flourish.

No government is perfect. One of the chief virtues of a democracy, however, is that its defects are always visible and under democratic processes can be pointed out and corrected. The Government of Greece is not perfect. Nevertheless it represents 85 percent of the members of the Greek Parliament who were chosen in an election last year. Foreign observers, including 692 Americans, considered this election to be a fair expression of the views of the Greek people.

The Greek Government has been operating in an atmosphere of chaos and extremism. It has made mistakes. The extension of aid by this country does not mean that the United States condones everything that the Greek Government has done or will do. We have condemned in the past, and we condemn now, extremist measures of the right or the left. We have in the past advised tolerance, and we advise tolerance now.

Greece's neighbor, Turkey, also deserves our attention.

The future of Turkey as an independent and economically sound state is clearly no less important to the freedom-loving peoples of the world than the future of Greece. The circumstances in which Turkey finds itself today are considerably different from those of Greece. Turkey has been spared the disasters that have beset Greece. And during the war the United States and Great Britain furnished Turkey with material aid.

Nevertheless, Turkey now needs our support.

Since the war Turkey has sought additional financial assistance from Great Britain and the United States for the purpose of effecting that modernization necessary for the maintenance of its national integrity.

That integrity is essential to the preservation of order in the Middle East.

The British Government has informed us that, owing to its own difficulties, it can no longer extend financial or economic aid to Turkey.

As in the case of Greece, if Turkey is to have the assistance it needs, the United States must supply it. We are the only country able to provide that help.

I am fully aware of the broad implications involved if the United States extends assistance to Greece and Turkey, and I shall discuss these implications with you at this time.

One of the primary objectives of the foreign policy of the United States is the creation of conditions in which we and other nations will be able to work out a way of life free from coercion. This was a fundamental issue in the war with Germany and Japan. Our victory was won over countries which sought to impose their will, and their way of life, upon other nations.

To insure the peaceful development of nations, free from coercion, the United States has taken a leading part in establishing the United Nations. The United Nations is designed to make possible lasting freedom and independence for all its members. We shall not realize our objectives, however, unless we are willing to help free peoples to maintain their free institutions and their national integrity against aggressive movements that seek to impose upon them totalitarian regimes. This is no more than a frank recognition that totalitarian regimes imposed upon free peoples, by direct or indirect aggression, undermine the foundations of international peace and hence the security of the United States.

The peoples of a number of countries of the world have recently had totalitarian regimes forced upon them against their will. The Government of the United States has made frequent protests against coercion and intimidation, in violation of the Yalta agreement, in Poland, Rumania, and Bulgaria. I must also state that in a number of other countries there have been similar developments.

At the present moment in world history nearly every nation must choose between alternative ways of life. The choice is too often not a free one.

One way of life is based upon the will of the majority, and is distinguished by free institutions, representative government, free elections, guaranties of individual liberty, freedom of speech and religion, and freedom from political oppression.

The second way of life is based upon the will of a minority forcibly imposed upon the majority. It relies upon terror and oppression, a controlled press and radio, fixed elections, and the suppression of personal freedoms.

I believe that it must be the policy of the United States to support free peoples who are resisting attempted subjugation by armed minorities or by outside pressures.

I believe that we must assist free peoples to work out their own destinies in their own way.

I believe that our help should be primarily through economic and financial aid which is essential to economic stability and orderly political processes.

The world is not static, and the *status quo* is not sacred. But we cannot allow changes in the *status quo* in violation of the Charter of the United Nations by such methods as coercion, or by such subterfuges as political infiltration. In helping free and independent nations to maintain their freedom, the United States will be giving effect to the principles of the Charter of the United Nations.

It is necessary only to glance at a map to realize that the survival and integrity of the Greek nation are of grave importance in a much wider situation. If Greece should fall under the control of an armed minority, the effect upon its neighbor, Turkey, would be immediate and serious. Confusion and disorder might well spread throughout the entire Middle East.

Moreover, the disappearance of Greece as an independent state would have a profound effect upon those countries in Europe whose peoples are struggling against great difficulties to maintain their freedoms and their independence while they repair the damages of war.

It would be an unspeakable tragedy if these countries, which have struggled so long against overwhelming odds, should lose that victory for which they sacrificed so much. Collapse of free institutions and loss of independence would be disastrous not only for them but for the world. Discouragement and possibly failure would quickly be the lot of neighboring peoples striving to maintain their freedom and independence.

Should we fail to aid Greece and Turkey in this fateful hour, the effect will be far-reaching to the West as well as to the East.

We must take immediate and resolute action.

I therefore ask the Congress to provide authority for assistance to Greece and Turkey in the amount of $400,000,000 for the period ending June 30, 1948. In requesting these funds, I have taken into consideration the maximum amount of relief assistance which would be furnished to Greece out of the $350,000,000 which I recently requested that the Congress authorize for the prevention of starvation and suffering in countries devastated by the war.

In addition to funds, I ask the Congress to authorize the detail of American civilian and military personnel to Greece and Turkey, at the request of those countries, to assist in the tasks of reconstruction, and for the purpose of supervising the use of such financial and material assistance as may be furnished. I recommend that authority also be provided for the instruction and training of selected Greek and Turkish personnel.

Finally, I ask that the Congress provide authority which will permit the speediest and most effective use, in terms of needed commodities, supplies, and equipment, of such funds as may be authorized.

If further funds, or further authority, should be needed for purposes indicated in this message, I shall not hesitate to bring the situation before the Congress. On this subject the Executive and Legislative branches of the Government must work together.

This is a serious course upon which we embark.

I would not recommend it except that the alternative is much more serious.

The United States contributed $341,000,000,000 toward winning World War II. This is an investment in world freedom and world peace.

The assistance that I am recommending for Greece and Turkey amounts to little more than one tenth of one percent of this investment. It is only common sense that we should safeguard this investment and make sure that it was not in vain.

The seeds of totalitarian regimes are nurtured by misery and want. They spread and grow in the evil of poverty and strife. They reach their full growth when the hope of a people for a better life has died.

We must keep that hope alive.

The free peoples of the world look to us for support in maintaining their freedoms.

If we falter in our leadership, we may endanger the peace of the world—and we shall surely endanger the welfare of our own Nation.

Great responsibilities have been placed upon us by the swift movement of events.

I am confident that the Congress will face these responsibilities squarely.

appendix B

The Sources of Soviet Conduct[1]

By George F. Kennan

The political personality of Soviet power as we know it today is the product of ideology and circumstances: ideology inherited by the present Soviet leaders from the movement in which they had their political origin, and circumstances of the power which they now have exercised for nearly three decades in Russia. There can be few tasks of psychological analysis more difficult than to try to trace the interaction of these two forces and the relative role of each in the determination of official Soviet conduct. Yet the attempt must be made if that conduct is to be understood and effectively countered.

It is difficult to summarize the set of ideological concepts with which the Soviet leaders came into power. Maximum ideology, in its Russian-Communist projection, has always been in process of subtle evolution. The materials on which it bases itself are extensive and complex. But the outstanding features of Communist thought as it existed in 1916 may perhaps be summarized as follows: (a) that the central factor in the life of man, the factor which determines the character of public life and the "physiognomy of society," is the system by which material goods are produced and exchanged; (b) that the capitalist system of production is a nefarious one which inevitably leads to the exploitation of the working class by the capital-owning class and is incapable of developing ade-

---

[1] Reprinted by permission from *Foreign Affairs,* July 1947, pp. 566–82. Copyright, Council on Foreign Relations, Inc., New York.

221

quately the economic resources of society or of distributing fairly the material goods produced by human labor; (c) that capitalism contains the seeds of its own destruction and must, in view of the inability of the capital-owning class to adjust itself to economic change, result eventually and inescapably in a revolutionary transfer of power to the working class; and (d) that imperialism, the final phase of capitalism, leads directly to war and revolution.

The rest may be outlined in Lenin's own words: "Unevenness of economic and political development is the inflexible law of capitalism. It follows from this that the victory of Socialism may come originally in a few capitalist countries or even in a single capitalist country. The victorious proletariat of that country, having expropriated the capitalists and having organized Socialist production at home, would rise against the remaining capitalist world, drawing to itself in the process the oppressed classes of other countries." [2] It must be noted that there was no assumption that capitalism would perish without proletarian revolution. A final push was needed from a revolutionary proletariat movement in order to tip over the tottering structure. But it was regarded as inevitable that sooner or later that push be given.

For 50 years prior to the outbreak of the Revolution, this pattern of thought had exercised great fascination for the members of the Russian revolutionary movement. Frustrated, discontented, hopeless of finding self-expression—or too impatient to seek it—in the confining limits of the Tsarist political system, yet lacking wide popular support for their choice of bloody revolution as a means of social betterment, these revolutionists found in Marxist theory a highly convenient rationalization for their own instinctive desires. It afforded pseudo-scientific justification for their impatience, for their categoric denial of all value in the Tsarist system, for their yearning for power and revenge and for their inclination to cut corners in the pursuit of it. It is therefore no wonder that they had come to believe implicitly in the truth and soundness of the Marxian-Leninist teachings, so congenial to their own impulses and emotions. Their sincerity need not be impugned. This is a phenomenon as old as human nature itself. It has never been more aptly described than by Edward Gibbon, who wrote in "The Decline and Fall of the Roman Empire": "From enthusiasm to imposture the step is perilous and slippery; the demon of Socrates affords a memorable instance how a wise man may deceive himself, how a good man may deceive others, how the conscience may slumber in a mixed and middle state between self-illusion and voluntary fraud." And it was with this set of conceptions that the members of the Bolshevik Party entered into power.

---

[2] "Concerning the Slogans of the United States of Europe," August 1915. Official Soviet edition of Lenin's works.

Now it must be noted that through all the years of preparation for revolution, the attention of these men, as indeed of Marx himself, had been centered less on the future form which Socialism [3] would take than on the necessary overthrow of rival power which, in their view, had to precede the introduction of Socialism. Their views, therefore, on the positive program to be put into effect, once power was attained, were for the most part nebulous, visionary and impractical. Beyond the nationalization of industry and the expropriation of large private capital holdings there was no agreed program. The treatment of the peasantry, which according to the Marxist formulation was not of the proletariat, had always been a vague spot in the pattern of Communist thought; and it remained an object of controversy and vacillation for the first ten years of Communist power.

The circumstances of the immediate post-revolution period—the existence in Russia of civil war and foreign intervention, together with the obvious fact that the Communists represented only a tiny minority of the Russian people—made the establishment of dictatorial power a necessity. The experiment with "war Communism" and the abrupt attempt to eliminate private production and trade had unfortunate economic consequences and caused further bitterness against the new revolutionary régime. While the temporary relaxation of the effort to communize Russia, represented by the New Economic Policy, alleviated some of this economic distress and thereby served its purpose, it also made it evident that the "capitalistic sector of society" was still prepared to profit at once from any relaxation of governmental pressure, and would, if permitted to continue to exist, always constitute a powerful opposing element to the Soviet régime and a serious rival for influence in the country. Somewhat the same situation prevailed with respect to the individual peasant who, in his own small way, was also a private producer.

Lenin, had he lived, might have proved a great enough man to reconcile these conflicting forces to the ultimate benefit of Russian society, though this is questionable. But be that as it may, Stalin, and those whom he led in the struggle for succession to Lenin's position of leadership, were not the men to tolerate rival political forces in the sphere of power which they coveted. Their sense of insecurity was too great. Their particular brand of fanaticism, unmodified by any of the Anglo-Saxon traditions of compromise, were too fierce and too jealous to envisage any permanent sharing of power. From the Russian-Asiatic world out of which they had emerged they carried with them a skepticism as to the possibilities of permanent and peaceful coexistence of rival forces. Easily persuaded of their own doctrinaire "rightness," they insisted on the

---

[3] Here and elsewhere in this paper "Socialism" refers to Marxist or Leninist Communism, not to liberal Socialism of the Second International variety.

submission or destruction of all competing power. Outside of the Communist Party, Russian society was to have no rigidity. There were to be no forms of collective human activity or association which would not be dominated by the Party. No other force in Russian society was to be permitted to achieve vitality or integrity. Only the Party was to have structure. All else was to be an amorphous mass.

And within the Party the same principle was to apply. The mass of Party members might go through the motions of election, deliberation, decision and action; but in these motions they were to be animated not by their own individual wills but by the awesome breath of the Party leadership and the overbrooding presence of "the word."

Let it be stressed again that subjectively these men probably did not seek absolutism for its own sake. They doubtless believed—and found it easy to believe—that they alone knew what was good for society and that they would accomplish that good once their power was secure and unchallengeable. But in seeking that security of their own rule they were prepared to recognize no restrictions, either of God or man, on the character of their methods. And until such time as that security might be achieved, they placed far down on their scale of operational priorities the comforts and happiness of the peoples entrusted to their care.

Now the outstanding circumstance concerning the Soviet régime is that down to the present day this process of political consolidation has never been completed and the men in the Kremlin have continued to be predominantly absorbed with the struggle to secure and make absolute the power which they seized in November 1917. They have endeavored to secure it primarily against forces at home, within Soviet society itself. But they have also endeavored to secure it against the outside world. For ideology, as we have seen, taught them that the outside world was hostile and that it was their duty eventually to overthrow the political forces beyond their borders. The powerful hands of Russian history and tradition reached up to sustain them in this feeling. Finally, their own aggressive intransigence with respect to the outside world began to find its own reaction; and they were soon forced, to use another Gibbonesque phrase, "to chastise the contumacy" which they themselves had provoked. It is an undeniable privilege of every man to prove himself right in the thesis that the world is his enemy; for if he reiterates it frequently enough and makes it the background of his conduct he is bound eventually to be right.

Now it lies in the nature of the mental world of the Soviet leaders, as well as in the character of their ideology, that no opposition to them can be officially recognized as having any merit or justification whatsoever. Such opposition can flow, in theory, only from the hostile and incorrigible forces of dying capitalism. As long as remnants of capitalism were officially recognized as existing in Russia, it was possible to place on them, as an internal element, part of the blame for the maintenance of a dictatorial form of society. But as these remnants were liquidated, little by little, this justification fell away; and when it was indicated officially that they had been finally destroyed, it disappeared altogether. And this fact created one of the most basic of the compulsions which came to act upon the Soviet régime: since capitalism no longer existed in Russia and since it could not be admitted that there could be serious or widespread opposition to the Kremlin springing spontaneously from the liberated masses under its authority, it became necessary to justify the retention of the dictatorship by stressing the menace of capitalism abroad.

This began at an early date. In 1924 Stalin specifically defended the retention of the "organs of suppression," meaning, among others, the army and the secret police, on the ground that "as long as there is a capitalist encirclement there will be danger of intervention with all the consequences that flow from that danger." In accordance with that theory, and from that time on, all internal opposition forces in Russia have consistently been portrayed as the agents of foreign forces of reaction antagonistic to Soviet power.

By the same token, tremendous emphasis has been placed on the original Communist thesis of a basic antagonism between the capitalist and Socialist worlds. It is clear, from many indications, that this emphasis is not founded in reality. The real facts concerning it have been confused by the existence abroad of genuine resentment provoked by Soviet philosophy and tactics and occasionally by the existence of great centers of military power, notably the Nazi régime in Germany and the Japanese Government of the late 1930's, which did indeed have aggressive designs against the Soviet Union. But there is ample evidence that the stress laid in Moscow on the menace confronting Soviet society from the world outside its borders is founded not in the realities of foreign antagonism but in the necessity of explaining away the maintenance of dictatorial authority at home.

Now the maintenance of this pattern of Soviet power, namely, the pursuit of unlimited authority domestically, accompanied by the cultivation of the semi-myth of implacable foreign hostility, has gone far to shape the actual machinery of Soviet power as we know it today. Internal organs of administration which did not serve this purpose withered on the vine. Organs which did serve this purpose became vastly swollen. The security of Soviet power came to rest on the iron discipline of the Party, on the severity and ubiquity of the secret police, and on the uncompromising economic monopolism of the state. The "organs of suppression," in which the Soviet leaders had sought security from rival forces, became in large measure the masters of those whom they were designed to serve. Today the major part of the structure of Soviet power is committed to the perfection of the dictatorship and to the maintenance of the concept of Russia as in a state of siege, with the enemy lowering beyond the walls. And the millions of human beings who form that part of the structure of power must defend at all costs this concept of Russia's position, for without it they are themselves superfluous.

As things stand today, the rulers can no longer dream of parting with these organs of suppression. The quest for absolute power, pursued now for nearly three decades with a ruthlessness unparalleled (in scope at least) in modern times, has again produced internally, as it did externally, its own reaction. The excess of the police apparatus have fanned the potential opposition to the régime into something far greater and more dangerous than it could have been before those excesses began.

But least of all can the rulers dispense with the fiction by which the maintenance of dictatorial power has been defended. For this fiction has been canonized in Soviet philosophy by the excesses already committed in its name; and it is now anchored in the Soviet structure of thought by bonds far greater than those of mere ideology.

II

So much for the historical background. What does it spell in terms of the political personality of Soviet power as we know it today?

Of the original ideology, nothing has been officially junked. Belief is maintained in the basic badness of capitalism, in the inevitability of its destruction, in the obligation of the proletariat to assist in that destruction and to take power into its own hands. But stress has come to be laid primarily on those concepts which relate most specifically to the Soviet régime itself: to its position as the sole truly Socialist régime in a dark and misguided world, and to the relationships of power within it.

The first of these concepts is that of the innate antagonism between capitalism and Socialism. We have seen how deeply that concept has become imbedded in foundations of Soviet power. It has profound implications for Russia's conduct as a member of international society. It means that there can never be on Moscow's side any sincere assumption of a community of aims between the Soviet Union and powers which are regarded as capitalist. It must invariably be assumed in Moscow that the aims of the capitalist world are antagonistic to the Soviet régime, and therefore to the interests of the peoples it controls. If the Soviet Government occasionally sets its signature to documents which would indicate the contrary, this is to be regarded as a tactical manœuvre permissible in dealing with the enemy (who is without honor) and should be taken in the spirit of *caveat emptor*. Basically, the antagonism remains. It is postulated. And from it flow many of the phenomena which we find disturbing in the Kremlin's conduct of foreign policy: the secretiveness, the lack of frankness, the duplicity, the wary suspiciousness, and the basic unfriendliness of purpose. These phenomena are there to stay, for the foreseeable future. There can be variations of degree and of emphasis. When there is something the Russians want from us, one or the other of these features of their policy may be thrust temporarily into the background; and when that happens there will always be Americans who will leap forward with gleeful announcements that "the Russians have changed," and some who will even try to take credit for having brought about such "changes." But we should not be misled by tactical manœuvres. These characteristics of Soviet policy, like the postulate from which they flow, are basic to the internal nature of Soviet power, and will be with us, whether in the foreground or the background, until the internal nature of Soviet power is changed.

This means that we are going to continue for a long time to find the Russians difficult to deal with. It does not mean that they should be considered as embarked upon a do-or-die program to overthrow our society by a given date. The theory of the inevitability of the eventual fall of capitalism has the fortunate connotation that there is no hurry about it. The forces of progress can take their time in preparing the final *coup de grâce*. Meanwhile, what is vital is that the "Socialist fatherland"—that oasis of power which has been already won for Socialism in the person of the Soviet Union—should be cherished and defended by all good Communists at home and abroad, its fortunes promoted, its enemies badgered and confounded. The promotion of premature, "adventuristic" revolutionary projects abroad which might embarrass Soviet power in any way would be an inexcusable, even a counter-revolutionary act. The cause of Socialism is the support and promotion of Soviet power, as defined in Moscow.

This brings us to the second of the concepts important to contemporary Soviet outlook. That is the infallibility of the Kremlin. The Soviet concept of power, which permits no focal points of organization outside the Party itself, requires that the Party leadership remain in theory the sole repository of truth. For if truth were to be found elsewhere, there would be justification for its expression in organized activity. But it is precisely that which the Kremlin cannot and will not permit.

The leadership of the Communist Party is therefore always right, and has been always right ever since in 1929 Stalin formalized his personal power by announcing that decisions of the Politburo were being taken unanimously.

On the principle of infallibility there rests the iron discipline of the Communist Party. In fact, the two concepts are mutually self-supporting. Perfect discipline requires recognition of infallibility. Infallibility requires the observance of discipline. And the two together go far to determine the behaviorism of the entire Soviet apparatus of power. But their effect cannot be understood unless a third factor be taken into account: namely, the fact that the leadership is at liberty to put forward for tactical purposes any particular thesis which it finds useful to the cause at any particular moment and to require the faithful and unquestioning acceptance of that thesis by the members of the movement as a whole. This means that truth is not a constant but is actually created, for all intents and purposes, by the Soviet leaders themselves. It may vary from week to week, from month to month. It is nothing absolute and immutable— nothing which flows from objective reality. It is only the most recent manifestation of the wisdom of those in whom the ultimate wisdom is supposed to reside, because they represent the logic of history. The accumulative effect of these factors is to give to the whole subordinate apparatus of Soviet power an unshakeable stubbornness and steadfastness in its orientation. This orientation can be changed at will by the Kremlin but by no other power. Once a given party line has been laid down on a given issue of current policy, the whole Soviet governmental machine, including the mechanism of diplomacy, moves inexorably along the prescribed path, like a persistent toy automobile wound up and headed in a given direction, stopping only when it meets with some unanswerable force. The individuals who are the components of this machine are unamenable to argument or reason which comes to them from outside sources. Their whole training has taught them to mistrust and discount the glib persuasiveness of the outside world. Like the white dog before the phonograph, they hear only the "master's voice." And if they are to be called off from the purposes last dictated to them, it is the master who must call them off. Thus the foreign representative cannot hope that his words will make any impression on them. The most that he can hope is that they will be transmitted to those at the top, who are capable of changing the party line. But even those are not likely to be swayed by any normal logic in the words of the bourgeois representative. Since there can be no appeal to common purposes, there can be no appeal to common mental approaches. For this reason, facts speak louder than words to the ears of the Kremlin; and words carry the greatest weight when they have the ring of reflecting, or being backed up by, facts of unchallengeable validity.

But we have seen that the Kremlin is under no ideological compulsion to accomplish its purposes in a hurry. Like the Church, it is dealing in ideological concepts which are of long-term validity, and it can afford to be patient. It has no right to risk the existing achievements of the revolution for the sake of vain baubles of the future. The very teachings of Lenin himself require great caution and flexibility in the pursuit of Communist purposes. Again, these precepts are fortified by the lessons of Russian history: of centuries of obscure battles between nomadic forces over the stretches of a vast unfortified plain. Here caution, circumspection, flexibility and deception are the valuable qualities; and their value finds natural appreciation in the Russian or the oriental mind. Thus the Kremlin has no compunction about retreating in the face of superior force. And being under the compulsion of no timetable, it does not get panicky under the necessity for such retreat. Its political action is a fluid stream which moves constantly, wherever it is permitted to move, toward a given goal. Its main concern is to make sure that it has filled every nook and cranny available to it in the basin of world power. But if it finds unassailable barriers in its path, it accepts these philosophically and accommodates itself to them. The main thing is that there should always be pressure, unceasing constant pressure, toward the desired goal. There is no trace of any feeling in Soviet psychology that that goal must be reached at any given time.

These considerations make Soviet diplomacy at once easier and more difficult to deal with than the diplomacy of individual aggressive leaders like Napoleon and Hitler. On the one hand it is more sensitive to contrary force, more ready to yield on individual sectors of the diplomatic front when that force is felt to be too strong, and thus more rational in the logic and rhetoric of power. On the other hand it cannot be easily defeated or discouraged by a single victory on the part of its opponents. And the patient persistence by which it is animated means that it can be effectively countered not by sporadic acts which represent the momentary whims of democratic opinion but only by intelligent long-range policies on the part of Russia's adversaries—policies no less steady in their purpose, and no less variegated and resourceful in their application, than those of the Soviet Union itself.

In these circumstances it is clear that the main element of any United States policy toward the Soviet Union must be that of a long-term, patient but firm and vigilant containment of Russian expansive tendencies. It is important to note, however, that such a policy has nothing to do with outward histrionics: with threats or blustering or superfluous gestures of outward "toughness." While the Kremlin is basically flexible in its reaction to political realities, it is by no means unamenable to considerations of prestige. Like almost any other government, it can be placed by tactless and threatening gestures in a position where it cannot afford to yield even though this might be dictated by its sense of realism. The Russian leaders are keen judges of human psychology, and as such they are highly conscious that loss of temper and of self-control is never a source of strength in political affairs. They are quick to exploit such evidences of weakness. For these reasons, it is a *sine qua non* of successful dealing with Russia that the foreign government in question should remain at all times cool and collected and that its demands on Russian policy should be put forward in such a manner as to leave the way open for a compliance not too detrimental to Russian prestige.

III

In the light of the above, it will be clearly seen that the Soviet pressure against the free institutions of the western world is something that can be contained by the adroit and vigilant application of counter-force at a series of constantly shifting geographical and political points, corresponding to the shifts and manœuvres of Soviet policy, but which cannot be charmed or talked out of existence. The Russians look forward to a duel of infinite duration, and they see that already they have scored great successes. It must be borne in mind that there was a time when the Communist Party represented far more of a minority in the sphere of Russian national life than Soviet power today represents in the world community.

But if ideology convinces the rulers of Russia that truth is on their side and that they can therefore afford to wait, those of us on whom that ideology has no claim are free to examine objectively the validity of that premise. The Soviet thesis not only implies complete lack of control by the west over its own economic destiny, it likewise assumes Russian unity, discipline and patience over an infinite period. Let us bring this apocalyptic vision down to earth, and suppose that the western world finds the strength and resourcefulness to contain Soviet power over a period of ten to fifteen years. What does that spell for Russia itself?

The Soviet leaders, taking advantage of the contributions of modern technique to the arts of despotism, have solved the question of obedience within the confines of their power. Few challenge their authority and even those who do are unable to make that challenge valid as against the organs of suppression of the state.

The Kremlin has also proved able to accomplish its purpose of building up in Russia, regardless of the interests of the inhabitants, an industrial foundation of heavy metallurgy, which is, to be sure, not yet complete but which is nevertheless continuing to grow and is approaching those of the other major industrial countries. All of this, however, both the maintenance of internal political security and the building of heavy industry, has been carried out at a terrible cost in human life and in human hopes and energies. It has necessitated the use of forced labor on a scale unprecedented in modern times under conditions of peace. It has involved the neglect or abuse of other phases of Soviet economic life, particularly agriculture, consumers' goods production, housing and transportation.

To all that, the war has added its tremendous toll of destruction, death and human exhaustion. In consequence of this, we have in Russia today a population which is physically and spiritually tried. The mass of the people are disillusioned, skeptical and no longer as accessible as they once were to the magical attraction which Soviet power still radiates to its followers abroad. The avidity with which people seized upon the slight respite accorded to the Church for tactical reasons during the war was eloquent testimony to the fact that their capacity for faith and devotion found little expression in the purposes of the régime.

In these circumstances, there are limits to the physical and nervous strength of people themselves. These limits are absolute ones, and are binding even for the cruelest dictatorship, because beyond them people cannot be driven. The forced labor camps and the other agencies of constraint provide temporary means of compelling people to work longer hours than their own volition or mere economic pressure would dictate; but if people survive them at all they become old before their time and must be considered as human casualties to the demands of dictatorship. In either case their best powers are no longer available to society and can no longer be enlisted in the service of the state.

Here only the younger generation can help. The younger generation, despite all vicissitudes and sufferings, is numerous and vigorous; and the Russians are a talented people. But it still remains to be seen what will be the effects on mature performance of the abnormal emotional strains of childhood which Soviet dictatorship created and which were enormously increased by the war. Such things as normal security and placidity of home environment have practically ceased to exist in the Soviet Union outside of the most remote farms and villages. And observers are not yet sure whether that is not going to leave its mark on the over-all capacity of the generation now coming into maturity.

In addition to this, we have the fact that Soviet economic development, while it can list certain formidable achievements, has been precariously spotty and uneven. Russian Communists who speak of the "uneven development of capitalism" should blush at the contemplation of their own national economy. Here certain branches of economic life, such as the metallurgical and machine industries, have been pushed out of all proportion to other sectors of economy. Here is a nation striving to become in a short period one of the great industrial nations of the world while it still has no highway network worthy of the name and only a relatively primitive network of railways. Much has been done to increase efficiency of labor and to teach primitive peasants something about the operation of machines. But maintenance is still a crying deficiency of all Soviet economy. Construction is hasty and poor in quality. Depreciation must be enormous. And in vast sectors of economic life it has not yet been possible to instill into labor anything like that general culture of production and technical self-respect which characterizes the skilled worker of the west.

It is difficult to see how these deficiencies can be corrected at an early date by a tired and dispirited population working largely under the shadow of fear and compulsion. And as long as they are not overcome, Russia will remain economically a vulnerable, and in a certain sense an impotent, nation, capable of exporting its enthusiasms and of radiating the strange charm of its primitive political vitality but unable to back up those articles of export by the real evidences of material power and prosperity.

Meanwhile, a great uncertainty hangs over the political life of the Soviet Union. That is the uncertainty involved in the transfer of power from one individual or group of individuals to others.

This is, of course, outstandingly the problem of the personal position of Stalin. We must remember that his succession to Lenin's pinnacle of preëminence in the Communist movement was the only such transfer of individual authority which the Soviet Union has experienced. That transfer took 12 years to consolidate. It cost the lives of millions of people and shook the state to its foundations. The attendant tremors were felt all through the international revolutionary movement, to the disadvantage of the Kremlin itself.

It is always possible that another transfer of preëminent power may take place quietly and inconspicuously, with no repercussions anywhere. But again, it is possible that the questions involved may unleash, to use some of Lenin's words, one of those "incredibly swift transitions" from "delicate deceit" to "wild violence" which characterize Russian history, and may shake Soviet power to its foundations.

But this is not only a question of Stalin himself. There has been, since 1938, a dangerous congealment of political life in the higher circles of Soviet power. The All-Union Congress of Soviets, in theory the supreme body of the Party, is supposed to meet not less often than once in three years. It will soon be eight full years since its last meeting. During this period membership in the Party has numerically doubled. Party mortality during the war was enormous; and today well over half of the Party members are persons who have entered since the last Party congress was held. Meanwhile, the same small group of men has carried on at the top through an amazing series of national vicissitudes. Surely there is some reason why the experiences of the war brought basic political changes to every one of the great governments of the west. Surely the causes of that phenomenon are basic enough to be present somewhere in the obscurity of Soviet political life, as well. And yet no recognition has been given to these causes in Russia.

It must be surmised from this that even within so highly disciplined an organization as the Communist Party there must be a growing divergence in age, outlook and interest between the great mass of Party members, only so recently recruited into the movement, and the little self-perpetuating clique of men at the top, whom most of these Party members have never met, with whom they have never conversed, and with whom they can have no political intimacy.

Who can say whether, in these circumstances, the eventual rejuvenation of the higher spheres of authority (which can only be a matter of time) can take place smoothly and peacefully, or whether rivals in the quest for higher power will not eventually reach down into these politically immature and inexperienced masses in order to find support for their respective claims? If this were ever to happen, strange consequences could flow for the Communist Party: for the membership at large has been exercised only in the practices of iron discipline and obedience and not in the arts of compromise and accommodation. And if disunity were ever to seize and paralyze the Party, the chaos and weakness of Russian society would be revealed in forms beyond description. For we have seen that Soviet power is only a crust concealing an amorphous mass of human beings among whom no independent organizational structure is tolerated. In Russia there is not even such a thing as local government. The present generation of Russians have never known spontaneity of collective action. If, consequently, anything were ever to occur to disrupt the unity and efficacy of the Party as a political instrument, Soviet Russia might be changed overnight from one of the strongest to one of the weakest and most pitiable of national societies.

Thus the future of Soviet power may not be by any means as secure as Russian capacity for self-delusion would make it appear to the men in the Kremlin. That they can keep power themselves, they have demonstrated. That they can quietly and easily turn it over to others remains to be proved. Meanwhile, the hardships of their rule and the vicissitudes of international life have taken a heavy toll of the strength and hopes of the great people on whom their power rests. It is curious to note that the ideological power of Soviet authority is strongest today in areas beyond the frontiers of Russia, beyond the reach of its police power. This phenomenon brings to mind a comparison used by Thomas Mann in his great novel "Buddenbrooks." Observing that human institutions often show the greatest outward brilliance at a moment when inner decay is in reality farthest advanced, he compared the Buddenbrook family, in the days of its greatest glamour, to one of those stars whose light shines most brightly on this world when in reality it has long since ceased to exist. And who can say with assurance that the strong light still cast by the Kremlin on the dissatisfied peoples of the western world is not the powerful afterglow of a constellation which is in actuality on the wane? This cannot be proved. And it cannot be disproved. But the possibility remains (and in the opinion of this writer it is a strong one) that Soviet power, like the capitalist world of its conception, bears within it the seeds of its own decay, and that the sprouting of these seeds is well advanced.

IV

It is clear that the United States cannot expect in the foreseeable future to enjoy political intimacy with the Soviet régime. It must continue to regard the Soviet Union as a rival, not a partner, in the political arena. It must continue to expect that Soviet policies will reflect no abstract love of peace and stability, no real faith in the possibility of a permanent happy coexistence of the Socialist and capitalist worlds, but rather a cautious, persistent pressure toward the disruption and weakening of all rival influence and rival power.

Balanced against this are the facts that Russia, as opposed to the western world in general, is still by far the weaker party, that Soviet policy is highly flexible, and that Soviet society may well contain deficiencies which will eventually weaken its own total potential. This would of itself warrant the United States entering with reasonable confidence upon a policy of firm containment, designed to confront the Russians with unalterable counter-force at every point where they show signs of encroaching upon the interests of a peaceful and stable world.

But in actuality the possibilities for American policy are by no means limited to holding the line and hoping for the best. It is entirely possible for the Unitied States to influence by its actions the internal developments, both within Russia and throughout the international Communist movement, by which Russian policy is largely determined. This is not only a question of the modest measure of informational activity which this government can conduct in the Soviet Union and elsewhere, although that, too, is important. It is rather a question of the degree to which the United States can create among the peoples of the world generally the impression of a country which knows what it wants, which is coping successfully with the problems of its internal life and with the responsibilities of a World Power, and which has a spiritual vitality capable of holding its own among the major ideological currents of the time. To the extent that such an impression can be created and maintained, the aims of Russian Communism must appear sterile and quixotic, the hopes and enthusiasm of Moscow's supporters must wane, and added strain must be imposed on the Kremlin's foreign policies. For the palsied decrepitude of the capitalist world is the keystone of Communist philosophy. Even the failure of the United States to experience the early economic depression which the ravens of the Red Square have been predicting with such complacent confidence since hostilities ceased would have deep and important repercussions throughout the Communist world.

By the same token, exhibitions of indecision, disunity and internal disintegration within this country have an exhilarating effect on the whole Communist movement. At each evidence of these tendencies, a thrill of hope and excitement goes through the Communist world; a new jauntiness can be noted in the Moscow tread; new groups of foreign supporters climb on to what they can only view as the band wagon of international politics; and Russian pressure increases all along the line in international affairs.

It would be an exaggeration to say that American behavior unassisted and alone could exercise a power of life and death over the Communist movement and bring about the early fall of Soviet power in Russia. But the United States has it in its power to increase enormously the strains under which Soviet policy must operate, to force upon the Kremlin a far greater degree of moderation and circumspection than it has had to observe in recent years, and in this way to promote tendencies which must eventually find their outlet in either the break-up or the gradual mellowing of Soviet power. For no mystical, Messianic movement—and particularly not that of the Kremlin—can face frustration indefinitely without eventually adjusting itself in one way or another to the logic of that state of affairs.

Thus the decision will really fall in large measure in this country itself. The issue of Soviet-American relations is in essence a test of the over-all worth of the Unitied States as a nation among nations. To avoid destruction the United States need only measure up to its own best traditions and prove itself worthy of preservation as a great nation.

Surely, there was never a fairer test of national quality than this. In the light of these circumstances, the thoughtful observer of Russian-American relations will find no cause for complaint in the Kremlin's challenge to American society. He will rather experience a certain gratitude to a Providence which, by providing the American people with this implacable challenge, has made their entire security as a nation dependent on their pulling themselves together and accepting the responsibilities of moral and political leadership that history plainly intended them to bear.

appendix C

Selected Chronology:
Strategic Arms Limitation Talks

PRE-SALT STATEMENTS

United States

Soviet Union

Early 1967

U.S. suggests to USSR that joint meeting be initiated to explore arms limitation agreement.

June 1968

Gromyko: USSR "ready for an exchange of opinion on this question."

August 1968

Czechoslovakia invaded by Warsaw Pact troops. Arrangements for arms talks broken off.

January 1969

Nixon in favor of strategic arms talks.

Bargaining chip: Secretary Laird supports Safeguard ABM system as means of improving U.S. bargaining position. ABMs could be disbanded if SALT successful.

January 1969

Soviet Foreign Ministry expresses interest in discussions to: (1) halt production of nuclear weapons; (2) reduce nuclear stockpiles; (3) ban and eliminate nuclear weapons completely.

June 1969

Bargaining chip: U.S. to test MIRVs for Minuteman III ICBMs.

April 1969

Bargaining chip: SS-9 ICBM testing.

October 1969

Bargaining chip: USSR has acquired 1350 ICBMs (300 more than U.S.) and is testing ABMs.

236

FIRST ROUND (Helsinki)
(November 17, 1969–December 22, 1969)

November 1969

Nixon: U.S. weapons levels guided by concept of maintaining "sufficiency" to protect self and allies; recognizes similar Soviet defense responsibilities.

Verification: Secretary Rogers states that U.S. will concede to USSR and not seek on-site inspection (verification to be by satellite photography, seismic monitoring, and technical intelligence collection).

December 1969

Definition of strategic weapons includes ABMs, ICBMs, IRBMs, and SLBMs. Did not include heavy bombers since USSR would include European-based fighter-bombers and aircraft carrier-based planes in Mediterranean.

November 1969

Semyonov: USSR seeking mutually acceptable solution without prejudicing own or other's security. USSR does not wish to place U.S. at military disadvantage.

Verification: USSR opposes on-site inspection.

December 1969

Definition of strategic weapons includes heavy bombers (of which they had relatively few) since they could strike USSR. Would not include their IRBMs which could not strike U.S.

SECOND ROUND (Vienna)
(April 16, 1970–August 14, 1970)

February 1970

Bargaining chip: Secretary Laird announces modified Phase II Safeguard ABM program.

March 1970

Bargaining chip: Secretary Laird announces Minuteman III to be deployed in June.

April 1970

Negotiations should attempt to limit deployment of both offensive and defensive weapons. Each nation should be permitted relatively small ABM system with numerical ceiling on offensive (ICBM and SLBM) weapons.

May 1970

Proposes that ABMs be limited to Washington and Moscow (100 ABMs each); freeze 1970 levels of ICBMs and SLBMs.

April 1970

Negotiations should attempt first to achieve defensive limitation. This is most realistic negotiating objective.

June 1970
Bargaining chip: Air force announces multiple warheads to be deployed for some ICBMs (creating MIRVS).

July 1970
Package proposal for freeze or reduction of offensive and defensive missile systems without restricting qualitative improvements:

(1) Overall numerical limit on strategic launching systems (land and sea-based missiles and U.S.-based strategic bombers); each side to arrange own mix within overall quota;

(2) Limit within ICBM quota on number of Soviet SS-9 or similar missiles developed by either side;

(3) Limit ABMs to low level (under 100 launchers) by either banning such systems or limiting them to ring of sites around Moscow and Washington.

August 1970
U.S. would give up ABM entirely if USSR limited number of SS-9s and scrapped 64-site ABM system around Moscow.

Bargaining chip: U.S. Senate supports ABM expansion.

"August 4 Plan":

(1) Includes ICBMs, SLBMs, and heavy bombers (one bomber equal to one missile). Total allowed each side under 2,000;

(2) No MIRV ban, no on-site inspection;

(3) U.S. not insist on including IRBMs if USSR excluded U.S. forward-based aircraft in Western Europe;

(4) Each nation have either four ABM sites defending ICBMs, or one site for capital.

June 1970
Proposes total ABM ban but interested in U.S. proposal. Incomplete ABM system already around Moscow.

July 1970
Will not consider MIRV limitation. This would freeze U.S. advantage (USSR had not tested MIRV).

August 1970
Objects to U.S. insistence that anti-aircraft defenses and radar could not be improved to point of becoming part of ABM system.

THIRD ROUND (Helsinki)
(November 2, 1970–December 18, 1970)

November 1970

Proposes that accords be restricted to strategic weapons systems.

December 1970

Mobile, land-based ICBM would complicate verification procedures, loophole for arms race to continue through refinement of existing systems.

November 1970

Proposes that accords include U.S. tactical air units in Western Europe.

December 1970

Permit both sides to deploy mobile, land-based ICBMs.

Proposes that offensive arms not be discussed and negotiations concentrate on ABM agreement.

FOURTH ROUND (Vienna)
(March 16, 1971–May 28, 1971)

February 1971

Bargaining chip: Nixon states that if Soviet SS-9 deployment continues, U.S. will order development of B-1 bomber and Trident-ULMS submarine.

March 1971

Nixon: U.S. willing to negotiate noncomprehensive agreement if "some mix" of offensive and defensive weapons agreed upon. Insists on offensive-defensive balance as proposed in "August 4 Plan."

March 1971

USSR continues to express interest in defensive agreement only as first step. Limit ABMs to national command centers (Washington and Moscow).

May 1971

Joint interim May 20 compromise: U.S. and USSR agree to concentrate on ABMs but include "certain measures" to limit some offensive weapons.

Also agree that issue of limiting arms in Western and Eastern Europe be turned over to entire membership of NATO and Warsaw Pact nations. European arms discussion include:

(1) IRBMs in "forward nuclear areas";

(2) 500 (or more) U.S. controlled fighter-bombers in West Germany;

(3) Nuclear arms carrier-based aircraft assigned to U.S. Sixth Fleet, Mediterranean.

FIFTH ROUND (Helsinki)
(July 8, 1971–September 24, 1971)

July 1971

U.S. proposes halt in construction of land and sub-based missiles:

(1) U.S. and USSR should choose between defending capital with 100 ABMs or deploying up to 300 ABMs, at 3 sites, to defend ICBMs;

(2) Establish cut-off date after which no new missile silos, SLBMs, or ICBMs could be constructed;

(3) Supreme national interest clause: either side could abrogate agreement if felt own security fundamentally endangered.

July 1971

USSR urges acceptance of plan to defend national capital.

Objects to SLBM halt because Soviet force smaller than American. If SLBMs included, should also include American fighter-bombers in Europe.

SIXTH ROUND (Vienna)
(November 15, 1971–February 4, 1972)

October 1971

Bargaining chip: Secretary Laird recommends B-1 bomber and Trident-ULMS submarine receive more funds. Secretary Laird also announces USSR testing SS-11, long-range SLBMs, and new ABM.

December 1971

Announces that if other elements of agreement asceptable, USSR would accepts U.S. ABM numerical edge of 150 ABMs to 100.

Favors freeze on land-based launching systems and resists inclusion of SLBMs.

February 1972

Prepares to accept 200 ABMs for two sites: exact parity. Each side free to decide where to deploy ABMs to any two sites.

February 1972

Prefers 200 ABMs (100 for Moscow and 100 for one ICBM site). Seeks parity with U.S.

SEVENTH ROUND (Helsinki)
(March 28, 1972–May 26, 1972)

Final Defensive and Offensive Arms Agreements
ABM Treaty

May 1972

(1) Treaty of unlimited duration;

(2) Required ratification by two thirds of U.S. Senate, but U.S. and USSR pledged immediate adherence to terms;

(3) U.S. and USSR limited to two ABM complexes, one for national command centers of Moscow and Washington, and second for one field of ICBMs. Each site to consist of 100 ABMs, with a total of 200 for each country. U.S. ICBM protection site at Grand Forks, North Dakota, Soviet's at unidentified site at least 800 miles from Moscow.

Offensive Strategic Weapons Agreement

May 1972

(1) Executive agreement (requiring majority approval by Congress).

(2) Limited all ICBMs to those under construction or deployed at time agreement signed:

   (a) USSR—1,618, including only 313 SS-9s;

   (b) U.S.—1,054, including 1,000 Minuteman and 54 Titan missiles;

(3) Froze SLBM construction at 1972 levels:

   (a) U.S.—710 SLBMs on 44 nuclear-powered submarines;

   (b) USSR—950 SLBMs on 62 submarines;

(4) Further construction could be undertaken only if an equal number of older ICBMs or SLBMs were dismantled.

INDEX